Praise for
Making Home

Making Home is quintessential Astyk. Which is why, when suggesting that "giving care is what makes us human", she is not only nudging our participation in the world's healing but, most strikingly, showing us exactly how it's done. Her legions of fans have come to expect just that and *Making Home* will not disappoint. Exhaustively researched and compassionately delivered, this tribute to home, family, community and place offers an honest analysis of the challenges we face and the skills, tools and heart we will need to take them on. Part call to arms, part siren song of love, *Making Home: Adapting Our Homes and Our Lives to Settle in Place*, is the new standard to beat.

— Harriet Fasenfest, author, *A Householder's Guide to the Universe*

Americans are born to be transient — Sharon Astyk has the prescription for dealing with that genetic disease, and building a healthy nativeness into our lives.

— Bill McKibben, author *Deep Economy*

True to form, Sharon Astyk has given us another thought provoking kick in the pants. No matter what your resources may be, or where you fall on the socio-economic spectrum, this book has something to teach about building resilience for a better future for everyone.

—Shannon Hayes, author, *Radical Homemakers* and *Long Way on a Little*

Global crises will be paralyzing unless we have made for ourselves a grounded home life that includes children, animals, soil, music, and daily chores—unless we have learned to respond to economic turmoil, peak oil, and climate change through the details of our daily existence. Sharon Astyk gives us exactly the eloquent, realistic encouragement we need at this moment in history.

— Richard Heinberg, Senior Fellow, Post Carbon Institute,
author, *The End of Growth*

Making Home is part how-to, part engaging memoir, part philosophy, and all wise and intelligent. Sharon shows us why the actions that prepare us for emergencies and energy descent are the right things to do no matter what the future brings, and she takes us through the steps to get there with certainty and good humor. She truly walks her talk, as this book shows, and is one of the clearest voices telling the much-needed new stories of the opportunities and challenges we'll meet as we continue to emerge from the fossil-fuel age. This book is another home run for Sharon Astyk.

—Toby Hemenway, author, *Gaia's Garden:*
A Guide to Home-Scale Permaculture

Making Home

Adapting Our Homes *and* Our Lives to Settle in Place

Sharon Astyk

new society
PUBLISHERS

Cover design by Diane McIntosh.
Cover image: © iStock (illuworld); label image © iStock Nic Taylor

Printed in Canada. First printing June 2012.

Paperback ISBN: 978-0-86571-671-1
eISBN: 978-1-55092-509-8

Inquiries regarding requests to reprint all or part of *Making Home*
should be addressed to New Society Publishers at the address below.

To order directly from the publishers, please call toll-free (North America) 1-800-
567-6772, or order online at www.newsociety.com

Any other inquiries can be directed by mail to:

New Society Publishers
P.O. Box 189, Gabriola Island, BC V0R 1X0, Canada
(250) 247-9737

Library and Archives Canada Cataloguing in Publication

Astyk, Sharon
    Making home : adapting our homes and lives to stay in place /
Sharon Astyk.

Includes bibliographical references and index.
ISBN 978-0-86571-671-1

    1. Simplicity. 2. Sustainable living. 3. Conduct of life. 4. Thriftiness.
5. Happiness. I. Title.

BJ1496.A87 2012   646.7   C2012-903261-1

New Society Publishers' mission is to publish books that contribute in fundamental
ways to building an ecologically sustainable and just society, and to do so with the
least possible impact on the environment, in a manner that models this vision. We are
committed to doing this not just through education, but through action. The inte-
rior pages of our bound books are printed on Forest Stewardship Council®-registered
acid-free paper that is **100% post-consumer recycled** (100% old growth forest-free),
processed chlorine free, and printed with vegetable-based, low-VOC inks, with covers
produced using FSC®-registered stock. New Society also works to reduce its carbon
footprint, and purchases carbon offsets based on an annual audit to ensure a carbon
neutral footprint. For further information, or to browse our full list of books and purchase securely, visit our website at: www.newsociety.com

To the
authors of
my first
homes,
my
parents

Contents

Books for Wiser Living
recommended by *Mother Earth News*

Today, more than ever before, our society is seeking ways to live more conscientiously. To help bring you the very best inspiration and information about greener, more sustainable lifestyles, *Mother Earth News* is recommending select New Society Publishers books to its readers. For more than 30 years, *Mother Earth* has been North America's "Original Guide to Living Wisely," creating books and magazines for people with a passion for self-reliance and a desire to live in harmony with nature. Across the countryside and in our cities, New Society Publishers and *Mother Earth* are leading the way to a wiser, more sustainable world. For more information, please visit MotherEarthNews.com

Acknowledgments

THIS PROJECT WOULD NOT HAVE BEEN POSSIBLE without the support and friendship of many people — first and most importantly, Aaron Newton, who, even if he didn't write the book, has worked with me on many classes and projects and who continually inspires my thinking on this subject. Miranda Edel's beautiful illustrations made the pictures in my head real. Thanks go to those who agreed to be profiled: Gerri Williams, Risa Bear, Lisa Coons, Michelle Kay and Kathy Harrison. Others not profiled gave advice from their lives, including MEA, Pat Meadows, Michelle Chandler, Maria and Fred Tupper, Bernard Brennan, Loren Brown and Pamela Talese, Beth Hook, Stephen Beltramini, Deanna Duke, Tammi Hodson, Robyn and Brian Morton, Tovah Gidseg, Kathy McMahon, Dave Perkins, Edson Freeman and Lonna Cunningham. Thanks also the participants in our Adapting in Place classes and to the commenters on my blogs, who immensely improved this book.

I built upon ideas from Toby Hemenway, Richard Heinberg, Dmitry Orlov, Wes Jackson, John Michael Greer, Kurt Cobb, Albert Bates, Shannon Hayes, Rod and Julie Dreher, Harriet Fasenfest, Gene Logsdon, the late Carla Emery, Peter Bane and Keith Johnson, Larry Santoyo, Pat Murphy and Faith Morgan, Jeffrey Brown, Philip Rutter, Megan Quinn Bachman, Stuart Staniford, Naomi Davis, Nicole Foss, Ilargi and, of course, Wendell Berry.

Friends who helped me work through the whole long process include Alice Oldfather and Jeffrey Gordon, Jesse Wertheimer and Rachel Olson Wertheimer, Bess Libby-Shannon and Chris Shannon, Jon Libby and Stephanie Gallagher-Libby, Sandy and George Lawrence, Ted Lichtenfeld and Miriam Midlarsky-Lichtenfeld, Deborah Gordon and Judy Weinman, Susan Scharfstein and Joseph Shiang, and Alexandra and Steve Schmidt. I know this list bears some resemblance to that of past books, and I'm grateful for their ongoing support of everything we do.

Ingrid Witvoet was the best editor ever, and bought me a heck of a lot of drinks, which did, I swear, help me finish. Ginny Miller talked me down after my crisis in this book. Sue Custance made it beautiful — I can't thank them enough. Scott Steedman's copyedit improved the book immeasurably.

My family and Eric's family have been incredibly supportive through all of this. The most important support, as always, has come from my beloved husband and my four wonderful kids, who remind me that it isn't the place, it's the people. I love them more than I can say.

— Winter 2012

One

Welcome home

One of the peculiarities of the white race's presence in America is how little intention has been applied to it. As a people, wherever we have been, we have never really intended to be. The continent is said to have been discovered by an Italian who was on his way to India. The earliest explorers were looking for gold, which was, after an early streak of luck in Mexico, always somewhere farther on. Conquests and foundings were incidental to this search — which did not, and could not, end until the continent was finally laid open in an orgy of gold seeking in the middle of the last century. Once the unknown of geography was mapped, the industrial marketplace became the new frontier, and we continued, with largely the same motives and with increasing haste and anxiety, to displace ourselves — no longer with unity of direction, like a migrant flock, but like the refugees from a broken anthill. In our own time we have invaded foreign lands and the moon with the high-toned patriotism of the conquistador and the same mix of fantasy and avarice.

That is too simply put. It is substantially true, however, as a description of the dominant tendency in American history. The temptation, once that has been said, is to ascend altogether into rhetoric and inveigh equally against all our forebears and all present holders of office. To be just, however, it is necessary

1

> *to remember that there has been another tendency: the ten-*
> *dency to stay put, to say "No farther, this is the place." So far,*
> *this has been the weaker tendency, less glamorous, certainly*
> *less successful.*
>
> —Wendell Berry, *The Unsettling of America*

B Y THE TIME I ARRIVED BACK HOME I'd traveled more than seven hundred miles by train, slept in four different beds, given three talks,
introduced thirteen speakers and met more than three hundred new
people, none of whose names I could remember. I was exhausted and
frazzled, held together by one thought, the thought that always sustains
me at the ends of these speaking trips — I'm going to be home soon.

I am greeted first by the goats, who call out to see if I have food for
them, and then by the dogs that frisk and leap around me, gently chas-
tising me for failing to provide their daily head scratchings. I open the
door and am greeted, not by a smooth and peaceful immersion into the
paradise of domesticity but by my real and ordinary life in all its glory
and chaos.

Our two-year-old foster son screams "Mama!" and leaps into my
arms, while my six-year-old hugs my back and three boys simultaneously
try and tell me everything that has happened in my absence. My husband
pulls away from the stove where dinner is simmering and kisses me across
a mob of children, while my eldest, dribbling a basketball, shoots me a
quick pass in friendly greeting. The house is not perfectly tidy. It is not
an oasis of peace. The kindest possible description of its aesthetic would
be "lived in." It is just home — and it is unutterably beautiful to me.

A neighbor has dropped off a load of hay and it must be shifted into
the barn, so we all troop outside on the chilly November afternoon to
work and play together. The younger kids climb on the bales, the goats
nibble at their edges and Eric, the big boys and I make short work of
eighty bales of hay. After days of using my brain to talk about energy, climate and economy, I'm back to using my whole self, and it feels glorious.

In some measure, my home is not a place so much as it is people
— it would be home if I were coming back to a high-rise apartment in
Chicago or a brownstone in New York as long as my children and spouse
were there. And yet, the particulars of place matter. As I came down the

road back from my journey, the landscape, shifting from autumn into winter, spoke to me and called me home. My trip took me to lovely places full of wonderful people, but they did not call to me as my home does.

Things are changing here from moment to moment as the cold of winter begins to settle in and the nights get longer. The children grow and change, the livestock multiply, the landscape evolves, the climate changes. And yet, in human terms, essential elements remain the same. The sight of my children racing outside into the late fall sunshine, oblivious to mud from copious rain, my husband emerging from the barn where he is checking on a rabbit due to deliver a litter of babies any day, is both old and new. This place has seen these stories before — other children, other animals have lived and played and birthed and died here.

The basic structure of my life is intimately tied to the rocky foundation of my hundred-year-old house, the old Quaker barn beams that crisscross my living room and the new addition that we built for Eric's grandparents six years ago. Eric's grandparents have passed away now, but their place, their garden, their memories and legacy, remain.

My home is in the dirty laundry, covered with garden soil accumulated as my children helped plant bulbs. It is in the garden beds themselves, in perennials I planted that are settling in for winter, and in spring's new growth to come, in the plants from last season returned to the soil. My home is in the pregnant bellies of my goats, carrying their burdens lightly, and in the promise of their new kids to delight us — and support our work. It is in the bees, huddled in their hives, and in the chickens, resting upon their nests in these quiet darkening days.

My home is on the bookshelves, filled to overflowing, in the music made by my son, laboriously practicing piano, in the music of the wind against the chimes left here by the previous owners. It is in the sound of my neighbors' horses neighing across the fields and in the feel of the worn flannel on the sheets of my bed.

My home is a sense of place, an attachment to one place, one house, one set of people, one relationship between myself and a bit of dirt. It is the conditions that make it possible for me to live here — my home is my home because I am fortunate enough to have a home. I live in a nation where more and more people are losing their places and losing them more and more rapidly. In 2009 more than three million households — one in every thirty — lost their home to eviction or fore-closure. 2010 was a little better, parts of 2011 worse. The very fact that I have kept my home and do not immediately fear its loss is becoming increasingly unusual.

Money is not the only thing that can frame our relationship to home. A few months earlier, two consecutive hurricanes were driven inland to my area of upstate New York, dumping twenty inches of rain upon us. Up here in the hills it was a minor disaster: we lost our gardens, our apple crop, a car and some other small things to fallen trees and deep flooding, but our house was safe, situated as we are on a hill. In the valleys below us, however, thousands of people lost everything.

There's nothing unusual about the way I love my home, or about the people it ties me to, or even my relationship to the land beneath it. What is strange and different about my home is that part of the reason I do not live in fear of losing it is that I planned for a situation like the one most of us now find ourselves in — an unstable economy, a job that might disappear, sinking property values.

In many respects my home is just like yours — the place where beloved people, familiar things and a sense of comfort come together, the place that feels good and safe and reassuring to me. In other respects, it is very different — it is designed to allow me and my family to live well in highly variable circumstances, to use less money and less energy and fewer resources. My home is designed to produce more of what I need and cost me less than most American homes.

It's a process we've come to call "Adapting in Place" — that is, using what we have to make our lives run smoothly whether things are good or bad. And we've come to realize over the years that it isn't just our family that will need to do this — that most of us have to face the fact that the world is changing radically. We can see it changing before our eyes, as surely as the winter comes and the seasons shift. We have less wealth, our climate is less stable, we never know what we'll be paying for food, gas or heat, we can't count on many old assumptions. We need our lives to have a kind of resilience, to work for us in the face of difficulty.

Ideally, of course, we'd all have the money and government support to smooth over the changes in our way of life. New rail lines and public transport would be springing up all over. Inefficient housing would be replaced with energy-efficient, tightly built housing. Safety nets would be strengthened for those who can't make it without help. But exactly the opposite is happening – we're not investing in the things that matter most. The vast majority of the infrastructure building projects subsidized by Barack Obama's first-term economic stimulus funds, for example, went to existing highways and pre-planned programs that didn't do much to make our lives work better — programs that propped up the status quo by encouraging us to drive rather than share transport. Meanwhile states are slashing safety nets for kids, the disabled and the elderly left and right because they can't run the kind of deficits the federal government can.

The conversion of an ordinary old farmhouse to work with a lot less grid power, a lot less heating energy and a lot less money (among other things) started out as a way for us to live well on a small budget, but became more than that. Eventually it became part of a long-term attempt to imagine a way of life worth having. And that project is a really important one — perhaps one of the most important things we can do. For the last three generations, Americans and other Westerners have spent their time exporting a model life that simply can't go on — and we know it can't. We know for a fact that seven billion people cannot live the way Americans do — but that's what our TV shows, our movies, our economic policies, our belief in endless growth have sold.

Now the world is telling us they want what we've had all this time — no matter how dangerous to future generations, no matter how polluting or depleting, no matter what the cost. That is, they want the right to disregard all those issues, just as we have. So we have to show them another model. Both morally and practically, all of us need to offer up a good and viable vision of a way of life that uses only a fair share of the world's resources.

We came to this project simply — we had little money but a strong desire for a good life for ourselves, for our children and for our extended family. We wanted to eat good food, drink clean water, breathe good air. We wanted a home and a place to call our own, a stable place where our kids could live and thrive. We wanted our children to grow up with family. We wanted elderly family to live well as long as they lived. We wanted relationships with good neighbors and reasonable comfort. We wanted to do as little harm to others as possible, and have as happy a life as we could. Someone, we thought, had to model what a life with less that produced more could look like. Why not us?

And so, having no idea what we were getting into, we set to it. We didn't begin with grand dreams of changing the American way of life, but we've come to think that if there is going to be an alternative to the high-cost, high-waste life, someone has to model it. Why not us? For that matter, if not you, if not me, then who?

In the decade we've been here, we've looked at almost every system in our lives that provides us with something we need. We've changed the way we create and retain warmth, the way we buy, store and produce food, how we get and use water, the ways we clean and dry our clothes and every other place we use energy, money and resources. But this hasn't been a purely inward-looking prospect, because we've also focused on the systems in our communities and our culture that shape our lives and provide assistance and care, and found ways to use fewer resources in every one.

We are not perfect, and we haven't created an ideal life. Still, we use significantly less than the average American, if never quite as little as we'd like. We are slowly reducing our personal share of greenhouse gas emissions, our dependency on oil and coal. We don't worry about storms or natural disasters much anymore — we can weather an extended power outage and live well at home if we can't get out. We don't panic if something breaks and we don't have enough money to fix it — in most cases we have redundant backup systems that work for us. We're not pure and we're not perfect — we're real people who screw up a lot. But we are trying.

We still worry about money, but years and years of living on tight budgets — usually less than forty thousand dollars for our family of six, seven or more, and often much, much less — has made us comfortable with the prospect of facing harder times. We haven't found the magic bullet, but we've been careful about debt and living as far as possible below our means, and we have a measure of insulation. Our household economy — the work we do at home — reduces our expenses as well as meeting some of our needs outside the money economy. We barter with neighbors and share with friends and find that we need less and less as we learn more and more.

We've done this on a farm in rural upstate New York, where we've learned a lot about how to deal with the particular challenges of our place, family, climate and culture. But I've also spent the last few years working with people all over the world who want to do the same thing in their homes — people who want to feel safe and hopeful and make a life that works well with less. Most of them don't live next door to me — they live in apartments in Paris or Brooklyn or suburban homes outside Cleveland or Toronto. They don't have farms — they have a quarter or eighth of an acre in a leafy suburb, or a small city lot, or a balcony in an apartment complex. They don't necessarily need the same things my family does — their kids are grown or they never had any, they are disabled and can't do heavy work, or they are single and living in a dorm. What they need is a life that serves them, a sense they are living a viable dream and creating something with a future.

As much as I've enjoyed living my own story, I'm not sure it would make that interesting a book. The answer can never be "do it like me" — instead, the answer is for people to find their own ways to accomplish the same ends — less resource-intensive, less cost, lower carbon, safer, more sustainable, healthier, happier and more resilient — but where you are, with the people you love, with the money and resource you have for them. Like my sense of home, what I'm doing is tied to one place but is not particular to it. Instead, I've developed a set of tools and strategies that can be applied wherever the desire (or the need) exists. There's nothing precious about it, nothing restricted to the affluent, the rural, the white, the privileged. I know this because I know literally thousands of people who are adapting in place right now — that is, making the place they live in work for them. You'll meet some of them in this book.

It would be easy to dread this change; living with less sounds pretty dire when you can't envision what "less" looks like. And that's the problem — we have a pretty clear vision of "the American dream" and know more or less what it entails. But we don't have a clear vision at all of our future, and that scares the heck out of us. We think about "less" and think "harder, more inconvenient, more painful, more frightening, different and I can't figure it out." That's why we need a picture, and a set of plans for getting there.

The process of adapting in place requires a new way of thinking about the idea of "home," of gathering up what we love about our places and our lives and preserving those people and things that matter most to us, and giving them a hope for the future. Because right now most of the presumptions inherent in our way of life involve us asking future generations to pay the price for our failures — for our inaction on climate change, for our borrowing against their future economically and for our reckless use of resources. Every human culture believes in protecting and preserving the future — and yet, somehow, we've become a people who, instead of making sacrifices to offer better to the next generation, devours their share of the world instead.

I don't believe most of us want that — and if we could see our way to something better, I believe we'd jump at it. But we live in a world full of people telling us that things can go on this way forever — even as things begin to fall apart. The only way to convince people to change is to give them a different dream to hold on to.

I'm not arrogant enough to think that I could invent a new dream or vision for all of us. But I do think that we can do it collectively, that we can provide something just as powerful as what we're sold by Madison Avenue — a new story to tell about ourselves. And if we can change our stories, and create a way of life that is both worth having now and that has a future, maybe we can change other things, too.

How do we do this? The first thing we have to do is understand the difference between the stories we have been told and the reality that we live, what it means to stay in one place and how we might begin to make a real home there. And that's what this book is about — about coming home to ourselves and our lives and giving them a future. What's miraculous about home is that once you live there, no matter how chaotic or messy or imperfect the future, it has that glorious quality of being home. Once we learn to fully live in our place, in our world as it is, we can feel at home there — and begin to build upon that.

What would such an experience of home look like, though? How might it be achieved? What might it mean to settle and stay in one place and build this new life in a world where those things were valued, and where the shared project of finding our way home might inspire us?

Wendell Berry wrote *The Unsettling of America*, quoted at the beginning of the chapter, before I was born. In it he articulated the tension in American identity between the impulse to stop and stay and the impulse to always go on to the next thing. Many of us now find that there is no next new frontier, that one place suffers from much the same gradual economic and ecological decline as another.

This is a slow and sometimes painful realization, that we are here where we are. It can be difficult to give up the notion of moving on, to recognize that the next thing may not represent a substantial shift in our fortunes, that the next move may not be to a better life. It can be hard to consider that we may have chosen without choosing to stay, because we can no longer sell or no longer afford to move. We are here. We are home.

I know that many of my readers are not where they plan to be, and many of us may move and seek something better. There are many particulars of migration and movement in our future — in fact, I suspect many of these movements may, in some degree, track a backward path past the frontiers of each stage in America. As climate change accelerates, perhaps the new call becomes "Go East, Young Man — at least there's water!" Others may be driven, not back but in wholly new directions.

We know that coastal population centers will have to be unsettled or moved, we know that outer exurbia may fall to high gas prices. And yet, I think there is a larger truth here — that what we have now may be the starting point for a new life — one with radically different priorities and emphasis, but building on our present infrastructure.

Hence, of course, the idea of Adapting in Place for both those who have chosen something optimal and those who have had their place thrust upon them. The truth is that even those who build their dream houses move — the average stay in a "dream house" is only seven years in the US. Those who chose the "perfect" place and those who did not choose at all may have more in common than they think. We must acknowledge that on some level, it is possible to organize people around the idea of staying here, wherever here may be, because we are here and the ground below us is at the root of what we have to sustain us.

Much of what I write about involves enlisting the people around you. This is an enormously difficult job for most of us — partly because of the anomie of our culture, partly because we are not accustomed to community, partly simply because we have not had to. For several generations each of us could live a fossil-fueled, private solution to needs once met collectively.

The tools we have to get our next-door neighbors to work with us are not easy ones — some people do it, others find themselves saying "OK, I'm here, but I'm fundamentally alone, and I can only go so far that way." Any hope of settling meaningfully — in the largest sense of the word, that of transforming our homes and nations, wherever they may be, into places where the dominant narrative is overturned and we are enlisted into the vast project of making our here livable — must begin with other people. How do you get them together?

Wendell Berry rightly insists that we do have in us, even here in America, a strain of thought to draw on that is about staying, about making the place you live in better, about committing to a piece of land and a set of people. Berry keeps reminding us of this, requiring that we see it in the overarching narrative of always moving for the better job, the bigger house, the next frontier, the final frontier.

We do have a history to draw upon — and that matters. In our book *A Nation of Farmers*, Aaron Newton and I wrote about the problem of choosing a history:

> The simple truth is that the glorification of our past makes us believe lies. Glorification of our State makes us accept unacceptable things. And yet, there is a United States worth believing in — moments in history in which competing forces of powerful and weak met and created something decent, something worth treasuring and admiring. It never happened without resistance, but neither was the story always a narrative of good people and evil leaders — it is far more complicated than that.
>
> All of us were taught a state- and hero-centered history that erased too many ordinary contributions and focused our national pride on the wrong things. But we did have that teaching; we did learn that nationalism. Perhaps a large part of our projects is the unlearning of the untruths, but smashing idols isn't enough — we need to give people who love their country a place to put that love, give those who derive hope and comfort

from their sense of the past a past to attach themselves
to.

James H. Kunstler has described the dangers of the "psychology of previous investment" when applied to our driving culture — he observes that we become so attached to the things we have invested ourselves in that we go on preserving them long after such preservation has become destructive. Still, perhaps this urge can work for us as well as against us, if we can articulate a past, a history, something worth preserving and staying for that lays the ground for a livable future. That history of staying, thrust upon us now as it is, may be something to hold on to.

In tribute, then, to Berry's *Unsettling of America* and his long call for resettlement, I have come to think of my/our project in terms of Settlement. And this invokes something else worth invoking — the Settlement movement of the nineteenth and twentieth centuries, conceived as a way to remedy class conflict and integrate immigrants into a society. Never have those two goals seemed more relevant than today. As I write this, the Occupy movement has class in its sights, while immigration takes a political center stage in the coming election.

The Settlement movement called for ordinary people to go and live among the poor, like the poor, offering what they could to remediate their circumstances — to live together, and from one another learn and build something better. Lillian Wald, Dorothy Day, Jane Addams — their focus on the idea of a settlement as a means to integrate rather than disintegrate, to help people learn to live where they were, seems eminently relevant to us as we move toward a world where most of us are poorer, less secure, moving off the frontier into a changing world.

We must do it in community, we must work with people we once did not need, we must adjust our way of life. We must, ultimately, settle, in the sense of finding a home in places we thought we were only resting in momentarily. We must settle, in the sense of finding a vision that accepts what is viable in a settled way of life, to shift our happiness and expectations to meet our new realities rather than obsess about the lost and destructive dominant discourse. We must settle, in the sense of going out among people we did not choose, whose common ground is that they too have entered the process of settlement with us.

It is settlement that I think about when I think about how to survive the economic instability that has always been here but is newly acute. It is settlement that I write about — and in the end, it will be settlement, if we can do it, that creates something worth having for our posterity. Settlement, in the end is not loss but gain — a moment in which we turn around and realize that, like Dorothy in *The Wizard of Oz*, we had within us the means to find our way home all along.

> *We are living in the most destructive and, hence, the most stupid period of the history of our species. The list of its undeniable abominations is long and hardly bearable. And these abominations are not balanced or compensated or atoned for by the list, endlessly reiterated, of our scientific achievements. Some people are moved, now and again, to deplore one abomination or another. Others ... deplore the whole list and its causes. Much protest is naive; it expects quick, visible improvement and despairs and gives up when such improvement does not come. Protesters who hold out longer have perhaps understood that success is not the proper goal. If protest depended on success, there would be little protest of any durability or significance. History simply affords too little evidence that anyone's individual protest is of any use. Protest that endures, I think, is moved by a hope far more modest than that of public success: namely, the hope of preserving qualities in one's own heart and spirit that would be destroyed by acquiescence.*
>
> — Wendell Berry, *A Poem of Difficult Hope*

I. On not outrunning the boom

As you can probably imagine, my husband sometimes has more than a bit to put up with being married to me. One of the things that bothers him the most is that I'm absolutely no fun at movies. If you remember the show MST3K, I'm like them — all the time. There's something about the darkened room that brings out the snarky comments.

Early in our marriage we realized that we were both happier if we limited our joint film excursions to one of two categories — truly great movies, which we both enjoy, or ones bad enough that Eric doesn't mind pitching in on the commentary. My absolute favorite movie for this second purpose is the ubiquitous "outrunning the explosion" deus ex machina flick, in which our hero(ine) — who in any rational world would now be maimed, dead or otherwise out of the public eye — manages to suspend the laws of physics long enough to run faster than an exploding bomb.

Every thriller or disaster film on the planet has an ordinary outrunning of the boom, but I do like the variants composed by various filmmakers. Consider "outrunning the temperature extremes" in *Day After Tomorrow*, "outrunning the laser beam" in various space operas, "outrunning the meteorites" in *Deep Impact* and *Armageddon* and my newest fave, "outrunning the Yellowstone mega-caldera" in *2012* (which is particularly awesome because it is followed by "outrunning the caldera ash cloud," which apparently can be done, as the cloud overspreads Washington DC, by remaining comfortably in Las Vegas, where it is sunny and beautiful).

The convention is almost unworthy of comment, like the rule that knocking people on the head always knocks them unconscious but never gets our hero(ine) up on murder charges for causing accidental death, or the fact that heroic children in movies never feel the need to eat, whine or go the bathroom. The only reason I mention it here is that we accept it as ubiquitous — we know it is ridiculous, of course, but we are also so accustomed to this association of "disaster, suspension of the laws of physics and running super-fast" that on some level, it permeates our consciousness. The thing is, the ubiquitous does matter, even when we know deep down that it is false.

That's troubling because the truths of the disasters we are actually already undergoing is precisely the opposite of what film tells us. First of all, the laws of physics, instead of being conveniently suspended whenever they are really, really unpleasant, are in fact fundamental and definitive. That is, when something is not sustainable, it turns out that it doesn't go on forever. This, we are finding out, applies to burning fossil fuels in several respects.

If you know something really can't scale, it usually turns out that it doesn't. If it looks like material, physical limitations are closing in on you, it turns out they actually are. The laws of physics do not, in fact, go on holiday just because we would very much like them to. This may seem obvious, and yet many millions of people assume that these laws don't apply to them. And many millions more who do intellectually understand that the laws do apply to them choose not to grasp the real implications all the way to the bottom.

Despite the fact that we know we are burning fossil fuels unsustainably and that costs will go up and availability come down after the first half is gone, we keep doing it. Despite the fact that we know we are warming the planet, we keep on doing that too.

The second thing to learn from the movies is that running away is not the answer. We now know that in the near future, many people will likely have no choice but to leave places they want to stay due to climate change and energy depletion — the UN estimates of refugees come in the billions. If, however, there is a partial solution to the multi-pronged ecological disaster we're undergoing, it is this — don't run, stop and stay. The refugees themselves will eventually have to find a place — or someone will have to make one for them.

In disaster films, our hero (it is usually a guy, either literally or metaphorically Bruce Willis) has insider knowledge — he calls it the minute the disaster happens, and unlike the rest of the bit players who die in the background, he races away to the only safe spot, usually saving some adorable moppet and a beautiful woman or two. From this experience, he comes to understand (through intervention of attractive female and adorable moppet) what is truly important in this life. It turns out what is really important is home and family and kids, apple pie and cuteness, but he could only learn this by watching the world end, through an external crisis journey that implies that he must have been on some kind of inner journey too (disaster movies are too busy toppling cultural icons to actually build characters with depth).

Now consider the reality. In fact, our carbon problem is very simple. We can't burn all the carbon we do have, and we don't have enough to build our way out of burning it. We have to use less. What are the obvious ways of using less? Well, for starters we could stop running, stay home and get out of our vehicles.

Because we cannot run away from it. Climate change will not come equitably to every place, but it will come everywhere. Energy depletion

too will come unevenly, but it will come, and so will the financial consequences of both. The ways to mitigate them are the exact opposite of
running away to discover what we should have known already — we
need to appreciate what we have here, and slow down further.

Slow down long enough to plant more trees that mitigate climate
change, lower temperatures and respire water. Slow down long enough
to know the people around you, rather than relying on a single, heroic
gesture. Inaugurate the heroism on the ordinary acts of human generosity that are the foundation of community. Slow down enough to
know that there really is nothing heroic at all about abandoning the
great masses to their fate while you and the privileged few who accom-
pany you escape — that unlike in the movies, people dying around you
are not stock characters who rise again, but lives for which you bear
some responsibility.

Moreover, we are conditioned by film to believe that the disaster is
not real until icons topple — the head of the Statue of Liberty toppling,
the monument falling, the waves washing away the city. Sometimes it
does happen that way — the crisis in the New Orleans Superdome or
the collapsing towers of the World Trade Center do look a lot like scenes
from an action movie. But disasters are slow as well, sometimes imper-
ceptibly slow. The disaster comes when the birth of young birds and the
cycle of the food source they grow on no longer coincide, when the ordinary costs of food, gas and housing rise beyond the means of ordinary
people, when the waters are unfishable and jobs to buy food not forthcoming. Catastrophes are measured in real income declines, expiring
unemployment, foreclosures, tropical disease, species extinction — the
loss not of one vast monument but of the ordinary anchors of our world.

When confronted with disaster, our impulse to run is real — but for
the most part, it isn't the answer. If our places remain habitable, if our
world has a future, it is because we stay — stay to build the sea wall,
stay to plant the trees, stay home and out of our cars, stay to talk to the
neighbors, stay to mend and repair rather than buy new, stay to share
and protect. In some profound way, we know that we cannot truly out-
run the boom, but it has not yet fully penetrated that running is the
wrong answer for most of us, that they serve best who stand and wait —
and work where they stand.

II. Settling, occupying, stepping up

In the circles I run and write in, it is a common device to claim that other thinkers and writers have failed to understand the real, deepest cause of our problems, and have instead embarked upon too superficial a narrative explanation.

What's fascinating about this is that the thinkers doing so are almost always correct — that is, they are nearly always right that someone has missed a deep underlying cause. The reason for this is that causes are nearly as ample as effects. Thus the person who laments America's dependence on foreign oil can be usefully corrected by someone who observes that the problem is everyone's dependence on a finite resource, rather than a geopolitical error of resource development. The same person speaking of finite resources can then be corrected by someone who observes that a growing population is the "real problem" — that with few enough people, resource constraints would not be an issue. The person arguing in favor of population as the central underlying issue could then be corrected on several grounds — one might, for example, argue that the fundamental problem is the lack of equity between men and women, in which women lack the means and freedom to control their fertility or personal economies. Or you might argue that the fundamental problem is not population but social inequity — that the poor have access only to children as a source of improving their well-being. Both of these critiques (and plenty of others) would, in fact, be correct, and both would also be subject to further correction. It is, as they say, turtles all the way down.

I am cautious, then, of trying to identify first causes, because they are so easily overturned. At the same time, however, I find the articulation of origins, if transient and uncertain, to be valuable in that each exercise in imagining a root cause allows us to see our errors in new and useful ways. So recognizing that someone will inevitably argue that something else is truly the root cause and my own articulations are mere symptoms, I would like to suggest that we do not have a resource problem, or a climate problem, or an economic problem — we have a way of life problem.

Several years ago I was invited to attend a protest march on the coal plant that supplied the capital with energy. Many other people, including Wendell Berry, attended, marching to demand we stop warming the planet with coal. I wished to join in but couldn't, and when I talked to some friends who were planning to attend, I felt that there was a gap in their understanding.

Many of the younger people I met who were excited to bus down to Washington understood very well the dangers of coal — of mining and mountaintop removal, of contamination of water or destabilization of the climate — and were courageously willing to stand up to stop coal consumption. What was missing from this protest in some cases was a sense of the connection between that and how they would live. Coal is the single largest source of electricity in the US — how many of them were prepared to live with about half as much electricity?

Some undoubtedly were. Wendell Berry, for example, has tried for decades to convince Americans that the pre-electric past was not hell. But most of the young people I met on their way to the protest, and even some of the older ones, were not. They felt that we should replace our coal with renewables, and if they understood the technical and resource challenges in doing so, assumed (or preferred to believe) that we could do this rapidly without substantive sacrifice or personal constraint. They saw the merits of the protest and of closing the coal plant, which were manifest. Without the corresponding grasp of a daily life, a new American dream that consumes far, far less, however, such protests are doomed to failure, because we do not really want them to succeed, do not really want the life we would get if anyone took us seriously.

As the Occupy movement rose up in America, I was struck with the same disconnect — the attacks on corporate capitalism were absolutely correct, compelling and right. The protesters recognized that we have lost ground and control in ways that are deeply disturbing. But most of the ones I knew failed to fully grasp the way their dependence on the same corporate interests for their most basic needs — the banks for the mortgages that shelter them, large agricultural and processed food corporations for the food they eat, and onward — undermine their protest. I met few people fully prepared to live without the corporations they deplore.

I believe strongly in political action. I took part in my first protest as a teenager, I have been arrested for political reasons, and I feel public protest is good for the soul, not just for drawing attention or making change. I did not occupy or fight the capital coal plant, however, because I had to stay home — my son was nursing, my husband was working, the farm needed me — and I have come to think that this staying home had its merits as well. I do not say this to devalue public protest, which I think has an important role. But I do think that protest must be tied to the creation of other kinds of daily change.

This prioritization of protest over the emergence of an ordinary, sustainable life is understandable in a society that prefers the large and shiny to the small and domestic, and that demeans daily personal actions and ways of life as unimportant. I have in much of my other work attempted to articulate the ways in which our personal actions are, in fact, political. I have pointed out the many ways in which the conventional distinctions between personal and political are intellectually bankrupt, and while I may have made a modest fame in doing so, I've mostly failed so far.

This is problematic because it is precisely the emergence of a life worth living — and that can be lived by all the seven to nine billion people who will share our planet in the coming years — that is most urgently necessary. If creating and modeling some sort of preliminary life of this sort is my project, I come to it well after Berry, and less gracefully. Still, such a vast project with so few participants can always use one more.

In many ways, the story of the twentieth and early twenty-first century has been the overturning of one way of life (very broadly construed) and the emergence of another throughout the world. The consequences of this way of life and its variants are evident — we consume more of everything, so much so that we are using more than the planet can sustain, and rapidly making the future resources of the planet less available. There simply is no alternate calculation, no sleight of hand that makes the American way of life viable on a crowded planet.

This way of life had some true merits, and I don't want to deny them. Its greatest virtue (and great flaw — how often our great strengths and flaws are one) has been the recognition of the value of at least some of the people who are here now, a prioritization of the present.

I am inclined to be somewhat kinder to this prioritization than Berry is above (and Berry is, of course, more nuanced than any single quote could properly indicate) and argue that in many ways the people of the present were calling out to be recognized. Our prioritization of the present has brought great good to many individuals — the children who did not die before age five, the mothers and fathers who got to keep them, the recognition that it was not enough to wait for heaven's justice, if such a thing exists, to provide freedom and justice for people of color or women, that those who were here now deserved such things. The sense that the people who were here now deserve more and better now is not inherently a bad thing.

The difficulty is that our virtue became the single most destructive flaw of all time. The recognition that those who were here now deserved more became, as such things often do, pathological. Not only did we deserve clean water and children who would not die before age five, but also electricity, private transportation, college education for everyone, a personal computer in every home, etc, etc. We moved rapidly beyond what could actually be achieved by every person, while wholly abandoning the project of preserving enough for any future generation. And the prioritization of the present meant an increase in struggles between multiple presents — the conflict between America and China for supremacy (now largely over and largely lost by the US) can be seen as a conflict between two presents, whose needs cannot simultaneously and equitably be met. Most of the rest of the world was never even in the running — and that was the great underlying lie of all of this, because implicit in the increasing catalog of needs was the reality that when some people got so many of their needs met, more die as a result.

Most of all, the story that prioritizes those who are here now erases those who will be here later — they have no claim. One could trace the history of the twentieth century as a narrative in which a way of life that, for all its limitations, presumed that the future had some rights gave way to a new way of life with no future, a pact in which one person's posterity cannot be connected to ours, so we cannot be responsible for them.

First we altered the material space in which we lived so that generations of people who expected to live and work in approximately the same places as their parents and be followed by future generations no longer had any connection to place. We prioritized mobility and separation, so much so that the "generation gap" of the 1960s and the snide jokes about grown children living in their parents' basements came to convince us that the highest goal of adulthood was to get away from your past in a literal, material sense. Why preserve what you have? Why hold on to the old house, the old farm, the land, the family history? If you have raised your children to erase any connection to their past, taught / encouraged them to grow beyond their history, to abandon and dismiss those things, why preserve them? Why limit consumption just because it takes from the future? What certainty do you have that you will have a future, or that your grandchildren will come to visit? Why think seven generations ahead after seventy years of understanding at some visceral level that others could destroy the habitability of the world — is it not enough to hold what you can as long as you live?

It is, of course, also extremely profitable to consume a great deal and sell the future, so that has taken on its own life. It is even more profitable if you can also convince those who have lived quite modestly with fewer resources that they would be better off if they lived like those who have abandoned the future for the present, and this, appealing as it does to our most selfish and petty interests, is not difficult.

All of which is a complex way of saying that the problem is how we live — the "non-negotiable" American way of life (as a previous vice-president was heard to put it), which is now, with minor variants, the way of life most of the planet aspires to. No one, of course, is willing to take full responsibility for this — as we see in the battles over responsibility for anthropogenic global warming. China cannot constrain its emissions, we are told, because it is bringing its people out of poverty and into the way of life that we in America pioneered. America cannot constrain its emissions in part because China will not, and also because we must strive mightily to retain what's left of our economic standards. Thus we live in a global game of chicken with little hope of any actual restraint.

Except, perhaps this — we could change our way of life. We who became the global trendsetters, however inadvertently, tell an idealized story of how much better and happier we are through consumption, when we might consider telling another story. And if we told it compellingly enough we might just engage others, as our original story of freedom and happiness gained through the abandonment of future claims, future people and future rights.

In the quote I began with, Wendell Berry attempts to articulate the value of protest, particularly protest that is in many ways doomed to failure, by meditating on Hayden Carruther's poem "On Being Asked to Write a Poem Against the War in Vietnam." Since "protest doomed to failure" often describes the work I do quite aptly, I found his arguments compelling. Though I should add that I sincerely think we could — with protest and action and, most of all, the emergence of a new way of life — do a great deal to mitigate our circumstances.

That said, I do think that even were I — and the many others who have read the numbers and come to the conclusion that we cannot go on as we are — to be successful beyond even my wildest aspirations, we would fail, indeed have already failed, to save many lives, to protect species and places and the viability of future lives as well as present ones. This is the human condition, to be doomed to failure, and we are at the moment more doomed than ever — or as Berry says later in the same essay, "And what might have been the spiritual economy of Eden, when there was no knowledge of despair and sorrow? We don't need to worry about that."

Nearly everyone who thinks about these things knows that we are, to put it bluntly, plenty doomed enough, and it wears on us. I get several emails every day that essentially say, "I agree with you and try to do my part, I consume little and less each year, I grow a garden, I tend my place and my community, and yet I live each day surrounded by people who destroy what I do in a moment, who care nothing about all this. I feel that I bear all the disadvantages of this — I have less than they do in a culture that doesn't value less, I struggle more with my time in a culture that believes that all labor should be saved by burning fossil fuels, I live as rightly and honestly as I can, but it wears on me to always do the hard thing and have less. How do you live with this?"

Berry offers us one possible answer — that the point of our protest is not to change our neighbors or the world, but to create a world in which we have at least preserved the value of things. By valuing them, we have at least held inside ourselves the fact that these things matter. Which is small consolation when your dreams are grand and the necessities so vast and urgent.

I'd offer another consolation, however, because I believe there is another value to protest — and by this I mean protest in our lives as well as political protest. It is this — when protest is successful, on those

rare and remarkable and wondrous occasions when resistance is possible, it is successful not because of the pure, clear persistence of actors
who carry signs or passively protest or fight legal battles. Instead, it is
successful because political protest is chained not to doors or trees but
to the emergence of a new way of life. This way of life is not perfect or
sufficient, but the overwhelming emergence of something new and different in ordinary and daily ways is a hallmark of almost every successful
political protest.

Thus the success of the civil rights movement — which hardly eliminated racism or inequity but did make many things possible that were
not before, and did at least transform some of the ways that people lived
together — depended not just on protest but on the emergence of a new
way of daily life in which black and white people who had previously
lived together in one set of relationships began to tentatively develop a
new one, involving shared schools, meals and livelihoods.

The success of gay rights protests, from the Stonewall Riots to peaceful marches to legal challenges to the blood throwing of ACT UP, has
been linked to the emergence of a culture in which gay people are now
open and honest family members, neighbors, loved ones and friends,
and in which we expect to have Dave and Jim and their daughter over
for dinner along with Rose and Steve and their daughter.

I know about the daily acts and transformational changes of the civil
rights movement from those who have managed to capture the history
of ordinary life before, after and during this period of rapid change. I
know about the daily acts and transformational changes of the gay rights
movement because I lived within it — saw the ways that my mothers,
together at church, at my school, among our neighbors, changed the
way people thought.

It is much easier to draw attention to a parade, a protest, a legal
event, and these absolutely matter, but what mattered as much or more
were the everyday actions of ordinary people who went about the hard
work of developing a life in which black and white people, or gay and
straight people, lived together differently than they had before. It is
often assumed that the public protests created the way of life, but I
would argue otherwise — the public protests are an expression, a call to
action, a way of drawing attention. They matter, but they matter only

so much as they enable and support a profound transformation that is already underway.

This is the true value of protest, and why I am so very convinced that it matters that we both protest the totalizing, all-encompassing nature of our consumptive, destructive society, and also that we nurture and create and explore and develop the emergence of a new way of life. I know from watching the lives of my parents that this kind of work is tiring, and seems to have few public rewards. A protest is dramatic, it is exciting, you can attribute a great deal to it, but it is the life that underlies it that changes the world in the end.

I understand why it is frustrating to have less and use less, to be mocked or disdained or simply regarded as strange and outside the norm. In a society where public protest is regarded as "action" and living is regarded as "inaction," I understand why you might feel like you were accomplishing nothing or changing nothing.

At the same time, when I was eight and my parents came out to me, they were afraid. They were so afraid that they concealed their relationship, only revealing it to their children after a long time. They feared losing custody of my sisters and me, they feared loss of jobs, they feared physical attacks, and they had reason for fear. We could not let people know.

Seven years later, my mother and stepmother were foster parents, caring for other people's children, implicitly recognized in many quarters as better parents than a significant number of straight people. They were still frightened sometimes, but things were better. Nine years later, my stepmother came and spoke to my high school class about being a lesbian and gay and lesbian issues, with the full support of my school principal. Ten years later, my mother and stepmother were married in their church, in a celebration that included their grown children, their forthcoming first grandchild in utero and most of their congregation. A few years after that they were married at city hall in the town they had resided in for nearly thirty years.

There were a few moments in my childhood when I looked and said "things are changing." But for the most part, I was barely aware that my mothers and I and my sisters and millions of gay families were engaged in the creation of a way of life that made space for people who had once been marginalized. I knew many people who despaired at various points, who said "we will never be able to...." And some of them were right, they still aren't able.

Yet many of them were wrong — now they can. Saying that we have not solved it all, that gay people still suffer discrimination, that gay kids still kill themselves, that the beatings have continued although morale has improved, is entirely true — but it doesn't change the fact that the world is different, that gay lives are better, and there is more to be done, but what has been accomplished was worth accomplishing and mattered enormously.

We know it is possible for people to use vastly fewer resources, produce vastly fewer emissions, live with much less than we do and still have good and worthwhile lives — we know this because our great-grandparents did it and because people in the world are doing it now. We know there are things in our present that we need to preserve for our future, and things that we must and can abandon. What those are and how we do this is our project in the world. Whether you call it adapting in place or creating a new life or a quiet domestic political protest or anything you want, this is the only thing left that can save the world — or at least a little piece of it. The political process will follow the emergence of a new way of life, and there will be plenty of things for us to chain ourselves to, to march against, to speak out for, to go to jail for, to challenge in a court of law. All of those things, however, must be subsequent to this — that we make a life worth living, that allows us all to live, and that makes a place for posterity.

It isn't an easy project in a world that assumes a great deal of energy and emissions, that says freedom is consumer choice and participation is mandatory and wealth is our goal. So when you are in your garden, when you ride your bicycle or walk, when you explain to your neighbor yet again why you don't want their lawn chemicals on your yard, when you hang out your laundry, when you deliver a meal to a neighbor who is ill, when you say "no, we don't do that," when you teach your children who you are and why you do the difficult thing, when you try and convince yourself that you aren't too tired, when you get up in the morning and it looks like all you've done is pointless, remember this — you are doing something hard and vast and new. Without your work and courage there is no hope at all for all of those with the courage to chain themselves at the gates. Without those who chain themselves at the gates, enough people will not know what you have done. With both together, change begins.

III. My house and Al Gore's house: finding a fair share

Not long ago I was out at a dinner of climate activists, at the beginning of a conference, and as we were climbing into the car of one of the program leaders, there was talk about whose car was messier. This is a competition I always win — I mentioned to them that not only do I have little kids in my car, messing it up, but I drive goats around in my Taurus.

Several people asked me why I drive goats in a car, which even to me seemed like a reasonable question. The answer is that I am a farmer with goats but no pickup truck, so when they go to be bred or to the vet, they travel in the back seat, sometimes with their heads hanging out the window (once we stopped for gas and the attendant asked us "what kind of dog is that?").

Why don't I have a pickup? Don't all farmers have to have a truck? I admitted a truck would be a nice thing. As it is, a few times a year we barter for use of a truck with a friend of mine; she trades it for use of our pasture for her sheep and donkey. It is a bit of hassle to have to put down newspaper for the goats in the car, and to be reliant on my friend's truck when we want to get hay or take poultry to the butcher. But we are trying to live a comparatively low-resource life, and I know that if we owned a truck, we'd use it a lot more than we do. By not owning one, we make sure that when we use a low-mileage vehicle, we really need to.

The other speaker, a scientist from the CDC and an expert on the medical implications of global warming, was kind of mystified and skeptical that the inconvenience was worth it. Like most climate scientists I know, he didn't seem to believe that personal actions matter that much — and there's something to be said for his case. In the great scheme of things, whether I have a truck or not isn't very important. I could drive my goats around with the a/c running and the windows down in a Hummer, and it wouldn't be a drop in the bucket in world climate emissions. And yet, I think it does matter — not just for me, but in general.

The very first time I was asked to do a public presentation on peak oil and climate change, one of the people in the audience, an older man, stood up and said to me, "Look, you may be right, this sounds right. But a lot of people sound right, and I just want to know why I should believe you. I don't know whose papers to read or how to read them for the science — I never took a lot of science in school, and that was fifty years ago. What I want to know is if it is true, why don't the people who say it is true act that way? I've been hanging my laundry out on the line for forty years and more, and my wife just got us a dryer. Now you are saying I shouldn't use it. And I won't if you can show me a climate scientist out there with his underwear out on the line."

Now logically speaking, whether any given climate scientist hangs his laundry, runs it through the dryer or delights in the feeling of damp shorts is really not the point. It doesn't make a bit of difference to whether his computer models are correct. Whether a climate scientist drives an SUV or takes the bus makes no difference to the data revealed by her ice core samples. This is a red herring.

And yet, it isn't just a red herring. The perception of fairness and justice is a really big deal for people, and to underestimate its importance, I think, misses a central point. This guy was saying that he'd consider giving up some of his luxuries — but only if he felt that the people who were demanding he do so were also giving theirs up.

There's considerable psychological research that suggests that fairness matters an awful lot to us. In one paper, a study used a "Prisoner's Dilemma"-type game in which one recipient receives painful shocks to show whether our empathy for people's pain is affected by how we perceive the fairness of their actions. All participants found less empathetic responses when the person getting the shocks was acting unfairly. In men, it was found that not only were they not feeling empathy, but they received pleasure thinking that someone was getting revenge.

Other research suggests that people will even act against their own interests to avoid perceived unfairness — in fact, we can see this in many debates on social welfare policies. Many of the people who oppose these programs are among those who would benefit the most from them — the American healthcare debate is a good example. But the sense that others would benefit unfairly or more than they is so troubling to them that they often oppose the program, despite the fact that it would help them.

Similarly, historical evidence suggests that things that seem completely impossible to us now, things that no one believes are politically palatable, actually could be politically palatable if they were reframed in terms of fairness. Amy Bentley, whose book *Eating for Victory* focuses on food rationing and the relationship of food to World War II, observes that food rationing was actually fairly popular during World War II. This sounds very strange to our ears — who believes that some form of rationing would be politically viable? And yet, it was — because it was largely framed in terms of fairness. Women worried that without rationing, limited supplies of meat or sugar would be bought up by others, or that prices would rise out of reach due to scarcity. Rationing ensured a fair share for everyone, to the extent that after it was lifted, a substantial portion of the populace felt it had been lifted too soon and was willing to consider reinstating it.

The same thing is true of 1970s' gas rationing — in areas where gas was rationed, people reported lower degrees of concern about gas access and greater degrees of happiness. No one liked waiting in line to buy gas, but what really worried them was the idea that someone would get there before them and they wouldn't be able to get any gas. A program that made sure they were being treated fairly increased their security.

And this is what I detect in the question that man asked me — this quest for fairness. This is what underlies the anger that many people feel about Al Gore's house — OK, they know that the former vice-president isn't going to live in a hovel, but they feel that if Gore is going to call for constraints and changes in their lives, that he should enact them himself, that there's something wrong with calling for restraint in others and not showing it in your own life.

This plays out beyond the personal level — it's precisely the battle that is going on at the international level. The question of how we are to distribute the burden of dealing with climate change may, in the end, be the deal breaker. Russia, China, India and other nations of the Global South call out "foul!" when nations like Britain, Australia, the US and Canada want to continue to emit vastly more per person than they do. The US whines that there's nothing they can do without China, because there are so many people there, and it isn't fair. And if someone seems to be getting off unfairly, well, we'll let the whole world go to hell rather than have that happen.

It is true that this doesn't really make much sense, but I'm not at all convinced that a rational argument about why things don't have to be fair will ever affect most people's deep-seated need for fairness. Assuming that we really should be rational beings all the time never has worked yet. Ultimately, I suspect that we're going to have to accept that, for a chunk of the population, perceived fairness will always outweigh everything. Even though climate scientists could reasonably say it is more important that they go to conferences and compare data than it is that Steve down the street go see Granny twice a year in Cleveland and taking his every-two-year trip to Cancun, the reality is that Steve doesn't see it that way. If we're going to ask him to constrain his flying, everyone has to do it, and the scientists will just have to video-conference. Even though it doesn't matter even a tiny bit for total emissions whether I fly to Georgia for my climate conference or take the train, whether my goat goes in the front seat or in the pickup, it does matter. And so I put my behind on the train for 22 hours, and put down the newspaper for the goat.

There's also a credibility factor here — the painful truth is that people look for confirmation when told things that are strange or disturbing. If you believe that climate change or peak oil could really transform the world, people believe that you should be living your life that way. If you aren't, they start to wonder — how serious is this?

It isn't fair that fairness counts so much — it makes it a lot harder for people. But that is the reality — that any strategies with any meaningful hope of social acceptance must come with the advantage of being fair and equitable. We're going to have to put our money where our mouths are.

Two

Planning for both a future and failure

"He'll never catch up!" the Sicilian cried. "Inconceivable!"
"You keep using that word!" the Spaniard snapped.
"I don't think it means what you think it does."
— William Goldman, *The Princess Bride*

A FEW YEARS AGO MY AREA OF THE COUNTRY had a major sleet, snow and ice storm. We had more than two inches of ice, plus another six of snow and sleet. In the end, almost two million people in New England and New York were without power, many for more than a week. When we heard about the storm, my family set to work making sure we were ready for it.

We moved some of the firewood that sits in our mudroom into the depleted wood boxes in the house, and began moving more wood into the mudroom, so that we wouldn't have to chip the wood we use to warm our house out from a sheet of ice. We checked the freezer to make sure it was full, and added a few bottles of water to keep it at capacity longer, which helps keep food cold longer. I took a quick look at my pressure canner, which I would use in an extended power outage to can what could be salvaged from our freezer so that we didn't lose our food. We already keep our refrigerated food on our porch in winter, making use of natural cooling instead of electric refrigeration, so no worries about that on such a cold day.

We made sure we knew where all the flashlights and the extra bat-teries were, put the solar lantern in the window to charge, threw on an extra load of laundry in case it was a few days before the next one could go in and generally got ready for a power outage. We reassured the boys by changing the batteries in their LED nightlights and giving each one his own flashlight. We put our extra rechargeable batteries into the solar charger on the windowsill, so we wouldn't run out.

I was doing a radio interview about one of my books as we were mak-ing these preparations, and I mentioned what we were doing that day. The interviewer asked me whether other people should do this, and when I said I thought they should, she argued, "But think about all the time and money you use up getting ready to be able to operate without power — and most of the time you don't need those preparations! After all, extended power outages for most people happen only once every few years — is it really worth the effort for most of us? Plus, you have to be thinking 'what if something goes wrong' all the time — isn't that depressing?"

My interviewer was playing devil's advocate, of course, but I think she articulates a pretty common viewpoint — the idea that thinking about failures and bad stuff is too depressing and that it isn't worth the time and energy to prepare for most contingencies. The reason-ing behind that is that most disasters — even minor disasters — don't happen very often. Of course, when they do happen, well, the sheer dis-comfort of being unprepared is pretty intense, but then we forget.

In fact, I'd go further than she did and say that the idea of contingency planning in the US comes with a taint of superstition — that ill luck will strike those of us who actually spend time thinking about what might go wrong. The fact that our culture's only vision of someone who is prepared is the survivalist curled up in a shack with his stash of guns suggests that, fundamentally, we think that preparation for negative outcomes is on the whacked-out side. I think this leads us to radically underestimate how often things go badly wrong — we tend to think that failure happens infrequently. In fact, it is more common than most of us acknowledge.

And this leads to a painful reality — despite the fact that winter power outages happen out my way all the time, we know for a fact that the extended outages there will leave us with people who are freezing and hungry, isolated and unable to cope. They won't have the batteries for their flashlights, or any strategy for cooking or eating. At best, they will come out of this traumatized and miserable. At worst, some of them may actually die.

But we also know that these folks will be deemed normal, and their lack of preparation will be treated as completely normal. Just as people in California who haven't prepared for an earthquake or folks in Florida who haven't prepared for a hurricane will be treated as normal. In our society, we treat a lack of preparedness as completely reasonable and rational, even expected. If you are in line at a Red Cross shelter because you have no food and water in your home 48 hours after a hurricane hits Gainesville or an ice storm hits Boston, odds are no one will even raise an eyebrow and ask why in heck you didn't prepare. We should see this as strange.

My point is not to pick on anyone — in fact, I think the reason we look upon the lack of personal contingency plans as so reasonable is that it isn't just personal. It's our society as a whole that has very few contingency plans, much less strategies for adapting to failure. We regard planning for anything bad as a sign of an unhealthy focus on the negative. We feel it is so unhealthy that at every level of our culture — from the purely personal question of whether we have a will to the international policy level, where we have only recently begun to ask serious questions about the consequences of many actions — we have no contingency plans. Not only do we not have them, but we often dismiss and deride anyone who dares suggest we should make them *before* there is a problem.

This lack of failure planning is an obvious problem when disaster does strike. In that case many of us might ask whether it made sense for us to think differently — so let's go all the way in that direction and ask, "What if we treated failure as though it was a normal outcome in our lives?" Would this lead to us spending all our time miserably preoccupied with the worst? Or might we reduce the likelihood of some kinds of failure, while feeling more secure in others?

For example, for a good bit more than a decade now, a large number of voices have responded to the idea of globalization with fears that the creation of a global economy might eliminate protections for the most economically vulnerable members of society, erase valuable cultural differences, lead to political hegemony and environmental rape and make economies more vulnerable to difficulties in ways that wouldn't have

affected other economies much before. It turns out that anti-globaliza-
tion activists were right in just about every particular. Globalization did
screw quite a lot of the world's poor, to put it bluntly, and its collapse
seems poised to harm billions more. Tying our economies together is
starting to look like it wasn't such a hot idea for a lot of folks, starting,
perhaps, in Iceland; and for the banks that bought US mortgage debt,
Oops! Globalization did result in unprecedented ecological damage —
which we now have to live with. It turns out that the depressing people
who kept saying "Umm ... don't we need a back-up plan just in case this
doesn't work the way you hope it will?" and "Shouldn't we maybe reconsider something that works even if things don't go well?" were right.

There have been similar groups speaking out about energy issues for
decades, or asking whether it might not be safer to not degrade the environment in the first place rather than relying on our ability to fix it when
problems become evident. And they too have been accorded precisely
the amount of respect you'd expect — not much. And they too turn out
to have been right.

It turns out that we may be spending one-fifth of global GDP (according to *The Stern Report* on the economic impacts of climate change)
addressing the consequences of catastrophic climate change. The only
way to avoid such costs is to arrest the progress of global warming. The
last time we tried, in Copenhagen in the winter of 2009, we failed miserably, which means that if we, as seems increasingly likely, fail in the
almost unbelievable challenge of arresting climate change, we're facing a
potentially permanent economic Depression. Our economy may well be
permanently impacted by declines in available energy supplies and our
failure to invest in renewable energies. Oops! It turns out that a lot of folks
pointing out overarching problems over the last decades were, well, right.

But along with the "Oops!" and the enormous chorus of voices calling
our current crisis unforeseeable — even, as Goldman's wonderful villain
Vizzini would say, "Inconceivable!" — along with the talk of black swans
and unpredictability is the fact that, as Yeats put it, things fall apart. And
they do so, not once in a great while but rather often, even when the falling apart is something we do not choose to conceive of.

Thus the war to end all wars laid the ground for the next one, and
the end mechanism of the subsequent war left us with the massive and

presently insoluble problem of nuclear arms. Similarly, as Jared Diamond observes, all of our most intractable present problems have been caused by the solutions we've sought to other problems — peak energy and climate change aren't just bad things that are happening to us, they are the logical consequences of our solutions to other problems: standard of living, transportation and food issues. In many cases, social problems follow the same course — the urbanization, for example, of Southern African-Americans during and after World War II really did free a lot of impoverished rural workers from poorly paid domestic and agricultural labor, and offer short-term increases in wages. It also destroyed cultural networks, stripped farmers of land and access to natural resources and created an urban poverty that may arguably have been more destructive than the rural poverty that preceded it.

Now it would be false to suggest that the problems we were solving weren't real — and that for a time, the solutions didn't seem better to some people. For many a Chinese peasant, eating meat twice a week is better than twice a month before globalization. From the perspective of someone who values the Great Northeastern Forest, the replacement of coal and wood for heating by natural gas and heating oil was a real improvement. The problem is that the "solution" didn't last that long, and the new dependencies and destructions make the fallback much harsher — so, for example, the peasant who left the land to work on the periphery of the big city may soon no longer have his job or his land, or if he can get the land, climate change and pollution may mean that it cannot support him any longer. Now the American Northeasterner is completely unprepared for disruptions in the price or supply of their energy — and adaptation is likely to cause even greater deforestation than before. That things look different through different lenses is inevitable — but each layer of solution and complexity seems to have more dissenters, and put us in line for a bigger fall.

This might seem an argument primarily for contingency and scenario planning, and at a minimum, it should be. But I'd like to suggest something else — something that works at the personal level as well as the level of societal planning. What if we assumed failure? What if, instead of no contingencies, or simply having a very secondary backup plan, we insisted that our society work not just when things are going well, but that the very solutions we choose serve us even when they fail in reasonably predictable ways?

My family uses this model in our planning for the reasonable contingencies of our lives. We aren't prepped for everything — no bomb shelter, no SETI system to keep out alien invasion, and if the world goes into a sudden ice age, I'm woefully short on Mammoth repellent. But we're pretty good when we talk about things like ice storms knocking out the power — because we know that happens. Because of our failure planning, my house works pretty well without grid power.

I have solar lanterns, rechargeable batteries and solar chargers, a couple of oil lamps, a manual water pump for when the well goes out, a wood cookstove, a solar oven and a composting toilet and a spare battery for the laptop so I don't lose too much work time. Our house works great during the vast majority of times when we have power — and if it goes out, well, we flip on a few battery lights, put dinner on the cookstove to simmer and go out and bathe standing up in the tub with a solar shower bag filled with water that warmed on the cookstove.

Now you could argue that getting my home ready to function this way took money, time and energy, and you'd be right. So is it really worth it? Sure — and this is why. The very tools that I use to ensure that I'm comfortable in a power outage also serve me when the power is on. The solar battery charger works great for my sons' nightlight and the flashlights. The down comforters that keep us warm when the only heat is coming from the woodstove also work great when we just don't want to burn fuel or spend money on heating oil. The solar lantern goes out to the barn with me, the cookstove allows me to use the wood that the ice storm is going to provide us with in fallen tree limbs. The solar shower bags are wonderful for that outdoor sluice-off in the summer when I'm covered with garden mud.

Now these adaptations could operate solely as contingency plans — and then they would be costly and energy absorbing. Having a wood cookstove that you use only when the heat or cooking facilities are out is certainly better than nothing, but it is an awfully expensive way to deal with a crisis. I certainly couldn't blame contingency planners for saying it might not be worth it. On the other hand, a cookstove or super-efficient rocket mass stove that makes good use of downed wood or waste biomass, cuts your energy bills and also gives you an emergency backup, well, that's not a bad solution. By working, not from the assumption that I ought to have an emergency plan for an unlikely contingency but from the assumption that complex systems fail regularly *and* that the best system is to build infrastructure that assumes failure but also functions well without it, I get the best of both worlds — it actually doesn't cost me very much to adapt.

How would this work on a world policy scale? Well, let's take energy as an example. Let's assume that more than thirty years ago, during the first energy shocks, we'd recognize that both absolute oil supplies (as characterized by the peaking of North American oil) and foreign supplies (as characterized by the OPEC cuts) were unstable and subject to failure. How would that have changed our energy and economic policy over the last thirty years? It is very difficult for me to imagine a scenario in which we did not begin seriously building out renewable energies then — or one that did not offer big improvements over our present situation.

Simply assuming that the oil supply could fail might well have reduced our overall economic growth (although that is by no means a given) compared to what we later had fueled by cheap oil. But among the economists I know, I cannot find one who thinks that even the very short-term economic impact would have been negative enough to offset the advantages — and many doubt the impact would have been negative at all. Similar scenarios are devisable if, for example, we were to have taken the information about global warming available to us in 1979 (copious) and said, "It seems pretty likely that continuing to burn fossil fuels would be a bad idea, so let's begin a gradual phase-out."

But, of course, hindsight is always 20–20 — what would such a policy look like right now? Well, in economic terms, having a policy that planned for failure would mean assuming that the economy is not necessarily going to rebound in 2012 or 2013, and that our investments in infrastructure must be concentrated on mitigating the suffering of people who are going to be poorer, not shoring up financial institutions bound to failure. Thus we'd be putting our billions into small businesses, not huge ones, into basic things like local food and insulation instead of big luxury items that bring in profits in good times but are useless in bad ones.

But the funny thing about this is that just like the example of the energy build-out thirty years ago, I think there's a compelling case to make that we would be richer in the long run, for example, if it took only a little energy to heat our homes and if we invested in small-scale agriculture. I'm not going to sit down and make this argument point by point today, because even if the great successes were smaller, historically speaking, the boom-and-bust cycle doesn't necessarily result in net improvements over a more stable model.

This may be a large part of our project of reimagining — to conceive a world in which failure is normalized, part of the narrative, expected, and in which we choose our strategies at home and at the community and policy level to bring positive returns even when things, as they say, fall apart.

I. What does the future look like?

Collapse is a scary word, and some people doubt it is even relevant to us. Obviously the previous section of this chapter should indicate we are facing some major challenges in this century. Does that mean collapse? What is collapse, exactly? When societies have collapsed, what actually happened? How bad is it? Are there ways of reducing the badness? While historic events can't give a totally accurate picture of the future, they can at least give us some ground to stand on.

When looked carefully, "collapse" is actually an extremely common phenomenon in nations and societies — they rise to a particular level of function and then run into hard limits, often ecological limits, as documented by, among others, Jared Diamond in *Collapse: How Societies Choose to Succeed or Fail* and Joseph Tainter in *The Collapse of Complex Systems*. This causes a sudden and radical decline in complexity and a drop to a lower level of function. How low is up for grabs, and depends on the kind of response the society makes. At times this level can be extremely low — there's Easter Island, for example, whose population went extinct. More recently Rwanda and Burundi have several times in my lifetime collapsed into untenable violence and endless civil war, with horrifyingly bloody consequences for the people, ones that don't look that far off of *Mad Max*.

On the other hand, we could look at the most recent society to collapse: Iceland. In 2008 and into 2009, the country, which had become enormously wealthy and prosperous, underwent an economic collapse, the effects of which are still playing out. The banking collapse in Iceland was the largest ever suffered, relative to the nation's size, in economic history.

What happened in Iceland is probably very reassuring for people who are worried about collapse — the situation wasn't at all pleasant for people, but compared to Rwanda, it was a walk in the park. There was rioting and the government was, broadly speaking, changed, and there were some suicides and emigrations. The costs of dealing with the crisis were enormous, there was widespread unemployment, interest rates shot up and imports stalled, there was a foreclosure crisis, many formerly high-paid professionals had to go back to the fishing industry (which led to prompt fish stock collapses), imported goods became expensive and people got a lot poorer. On the other hand, everyone's food supply was comparatively safe.

So the first thing we can say about collapse is that it is highly variable — you can have economic collapse, you can have an energy-supply-related collapse, a political collapse, collapse into civil war — and some collapses are better than others. Dmitry Orlov, author of the superb *Reinventing Collapse*, which compares what he believes is the coming US collapse with the collapse of the Soviet Union (which he in part witnessed), makes precisely this point in his very thoughtful and funny essay "The Five Stages of Collapse":

> Although many people imagine collapse to be a sort of elevator that goes to the sub-basement (our Stage 5) no matter which button you push, no such automatic mechanism can be discerned. Rather, driving us all to Stage 5 will require that a concerted effort be made at each of the intervening stages. That all the players seem poised to make just such an effort may give this collapse the form of a classical tragedy — a conscious but inexorable march to perdition — rather than a farce ("Oops! Ah, here we are, Stage 5." — "So, whom do we eat first?" — "Me! I am delicious!") Let us sketch out this process.

I admit, I find it enormously difficult to imagine a scenario in which the US does not collapse on some level — in nearly every available measure, it is in danger of doing so. While we trumpet that we've averted economic collapse, it would be more accurate to say we've pushed some of it off for a few years, and made it more likely that crushing economic burdens will fall more heavily on people under fifty and future generations. Much the same can be said of our energy crisis and of climate change. It is hard to imagine anyone who would deny that in all three areas our policies are short-term, designed to stop us from bearing a burden right now rather than actually averting a crisis.

What leads me to believe that these crises will be as severe as a collapse? Some fairly trustworthy and impartial analysts suggest that it's likely. For example, in 2005, the US Department of Energy commissioned the Hirsch Report to evaluate whether peak oil was a meaningful threat. Robert Hirsch, the lead scientist in the report, has since become a peak oil believer, but he didn't start out that way. The DOE report concluded that with twenty years of WWII-level investment, we could avert collapse, but that less than twenty years means a major crisis. That's not my conclusion, but the DOE's — and since we're not engaged in a WWII-level build-out of renewable energies and even the USGS predicts peak oil by 2023, simple arithmetic suggests that we are headed for some fairly serious problems. The US Army's JOE has also produced a report on peak oil with similar conclusions.

What about climate change? Well, as already mentioned, there's the Stern Review, compiled by Sir Nicholas Stern, on the economic consequences of climate change. Among his conclusions (based upon a now-out-of-date set of assumptions about climate targets and their viability — he assumes that 550 ppm avoids more consequences than it probably does) was that, unchecked, climate change could lead to mitigation costs of up to 20 percent of world GDP — a burden no economy could bear without, well, collapsing. Given that we show no signs of being able to stabilize our ecology at the lower levels we know are safe, it seems reasonable to assume we are facing high mitigation costs, with heavy economic consequences.

The same is true of my assumptions about the practical, material consequences of climate change. The predictions of the Intergovernmental

Panel on Climate Change (IPCC) and other studies suggest that among the logical effects of climate change will be large numbers of refugees, conflict over scarce resources, drought, lowered rates of food production, increases in disease, heavier storms and more natural disasters. Not only do these things have economic costs, they have material ones — they result in collapsed societies. New Orleans, for example, can be reasonably said to have collapsed to a much lower level of function for quite a long time, and it isn't totally clear that it will ever come back entirely.

I don't think I need to explain why I think an economic collapse could happen — we know that they occur all the time, and we know by most assessments that one nearly occurred in fall 2008. That is, we've already seen a stair-step down to a lower level of economic security in the US.

We also know energy supply collapses happen — often along with economic collapses. For example, former Soviet prime minister Yegor Gaider wrote a book arguing that the Soviet Union collapsed (under his watch, actually) due to its dependency on foreign energy exports and the shift of its population out of the countryside and into cities. For a long time, the Soviet Union was able to rely on energy exports to allow it to pay for food on foreign markets, but when energy prices collapsed, there were not enough farmers left to grow food for the population and the government could not hold.

We know that this caused some subsidiary collapses — Cuba collapsed, for instance, because the Soviet Union collapsed and stopped sending it oil. The country lost one-fifth of its energy imports, and societal structures largely fell apart — people went hungry and started eating fried grapefruit peels because of lack of energy to run their highly technological agricultural system.

What's interesting about the examples of Cuba is that it is further evidence to suggest that fairly small energy resource shocks can cause fairly serious consequences — one-fifth of all oil shouldn't have led to serious hunger. Most people would reasonably argue that waste in the system and proper allocation of resources should have been able to absorb this — or will argue that the fault was the Cuban government's. To some extent that last point is probably true, but we should remember that we have examples from the US that show that small energy supply disruptions can be extremely destructive — the oil shocks of the 1970s and the major recession that followed resulted from a reduction in imports of just over 5 percent.

So yes, I think we're on a path toward some kind of collapse, without necessarily assuming cannibalism or even roving gangs of white-suprem-acist kale-stealers. I would like such a collapse to be averted very much, but it seems less and less likely that we will do so. And the evidence is becoming compelling that we are going to be facing economic, energy and climate crises all at the same time — and that I find it hard to imagine us navigating successfully.

Is it impossible? Probably not impossible, but certainly improbable — the societal restructuring would be enormous — and would have to involve nearly all the things I'm suggesting anyway. Nearly everyone dealing with these issues talks about WWII-style build-outs and war footings — having to do something roughly equivalent to the 1940s build-out (Niels Bohr famously said that it would be impossible to develop the atom bomb without turning the entire nation into a factory, and then, in 1944, observed that we had). Doing such a thing while dealing with a multi-front crisis seems even less possible.

Our strategies must serve us when we fail and when we succeed, and they should also serve both those who have escaped the worst and those whose lives are already undergoing collapse — people who are out of work, are losing their homes, don't have enough to eat, have a medical crisis and no health insurance ... that is most of the things that I encourage people to do, including building up a reserve of food and strengthening social supports works for the *people* who are experiencing collapse even if their society doesn't officially get that label.

What are the common features of collapsed societies? I could go back to Rome, of course, but there's probably no need. There are some common features of modern collapses that we can speak of:

1. People get really mad at their government. This usually leads to some measure of civil unrest, and often changes of government, some of which are meaningful and some of which are not. Sometimes this is good, sometimes this is bad — it also, as we know, can lead to the government or others scapegoating someone or other, which is really bad. Generally the better outcomes occur when the government

seems to respond to the people, and also, when the government gets out of the people's way and lets them respond.

2. Crime rates go up and services like police protection are less available or privatized — one universal feature of collapsed societies is that they are more violent. But that doesn't tend to mean warlords killing everyone in their path — it tends to mean more street violence, robbery, rape and murder, sometimes along with for-profit kidnapping. It tends to mean that people are vulnerable, and afraid, and often can't trust the authorities — it could be rather like being African-American in many poor urban neighborhoods, or it could be like living in Baghdad. Generally speaking, you don't want your kids to go out very much, you tend to avoid going out yourself and safety becomes a serious issue.

3. Everyone gets poorer fast. When societies collapse, the percentage of people who are poor goes way up — in Argentina, for example, the 2001 collapse virtually wiped out the middle class and pushed poverty levels up from lows around 20 percent to nearly 57 percent. This, I think, is the one universal likely outcome, and of course, one that is happening now.

4. The cost and attainability of food becomes an issue. Accounts from Argentina, which was previously both stable and affluent, suggest that many desired foods, particularly imports, are often unavailable, and more importantly, widespread economic impacts make it harder to buy food. This, and a lack of medical care, impacts people's health, and depression and drug and alcohol use begin to show up.

5. Services and utilities are widely disrupted. Sometimes the disruption comes, as is common among the US poor, because people can't afford to pay the bill — tens of thousands of US households, for example, will have their utilities cut off on April 1, just as soon as it is legal (most utilities can't cut off a household in the winter). But people also endure service interruptions because of aging infrastructure and social disruption. You are much more likely to spend time with no power, have no trash pickup, run out of gas and have the delivery trucks not come through....

6. People are pushed together — whether they are herded into ghettos or lose their housing, extended families, biological and otherwise,

come to rely on each other. So do communities and neighbors —
when someone has food, you share; when someone needs a place to
stay, you let them in. A culture of sharing emerges, and it is extremely
useful to have stuff to share.

These are the near-universals — all these things happen in collapsed
societies pretty much inevitably. In some collapsed societies, your neighbors start murdering you, or gangs terrorize your neighborhood — but
this isn't inevitable.

Now the question is, if collapse is likely, where do you concentrate your efforts? Do you try and prevent it, even if that is increasingly
unlikely, or do you focus your efforts on, as Orlov puts it, stopping the
elevator to the basement? I think the answer is both, but that you should
emphasize strategies that are dual purpose — whenever you face a likelihood of major systems failure, multi-purpose strategies that both reduce
impacts and increase resilience are clear winners. I like to think that
most — not all — of what I advocate falls into this category.

If a collapse of some sort does happen, what helps? We know, for
example, that social supports make an enormous difference in a collapsing society. *Reinventing Collapse*, for example, finds that the major
factors in keeping the Russian people from disaster were a system of
social supports. Making medical care, food and shelter available to people in crisis keeps things from being too awful.

Faced with the "special period," the Cuban government, for all its
limitations, did some remarkable things, because they are precisely the
opposite of what America has been doing — they strengthened social
supports at the expense of potential growth. They expanded educational programs into more, smaller campuses, put more clinics out
into rural and underserved areas and expanded food support programs. As I argue in *Depletion and Abundance*, this is precisely what's
needed here — investment in healthcare, food security, education and
safety net programs for the elderly, disabled and children should be our
highest priority. What's useful about this as a political strategy is that
it turns out that all the things that people say they care most about
personally in the political sphere turn out to be the very things that
actually matter.

Unfortunately, that's not the culture we live in — Americans uniformly respond to economic and social crisis by beefing up government and military programs and by cutting social safety networks. We're already seeing this happen — which is one of the reasons I put so much effort on truly local safety nets, private (not in the sense of ability to pay, but familial and community-based for those within the community) and other smaller resources, rather than large-scale programs — such programs serve as a last layer of support for people who have fallen through the sliced nets above them, but are likely to survive even in the absence of federal or state funding, because they can operate on a fairly small scale. We also need to focus on programs like universal healthcare, funding LIHEAP, food stamps, WIC and programs for the disabled and elderly — but we will need to build local backups as well.

The other thing that matters to reduce the rate of descent toward the basement are self-help strategies. In Cuba, for example, small-scale agriculture in urban centers did a lot (not everything, imported staples also mattered) to alleviate hunger and nutritional deficiencies. In Russia, according to all contemporary economic analyses, there should have been widespread starvation — but there wasn't, largely because small-scale localized economics arose to replace what was missing. In Argentina, cardboard scavenging came to support forty thousand people — just barely, though. In the US during the Great Depression, an example of near-collapse in many ways, the number of informal economy jobs skyrocketed. In 1932, The *New York Times* observed that there were now seven thousand people, most of them adults, shining shoes in NYC, while in 1928, there had been less than two hundred.

Self-help/subsistence strategies and social support networks are not in conflict in these situations — both are needed, particularly when social support programs are under fire or overwhelmed, as they are in the US at present. Neither can meet all needs or mitigate all outcomes alone — but simultaneously, in the best-case scenarios, they can keep people alive and fed and reasonably secure.

On some level, it seems churlish, I think, to settle for that. Everyone wants better for themselves, their friends, the world, their children — I do too. If we are going to have better for ourselves, we have to find it in things that are not vulnerable to collapse — in beauty and community, in the pleasure of good work and family, in things that are low-cost, simple and available. We're going to have to find a new definition of better.

The good news is that other societies have proved that you can have things like good health, an education for your children, enough food, strong community, support networks for the vulnerable, the pleasures of home and family — all during periods of decline from one level to another. We know that this is possible — so our central project becomes ensuring that it is feasible for us, that we can offer our children something worth having, even if we have less.

Profile 1

Michelle, Chicago: the future of cities

Michelle picked me up at my hotel on a warm day in July, and the warmth of her smile was my first indication of how much I was going to like her. We had met previously over the computer, discussing the future. Few people have done as much to convince me that cities have a sustainable future as Michelle, who made a passionate case in their favor. Now I was seeing Chicago's future through Michelle's eyes.

In her mid-fifties, Michelle looks a decade younger. She is an immigrant from South Africa who lives alone in an older house in the West Walker neighborhood. She's thoughtful, energetic, passionate and funny, and I loved my tour of her city.

We toured through neighborhoods, looking for old and new infrastructure, through old ethnic neighborhoods and new immigrant communities. We visited garden projects in the city center and then headed back to Michelle's neighborhood, where she showed me the gardens of her neighbors, immigrants from a dozen countries, and the community garden she and others are building in their area and how it fits into a larger picture of food security for the city.

At Michelle's home, I saw the beauty of an urban homestead, from the solar panels on her roof to the beehives on her second-floor balcony. The basement of her home is a freestanding space that she imagines could be shared with others. Her garden makes use of every inch of space — and produces seedlings and herbs she sells at the local farmer's market. Her honey, too, is for sale. She told the story of a change-by-change transition to a productive household.

Her lot is just over three thousand square feet, of which a thousand is taken up by the house's footprint. She has more than a thousand square feet of edibles, and makes use of concrete space by covering it with container nursery plants. She notes that she "stealth" seeded another four hundred feet of land along the sidewalk as well, making use of public space.

Her solar panels generate not electricity but hot water and heat — 100 percent of her spring and summer usage and about 30 percent of what she uses in the winter. Between her careful use of resources and her solar panels, Michelle's home uses vastly less than an average city house — and most city dwellings use fewer resources than comparably sized suburban or rural homes.

Michelle and I met over a discussion of the future of cities. She believe that urban spaces have a vibrant and viable future, and standing on Michelle's balcony overlooking her gardens and the gardens of her neighbors, surrounded by active bees bringing home pollen, one can see the fertile possibilities.

Three

Choosing home

I. Changing the pictures in our heads

I KNOW A LOT OF PEOPLE WHO READ "shelter magazines" — which is just a fancy way of saying magazines full of pretty homes. I admit to liking to look at them in checkout lines myself, since they do help me beautify my house — just not the way they are supposed to. I think: "Wow, that's a gorgeous sleigh bed — I'd love that ... hmmm ... eight thousand dollars .... yeah, my futon's looking cozier and more elegant already!"

I confess, too, that I'm not totally immune to the call of the beautiful — I mean, who is? Aesthetics are important. They are also not something I'm naturally good at. One of my sisters is — she's one of those people who always looks cool and pressed, whose clothes are nicer than everyone else's even though she buys a lot of them used, and who just knows instinctively what looks good — she never has to make beauty a separate project, it just flows from her as part of her way of being.

Whatever portion of our genome that proceeded from, I don't have it. I am casual and sloppy by nature, and while I appreciate beauty, it feels like it takes a lot of effort to create, an effort I don't always have time or energy for. Instead of beauty flowing out of my actions, form is something that has to be added on top of "functional" for me most of the time.

Until then, I keep thinking that the best possible thing I might be able to do would be to start a shelter magazine for normal people trying to Adapt-In-Place. In my head I've been working on *Better Homesteads and Ratholes* (OK, that probably wouldn't be the best sales inducement, but it is just a working title) ... or maybe, more seriously, *Working Home Magazine* — a magazine that would aestheticize function and sustainability — not in the way that fake sustainability magazines like *Real Simple* and *Natural Home* do it, with $7,000 eco-mattresses and 4,000-square-foot green-built homes with a $30K solar array on them, but the real thing.

Transforming our sense of what is beautiful, elegant, cozy, etc. is going to be such a big project. Some of it will come, as we are impoverished, by necessity. But some of it is still required. We have to learn to look at what we are creating as in itself lovely. And yet, that's hard — really hard. I know intellectually all the arguments for the pointlessness of lawns, of course, and yet I still cannot help seeing my tall flowering grasses through the eyes of someone trained to see cut grass as tidy and neat, and my yard as a mess. And if I can't always see the beauty of my meadow, how can someone who has had the mantra that "lawns represent beauty, neatness, order, affluence " banged into them since infancy?

The reality is that we're going to have to offer other images of beauty, neatness, order and affluence to help people change what's floating in their heads. And one of the things we may have to point out is this — a working home, whether rural, urban or suburban, does not look like a showplace. It should not. It cannot. So creating images of homestead beauty — beauty that can exist within the realities of a home that is used — is an important project. All over the country, zoning prohibitions have arisen to prevent people from actually using their homes to save or make money — no front yard gardens, no clotheslines, no rain barrels, no cottage industries. We are so convinced that the home is supposed to be a showplace that we've forgotten what that home is for — that it is to serve us, rather than we it.

How can you tell if you have a working home, rather than a showplace home? Well, first of all, you are there a lot. Whether you own or rent, have a private place or a collective one, a working home is a place where you really live. You want to be there, and as much as possible given the realities of your life, you arrange your world to be there.

At a minimum, this means that you invest your time and energy into the place, to adapting it to you and you to it. In aesthetic terms, that means there's almost always a project getting done, and the accoutre-ments of that work-in-progress about. Your hoes and shovels don't come out once in a while, there are tools and sawdust around, furniture being moved about, and most of your home tours include the sentences "even-tually that will be..." or "that's a work-in-progress."

The other reality is that you probably use your home more than most people. Maybe you work full time, but you spend your evenings gar-dening and cooking and building things. Or maybe you have a cottage business, or work from home. Maybe you homeschool, or your kids spend more time at home and playing in the neighborhood than they spend at camp and more structured programs, because they are learning home-based skills.

That also, frankly, means that your home does not look like a maga-zine spread — remember, in those shelter magazine pictures, people are always lounging around or having a barbecue — I'm sure you do some of that too, but the reality is that you are going to have your office full of work, or your barn full of boards, homework spread all over the din-ing room table, tomatoes on the counter — not a bowlful, decoratively laid out, but buckets of them, waiting to be canned.

The major feature by which a working home differs from a home that just consumes is that more and more of one's needs are met at home, rather than elsewhere. That does not mean we live in caves and never come out into the light — but it does mean we're more likely to eat with our friends at our own table than at restaurants, or replace trips to the store with trips to the garden, a fabric stash or the accumu-lation of "potentially useful salvage." Not only does this mean projects, but it also means storing stuff (for some people; others like to come at this lightly).

All of which means there is exactly no chance that your house will look like a magazine. Some people's do, of course, but except for the homes of those rare people with the instinctive gift for making things purty, that's mostly because no one is home — adults work, kids go to school and to activities if they are middle or upper class, or to jobs if they are older and not. Our standards of cleanliness and perfection can be so high precisely because homes are expensive spaces in which we do not ordinarily live.

The other thing that makes a working home is attention to one's place, and for one's larger community. Many of the things typically used to meet modern aesthetic standards are toxic, unsustainable and dangerous to the environment. Now in some cases it is possible to find a replacement — you can get rid of the bleach in your laundry and use the sun or natural whiteners, get rid of the power mower and switch to the push mower, and achieve much the same effect. On the other hand, without a dryer, your towels simply won't be as soft, and without chem-lawn and a sprinkler, your lawn won't be that scary, shiny green. The imperfect lawn and the crunchy towels are the better choice by far — but it is hard to get people with strong aesthetic assumptions to grasp the shift — to find the weedier lawn more beautiful, or even better, the beds of vegetables or appropriate natural plantings.

Wealth itself is unsustainable. This is a hard message for people who have lived their whole lives being told that affluence is their goal. It's a practical and painful reality that the world cannot afford rich people anymore. By rich, I do not mean the absurdly wealthy, although certainly those too — I mean people who are simply well-off by developed world standards. That does not mean we cannot afford ornamentation, beauty or elegance — after all art, ornament and beauty are a part of many societies that live far more sustainably than we do — but it does mean that each of us cannot have our own private palace, decorated with expensive (in both ecological and monetary terms) consumer items.

The deep fear of "looking poor" that underlies so much of our actions is one we have to deal with — it is a tough thing to navigate, because it is much more complex than wanting to "keep up with the Joneses." That is part of it, of course, but there are other impulses — the desire not to have to apologize for not meeting the conventions of hospitality or neighborhood aesthetics, the fear of pity or contempt from others if they think you can't afford "normal" things. There's the fact that we too were taught to think of homely things as, well, homely.

I find myself apologizing to people, and warning them before they come to my house. I'm afraid they've read about what we do, and they hold in their head an image of what it should look like. A visiting friend of mine recently said to me, "Don't worry, the real farms are never the pretty ones." I know she's right in some ways, and being kind in others, but what I wanted her to say is, "Your farm is beautiful." And parts of it are — the woods are beautiful, the pasture dotted with sheep are beautiful, the gardens are lush. But the kids' bikes are scattered around the yard, we still haven't stacked our wood and the rabbit hutches on the porch are home-built. There is enough squalor here to read "squalor."

Some of it truly could be a lot prettier than it is — we could stack the wood faster, we could cut the grass more often — it is just that doing that would come out of something else. Right now the wood is sitting where it is because, well, we haven't gotten to it yet — I've been making the cherries into cherry jam instead. I can make beauty blossom on the shelves in my kitchen as red jars fill the shelves — but only at the price of the rathole look out on the driveway.

Thus I find myself dreaming of the day I can go up to the checkout stand and see *Working Home* magazine, with pictures of real people in their gardens, the old wooden tools and the bursting eggplant alongside the real gardeners, who do not look like the people at the barbecues in the magazines, showing what life looks like in a real and functional home. There is so much in the rich potential for beauty in made-over and made-do, in homegrown and home-cooked, in mended and patchwork, in home-built and fresh-made, and the art of hybridity — the transformation of an ordinary suburban ranch or an apartment in the Bronx into a place that is full of art, and life.

Meanwhile, my personal project is to stop apologizing for my home being what it is, and to try harder to make other people see it as I do on the good days. I like the exuberance of our lives, the piles of books and musical instruments, the discarded bikes that say "my children are learning to make their way in the world." I like the full pantry and the richly colored jars, but also the canning kettle out on the counter. I do need to work on the dirty dishes and the stacked wood, on prettying things up, simply because I like it that way. But I also want to stop letting myself see it through old eyes, and invite others to see it the new way, too.

II. Binding beauty and utility

Think about how you react to beautiful spaces — the deep release of breath that beauty brings to most of us. Think about how much of what we're doing involves going home and staying there — shouldn't we also enjoy that? Moreover, many of us first come to this project of making a real home through our desire for a beautiful place to live. Many of our aesthetic visions for our homes are based upon functional ideas of beauty — the Shaker or country aesthetic, for example. What we love about Shaker or country homes are the visuals associated with lives of great functionality.

These things are beautiful precisely because they are functional, but in modern design, function is often emptied out, and so is the spirit and depth. A country kitchen is beautiful, not because you've found the perfect old implements to hang on the wall but because those implements are useful, because that antique eggbeater can still make a mean whipped cream. The Shaker chair is beautiful, as William Coopersthwaite says, "because it was built by someone perfectly capable of believing that an angel might come and sit upon it."

The problem with beauty is that we've been told for a long, long time that aesthetics are the product of our "personal style," which involves the project of putting together mass-produced commercial objects or expensive antiques in such a way as to articulate our personal, tiny variation on the range of mass-produced aesthetics available to us. That is, we can be "country" or we can be "modern" or "Shaker" or "retro," but one way or another, we have a limited range of options, ones carefully dictated to us by TV, books, design magazines. And again, these have nothing to do with our actual lives as they are lived.

Now despite being an innate slob, I'm not at all immune to this — I find the pretty pictures in magazines as enticing as anyone else. When we were working on the house addition, I found myself gravitating to the design books in the library. But while I was whisked away by certain visions, I also observed some things about them. For example, have you noticed that unless they are showing a modernist media room, there's never, ever a TV in the pictures of fancy household living spaces? Again, unless you are seeing a super modernist or explicitly retro kitchen, or an ad for a particular small appliance, have you noticed that there's never a regular plastic toaster or blender on the counter of the dream kitchen? If a toaster does show up, it will be a fancy stainless steel one or a 1950s original in perfect condition, both of which cost as much as a cross-country flight.

This, of course, is because plastic is ugly, as are many of the accoutrements of modern life. There's no way to make a TV beautiful, so they don't put them in pictures of beautiful homes unless they are showcasing a "media room" and have no choice. Toasters mostly aren't pretty either, so when the people come to shoot the fancy home (of wealthy people with no children, generally), the toaster goes under the sink, where it does not ordinarily reside. And this isn't just cleaning up for the photographers — the net effect of everyone hiding the actual realities of daily living (how often do bathroom spreads even show a toilet?) is that we are given an image of beauty at home that most of us could never achieve.

But what if we could come up with a vision of beauty that didn't force us to hide the realities of our lives in the closet whenever anyone comes over? That's the beauty I long for — one that doesn't disappear the first time I make breakfast or the kids tromp into the house, enduring beauty that lasts more than two seconds and feeds our need for grace and peace all the time, rather than once in a while.

And that means a new relationship to our stuff. Because most of the stuff we own and use isn't beautiful — and it can't be made beautiful. Try and look at a parking lot full of cars and say "oh, how breathtaking!" Yeah, right. Seriously, there is no such thing as a pretty car (although some are uglier than others), and a sweep of them are nothing but butt ugly. Yes, manufacturers can try and make one car look OK with a half-naked woman and an expanse of mountains, but it is the woman and the mountains that are attractive. And when the photographers come to take pictures of your yard, bet you a million bucks they want the car out of the driveway to make things look pretty.

Having a beautiful home means making sure that your daily tasks are done with things that look nice to you. You shouldn't have to hide the evidence of your actual life before people come over. For me the shift to a human-powered, manual life does a lot to improve my aesthetic situation. Old things that were made well enough to survive and be passed down to me are often more beautiful than newer ones, and the best-made ones will often last several lifetimes — I still use tools that were owned by my grandparents and my husband's grandparents, many of which came to them secondhand. My family serves bread on a 150-year-old platter that has outlasted many cheaper dishes, for example. It was not expensive when it was made, but it was well made. Things made of natural materials are often more beautiful than things made of plastic.

Many good tools also look beautiful, as well as being highly functional.

The realities of this life I live require that I not have to hunt under the sink every time I want a piece of toast. Beautiful isn't a picture you take once — it is something you want to live in, like a fish in water. No one invites guests over and says, "Here, come look at the one moment the house was pretty."

The tools I'm finding for a beauty I can live with are cleanliness (not my strong suit, but I'm working on it), space for the reality of our lives (i.e., finding a way to either reduce our clutter or increase our organization or both, so that things fit into the spaces for them) and tools that are both beautiful and useful. If I can't find a beautiful version of something, perhaps that's a clue that maybe I should begin thinking of ways to replace it with something that is beautiful.

The more my life moves toward utility, the more my home becomes the space in which I work and live, and thus, the space that serves my present and actual needs, the better I like it. That doesn't mean that there aren't things about my house I think are ugly (the pink tile in one bathroom's days are numbered) or that I wouldn't change, but gradually I'm finding that as a consequence of designing a home to work with less or no power and meet the actual needs of my family, it looks more beautiful.

We took the fridge out of my kitchen. I'm not perfectly immune to the lure of those all-steel ones, but since we didn't use it anymore (more on this in Chapter 6), we simply removed it and used the space to build in shelves and a permanent place for my grain grinder. It looks a lot better than the plastic-sheathed white fridge used to. Again, I noticed when I read design magazines at the doctor's office that the only fridges I saw were those stainless ones in the perfect modernist kitchens, all pure, all perfect. But I only know one person who actually owns one of those — so most of us start behind when it comes to meeting standard conceptions of beauty. The only hope is to change them altogether.

I suspect that difficult times may put my family in our home even more than we live in it now, that our options for pleasure activities may become more and more "visiting people in their homes and them coming to us" — which to me means that it is important to consider aesthetics. I do not mean this in the sense of investing lots of money in expensive beauty. But cheap beauty is cheap. A can of paint is not so terribly expensive, and old things, used things, free things are often beautiful — or can be made that way with small investments. A functional home, designed for work and pleasure, tidy but lived in, is beautiful in many cases simply because it is. And that's something we can work toward — the unification of our forms and our new and necessary functions.

III. Best two falls out of three: wrestling with temptation

When we were first planning on moving to a farm in this area, we came very close to buying a gorgeous little farm in an Amish neighborhood a bit west of where we live now. The house was Amish built and fairly new pole construction, with four small bedrooms and large open public spaces (it looked pretty much like every other Amish home I've been in), with a medium-sized pole barn and ten acres, fenced for livestock. It was lovely. It was under $25K (yep, you saw that right!). I wanted to buy it — and my husband said, "No way."

But, I argued, we can add electricity and indoor plumbing gradually (it came with an outhouse and no electricity, obviously). I appealed to his innate cheapness — we'd have no debt, we'd have money to put into the house straight off. We'd adapt. My husband's reaction was not just "no," but "No!" And we ended up spending considerably more money for the house we have now (which is wonderful and lovely too). In the end, a house without power and running water was simply too weird for my spouse.

Now cheapness was only part of the reason I wanted this house so very much. There was a deeper reason. You see, self-discipline is not my middle name. My reaction to "Would you like a cookie" is almost always "Sure." I can justify all sorts of things with the reasoning that "this time is an exception." And of course, I start noticing after a while how often the exceptions add up. And my husband is not too different from me — he particularly hates raining on anyone else's parade, so he'll happily say, "Well, of course, honey, if you're tired...."

This lack of natural capacity for self-denial means that I work best if there are firm, hard rules, no exceptions (outside of the usual extraordinary circumstances) and mechanisms for enforcement. Ideally those mechanisms are external, because the problem with making the rules for yourself is that you know the person who made them. I know there are people who can always take the right path without firm direction. I'm just not one of them.

What I really wanted the non-electric home for was the experience of not being able to flick on a light, not being able to turn up the heat, not being able to do things the easy way. I knew we would probably add electricity at some point, ideally renewable energies, but I felt that we might be able to add only those things that really mattered to us, very gradually, and to carefully pick and choose what was essential to us.

I was fairly sure this would be a useful exercise. For a long time I didn't have a lot of conveniences — I was a poor graduate student. I had no car, no washing machine, very little money. So I did laundry quite infrequently — I washed out underwear in the sink, wore my clothes a fair while, and when I could work up energy and money, I piled all my laundry in a sack, slung the heavy load on my back and hauled it a long quarter mile to the laundromat and back, often cussing all the way.

But the funny thing is that if you'd asked me whether my laundry situation was a major burden, I'd have laughed. Ninety-nine percent of the time I never thought much about what a pain it was to do the laundry — and the other 1 percent, well, it was annoying, it was a pain, but it didn't really matter that much, even when it was cold, even when the laundry was heavy, even when I didn't like it. After all, every life has bits we don't enjoy, right? Sometimes those bits really are a drag, but more often, they really aren't that big a deal. Now for some people, this might have been a more significant issue — someone who couldn't haul their laundry or pull a cart or who was cloth-diapering several young kids might find this a struggle not worth bearing. And yet, I think about all the folks in New York City who do just this — perhaps for some it is a huge burden, but don't they also suggest that a surprising number of us might be able to find ways to do with less?

Well, the first time I lived with an actual washer-dryer in my own house and didn't save up coins, I was amazed by how wonderful it was. And ... how often everything suddenly seemed to need washing. Now I knew I hadn't always washed my clothes that often, and as far as I could remember, people didn't sidle away because I smelled bad. I knew my towels had usually been washed monthly. But somehow, no matter how I tried, I never could get my laundry down to the level of washing that

I did before I had a machine. I still can't — and I've been trying for a long time now.

The same thing is true of life without a car. It had its hassles and hardships, and I used to walk long distances quite routinely, sometimes in terrible weather. I know that I'm perfectly capable of covering a few miles on foot without any major hardship — but even allowing some level of adaptation for children, I find it very hard not to use the car on occasions when it would be somewhat inconvenient not to. That is, I find it hard to live in the mindset that allows me to make enough time to put the kids in the strollers and walk the four miles to the library. More often, I find myself rushing about and saying, "Oh, gosh, we're late, we have to take the car."

I do it sometimes — we keep our driving quite low, using just over 80 percent less gas than the American average. And I wash probably less than most people in the US — much less. But I also know that in the absence of the option of driving, I would make time to get there on foot. In the absence of the washer, I would find less laundry.

I know there are people out there who can simply say, "Well, we park the car and use our bikes every time." For me, it is more like, "we park the car and use our bikes about half the time it would be possible to." I'm always impressed by people who manage to have the "out" sitting right there and say no to it — sometimes I do, and sometimes, I don't.

For the first decade of my adulthood, we lived without a car. When we moved to the country, we "had to" have a vehicle. We've struggled to find good ways to balance the mobility we really need with the mobility we simply want — and to find ways to reduce temptation while upping our self-discipline. At one point, we were able to barter with neighbors to share a car — and knowing that we only had the vehicle on specific days made us more careful with our use. For a long time since that, we've only had one small car — the six of us cram (safely) into a Ford Taurus. We look like clowns getting out of our tiny car — but it means we use less gas, and have to seriously consider whether it is worth being crammed to make longer trips. It encourages us to use public transportation for visiting family and to skip unnecessary trips.

And sometimes I wonder if we really "have to" have a vehicle — could we combine two electric-assist rickshaw bikes, a barter arrangement with our friend with a truck (for when the goats or hay must be hauled) and a shared commute for Eric? I'm tempted sometimes to try it — and a little cautious about giving up my conveniences. It isn't that I'm never in favor of keeping something that makes life easier — I just want to know what the realities of the trade-off are.

Culturally, we tend to not have a lot of respect for people who lack self-discipline, and a lot of concern about temptation. We have decided, for example, that rules about avoiding sexual temptation are outdated — we should, instead, rely primarily on our own self-discipline. The same thing is true with technologies — we are told that there's no point in objecting to a technology, or suggesting we shouldn't go down certain technical avenues — no one has to have a cell phone or a car or a whatever. The problem is that a narrative that says so presumes that we have a cultural basis for self-denial, that we've been taught how to say no, how to think critically about our technologies or, for that matter, about sex. It assumes that we've been taught to value self-restraint.

There are real merits to self-denial and real pleasures in it, and not just austere ones or the pleasures of self-righteousness. I genuinely think my life without a car would be better, more enjoyable, more fun. The economic, personal, time and social costs of the car — and certainly, the costs of a car-based society — are simply too high. For example, in *The Logic of Sufficiency*, Thomas Princen suggests that the average American spends about two months a year working simply to support their cars — car payments, gas, tolls, repairs, etc. We think cars get us places faster — but what could you do in those two months?

Not only do most of us not realize that cars actually take more time and money than they return to us, but most of us have never in our lives been asked to think about what self-discipline might do for us, whether it has any merits other than the ability to sniff down your nose at someone not as austere. In fact, the accusation of self-righteousness often completely undermines any discussion of self-limitation, simply because we cannot imagine that there are other merits involved.

There is certainly plenty of truth in the statement that I need more personal self-discipline, or that I can't blame the fact that I eat too many cookies on the culture as a whole. And I don't. But in a culture that dismisses the idea that temptation is a problem, that we might begin addressing our deepest social problems by restricting our capacity to give way to our worst selves, it is very hard to even begin to find a way at those problems.

I don't know how many people struggle with this question of self-discipline, but I suspect a lot. Figuring out solutions for my family and myself involves a range of strategies. First, some creative deprivation — often the best way to use the minimum is not to have any choice. The one bright side of our current economic crisis is that many of us may get some chance to explore creative deprivation. We saw that last time we had a Depression, the habits of thrift and care lasted far longer than the Depression — our grandparents kept living the way they had to, in many cases simply because they couldn't imagine anything else; everything else seemed too extravagant.

The second shift is the need for self-discipline — sometimes it isn't good to take the cookie. I need to work on the ability to "say no" and to find the immutable wall in myself that says "these rules aren't just mine." Sometimes I get there by realizing the rules are part of a moral or cultural or religious code I've chosen to adhere to, sometimes by realizing that my actions affect other people, sometimes by simply promising that there will still be cookies later, and that I'll be happier this way. I'm working on the idea that self-denial has its own pleasures and satisfactions.

It is certainly unnecessary to have a religious faith to exercise self-denial, but I do think that religious rules represent ways that people externalize their rules — the idea that there are limits that are not of your own personal setting, and the creation of a community to explore them in, is useful to me, at least. And I'm reminded of a story that Scott Savage tells in *The Plain Reader*, when he writes:

> A story that appeared a number of years ago in the Amish publication *Family Life* told of a busload of tourists who visited an Amish farmer. The group consisted of people from many religious denominations. One of them said, "We already know all about Jesus Christ, but what does it mean to be Amish?" The Amish fellow thought for a minute and then asked for a show of hands for how many in the tour group had televisions. Every hand went up. Then he asked how many thought

that maybe having a television contributed to a lot of social and spiritual problems in society. Again, every hand went up. In light of this, he asked, how many would be willing to give up having television? This time, no hands went up. He went on to explain that this was the essence of being Amish: a willingness to do without something if that thing is not good for them spiritually.

The Amish exercise self-denial with both the force of community and the force of faith behind them. My own suspicions that I'd be better off without a car exist, not in complete isolation, but outside a unified cultural sense that cars are harmful — even though we know they are. We are not all going to share Amish religious convictions — but I wonder if there is a way to translate some of their culture of self-limitation into a secular reality?

I know that the Amish relationship to the technologies they choose to use and those they do not is probably not the right one for most of us — I'm not saying we should all be Amish. But the idea that we should look at our possessions, our technologies, our work and everything that structures our lives and ask ourselves whether it is good for us, is, I think, right.

But that's not enough — the best and most ethical of us will find it hard to do this in isolation. By ourselves, on our country road, it is painfully hard to imagine asking others to help us live without a car — or simply use ours less — even if we were to trade or barter with them. The burden of inconveniencing others in a project that they do not share or value seems high, perhaps too high. In a community where many people wanted or needed to use their cars less, or even get rid of them, we could feel ourselves full participants, share strategies for reducing temptation, give back as we get. It is a conundrum and a nut we have yet to crack.

I don't know all the answers — I do know that the problem of temptation in our society needs some exploration. We need to find ways to begin our discussions, not from the point that all of us ought to live as perfect paragons of self-discipline but from the idea that we might, at the same time we improve our practices and explore the pleasures and merits of self-denial, also wrestle with the enormously vexed question of managing temptation.

Four

Triaging your situation

I. First steps

THE FIRST QUESTION TO ASK is whether we should take Adapting in Place seriously at all. Shouldn't we, ideally, try and choose the best possible place to deal with the coming crisis? Some analysts suggest we will have to have vast population migrations out of suburbia, say, to more densely packed and walkable cities, while others propose re-ruralization. My suspicion is that both of these will probably occur to some degree — but that the progression will be intermittent and not very well organized. And plenty of people will stay in place, either in their homes and apartments or by settling in property known to them, owned or rented by family or close friends.

Why will they stay? Well, for millions of people who own a home but aren't in immediate danger of foreclosure, the option of selling, even if they are not "underwater," is problematic — with home sales at historic lows, most of us will be staying put, if we don't lose or abandon our properties. They can't afford to change jobs, because they will lose seniority and potentially get the axe. They can't afford the additional costs of moving, buying a new property or paying first, last and security.

And if they do move? Some of us will migrate, but a lot of us have compelling reasons to live where we do — community, culture and family. What most of us will probably do in dire circumstances is simply consolidate resources with people we can trust — we'll take in boarders or move in with family or friends. In tough times, we are likely to need family and community more — thus staying close to elderly parents or grandparents who can help with childcare while parents look for work becomes more urgent.

Some of us may also decide that where we are is the right place — it isn't just a matter of not being able to move, but of believing that we are best in places we know. The time for the radical changes picking up and moving and starting over require may have been a few years ago. More familiar projects may be wiser and better for many of us.

Some of us may have an investment worth keeping in our homes — by improving soil, starting cottage industries, building strong social, familial and community ties and local economic initiatives, we will also build in strong incentives to stay in place. We may see the common pattern of Global South employment in which some family members are sent where formal jobs are available to work, while most of the family remains together, anchored in one place. With more people per household, mortgage and property costs may become manageable, while the benefits of family and community are increased by our lack of fossil fuels.

Triaging your situation

This does not mean that everyone can or should stay in place. We will talk in the next section about who should not stay where they are. But I suspect many people, at least for a time, will need to stay put, or will move to a place where they intend to stay in the long term.

So it is worth asking — what are the first steps if you've decided to remain in your home, with all its imperfections and disadvantages (and its perfections and advantages — remember, there is no perfect place)? Your goal is to be able to handle what is thrown at you, crises economic, energetic, ecological or political — or all of the above. And the first step, as always, is triage — setting priorities.

First steps

We all need to get ready to deal with the kind of short-term crisis that affects almost everyone sooner or later. Given the fragility of our systems, more and more of these disruptions are likely. Thus our first project is a medium-range systems problem — something that can be caused by ice storms, blizzards, hurricanes, tornadoes, flooding, geopolitical crisis, blackout ... you name it. We need to be ready to get along for a few weeks to a month in a very messed-up short-term situation. This is useful even if what we face is a very messed-up long-term situation.

That means moving first, to get basic needs met. Thus we concentrate on first-tier solutions. The qualities that these first-tier solutions must have are these:

> — They keep you alive and healthy. They are simple, accessible and not too expensive — since everyone needs these, regardless of income.

You need a reserve of food, and a way to cook it without power. You will require lots of warm clothing and blankets if cold is a potential problem, or sufficient water and ways to keep cool if heat is the issue. You need stored water and a backup source of water. You will want some basic lighting and a way to manage toileting and hygiene issues, and keep bodies and clothes clean. You need a way to keep aware of events and communicate with family and community.

Other than the food, medications and water, the emergency measures could be quite cheap, because they don't have to be comfortable and pleasant — for a few weeks, you can winter camp in your house even if you are cold, and pee in a bucket or use a home-dug latrine even if you'd rather not. For a few weeks you can do laundry infrequently in another plastic bucket, light your evening with your headlamp and rechargeable batteries, communicate with your neighbors by trekking out to a knocked-together neighborhood bulletin board. That is, you can be uncomfortable and/or inconvenienced for the short term, in most cases. That doesn't mean all the short-term solutions are unpleasant — in fact, sometimes you'll be surprised by how minor the inconvenience is — but the most important thing is that you have a way of meeting those needs, not that the methods be perfect.

For those who can't tolerate much discomfort or inconvenience because of health problems, age, disability or simple intolerance, you will need to move up a little in the list to the next steps, the long-term solutions. You may need solar panels, expensive equipment or a generator, which come with attendant costs. But for most of us, the first-tier inconvenient but survivable solutions get us part of the way there, and we could use many of them for longer if we had no choice.

But we all know that short term isn't everything. What happens if we can't afford electricity or gas anymore? What happens if we're suddenly in the Long Emergency, not the short one? The preparations you've made for a short-term crisis will get old really fast — but most of them will still serve you if you don't have, or can't afford, better. That is, you will not like lighting your house with only a headlamp and two flashlights, and you will not like going to bed when it gets dark in December in the north, but you can do it if you have no choice. Some of us may already have second-tier solutions in place — we might have a wringer washer already and not need the plastic buckets. Still, I recommend that you have the equipment or ability to use these minimal backup solutions, if only so you can teach others in your community — your neighbor down the road may need to know how to do laundry in a crisis too.

The second tier

The next level of preparations is partly about survival, but more about creating a life you can live with in the long term. If you have money, these are easy changes to make. If you don't have money, it will take time, and saving and scavenging to manage these systems — and you may be stuck with the original, inexpensive backups at times. Only you can decide what you can afford and have time to do, and what portion of your resources you can devote to improving your comfort and gaining more time. My own observation is that those accommodations that free up time and increase comfort increase rapidly in value in tough situations.

This is where you begin going step by step through the systems you depend on, figuring out what you can do to allow you to live decently and comfortably. Step by step, you start replacing, adding or converting to sustainable systems that will serve you in the absence of existing infrastructure, and will also be useful in other ways in your life now. My own belief is that while renewable energy systems are an excellent supplemental second-tier system if you have the money to afford them (and they are often expensive), even those who can afford them should create primary systems at a technological level they can fully operate.

That is, even someone with a solar system large enough to run their washing machine should have a bucket at a minimum, and might want a small pressure washer. Even someone with a generator for their well pump might want a manual pump on their well or rain catchment. Someone with a chainsaw still needs an axe and bucksaw. The reason for this is that things break, supply lines can be disrupted, replacement parts may not be available. Redundancy is healthy — and can be essential. And if you must choose between the solar panels and the manual well pump, my own feeling is that you should prioritize a system you can manage, repair and fully understand, whichever that may be.

For those without much money, it is often much easier to convert permanently to the alternatives than it is to maintain both "normal" and "backup" systems. That is, it is hard, if you are poor, to afford solar lanterns — unless, of course, you use them as a lighting source and save money on your electric bill. Sometimes if things seem too costly, the problem may be that you are imagining them as a backup, not a conversion to a new way of life. You may prefer the old way, but if you are serious enough about your concern for the future, converting early isn't the end of the world — our family has made this choice a number of times, in fact.

Some of the choices are easy and cheap — turning your lawn into a landscape of edibles can be quite inexpensive, if you can get slips and starts and divisions from people and buy plants and seeds from your cooperative extension, and it's also fun. Converting to a composting toilet is inexpensive and can save you a lot of money on your water bill if you have enough land to do so. Switching to buying in bulk and eating out of your food storage can save a lot on your food budget. Sometimes you can do things on the cheap if you have time — but if you have neither time nor money, things get difficult, so you need to prioritize.

II. The order and ethics of things

There are two good ways to prioritize — by urgency and by availability — and honestly, it makes sense to do both simultaneously. Generally, you should concentrate on the things that will matter to your happiness and comfort the most. For a family with two kids in diapers, this might be not having to do laundry in a bucket; for someone who is always cold, a good heat source. But don't forget (and this is a great chore to delegate to elderly relatives, friends who want to barter or teenagers) to keep an eye on Craigslist, Freecycle and garage sales and to talk about what you are trying to do with others, so you can take advantage of opportunities. Try and have a list of all the stuff you'd like to do, so that when that old hand washer or treadle sewing machine shows up, you can cross it off your priority list.

While you are finding comfortable ways to keep cool, refrigerate food, keep safe, go to the bathroom and the rest, you can also begin thinking about the long-term sustainability and community implications of these projects. That is, if you are going to burn wood, you need to be planting trees and harvesting carefully. You are just as vulnerable to diseases caused by human waste disposal problems as your neighbors — even if you don't contribute to them, you may get sick when your water supply is contaminated. So after you deal with your own water system, share your knowledge. Renewable and lasting systems are central. If your private solutions are likely to contribute to the long-term problems, pick different solutions.

In peasant economics, we find that most wealth accumulated by families is passed down through generations. Thus, as Shanin observes, a bicycle for a family may be expected to last until the family's father is too old to ride it and the daughter can take over. Land and property are passed down, and mostly stewarded — they are not disposed of lightly, because they imply an obligation to future generations who are not expected to have enough wealth to replace what we are careless with now. It would behoove most of us, as we make our adaptation plans, to ensure that our strategies serve not just our present, but our future — if our adaptations destroy future capacities to warm, feed, protect or slake the thirst of other people, perhaps we need to find new strategies.

Finally, you should practice. That doesn't just mean trying the solar battery charger once or making sure you know how to cook on your woodstove — try living with these systems routinely, and turning off the ones you've depended on up until now. Consider a test run, where you turn everything off in the winter for a week or live on nothing but your stored and garden food for a month. These tests will tell you really basic things you need to know, and show you the holes in your system while you still have a chance to plug them.

III. When not to Adapt in Place

The very first activity we do when I teach Adapting in Place in classes is to sit down and make a list of what our alternatives would be if we had to leave your present place. The reason we do this is because things like that happen — people lose jobs or homes, they are hit by fires, they are forced out by climate changes or environmental crises — sometimes you can't stay where you are. Many people reading this book will probably want to stay where they are — and that's OK — but we do have to think about the alternatives. I would advise everyone to sit down for a few minutes and make a similar list. Ask yourself, where would I go if I had to leave?

For some people, getting out of Dodge is the way to go. And it shouldn't just be hypothetical — I think some people should absolutely consider leaving where they are, and doing it sooner rather than later, because they have little or no hope of successfully remaining in place.

Now some of this comes down to long- versus short-term issues, and there are balances to be struck. For example, let's say you live in a place that may be underwater in a couple of decades. You love it, you are in your fifties or sixties, your kids are here. Do you have to leave?

No, you don't have to, but you might want to think about your choices. For example, do you want to have to evacuate your home regularly because of coastal storms in your eighties? Do you have a support network that will make that possible, that will help you? If you plan to move when things get more acute, how likely is it that you will be able to sell your house, as areas look increasingly difficult to inhabit? Do you need to sell it? If you have family inland that would take you in, maybe risking having to walk away is OK — or maybe it isn't.

Our homes are our homes, and our right to stay and choose them sometimes seems inviolable — but it isn't. In the next decades there are going to be a lot of migrants — and any of us may be one of them. Migrating now and settling in a reasonably livable place might be better — or it might not, and you might want to wait and see. But don't do it in ignorance — find out all you can. The reality is that many of us do more research on what movie to see than we do about our future, and the risks and benefits of the locations we choose.

So here's my list of when to think seriously about getting out. There will be exceptions in every case — my claim is not "you definitely must go" but "think hard about what you are choosing."

1. If you have an adjustable rate mortgage and can't reset it, are already facing foreclosure or have no reason to believe you'll be able to pay for your house, or if you bought your current house near the market peak and require two full-time incomes to pay for it.

   The odds are good you aren't going to keep your house in those circumstances — and the worst possible scenario for you may well be frantically going into debt trying to keep your old way of life open, which closes off other options. If you have a better choice, one that can provide some stability, or there is hope of selling and getting out from under, seriously consider it.

   If you do end up in full foreclosure, remember the magic words — "Produce the Note." Force the company to do full due diligence and stay in your house as long as you can — you might as well save up rent for the future. And unless your loan is a recourse loan (be very careful with state-assisted refinances, since many of these turn no-recourse loans into recourse loans that you are responsible for even after you leave your home — you do not want to be paying for this forever), you can walk away. Do me a favor, though, and don't trash the place on the way out — someone else, even you, may eventually end up renting a foreclosure, so don't trash what assets we've got indiscriminately.

2. If you have young children or are elderly, have close ties somewhere but are living far away from them in a community that you are not invested in.

   Not everyone has people (family, biological or chosen) who will give you a place at the table, thin the soup to make it stretch, let you sleep on their couch and otherwise cover your back. But if you do, recognize that these people are the beginnings of your tribe. Not all of us have tribes in one place — and some of us have multiple tribes. But if you aren't rooted where you are in some deep way, if you live there primarily for a job and you can get back to your people, think about it seriously.

The people who will most need family support are young families struggling to make do and older people who may need some help. Sometimes these two categories of people are related to one another. Not all family is good, not every friendship can go this far, but if you have these ties, they matter — in fact, they are essential.

3. If you have children or parents you need to care for far away.

   If you are going to be dealing with your parents' decline, or if you don't have custody of your kids but want to spend time with them, you need to set it up in a way that doesn't make anyone rely on airline or other expensive long-distance travel arrangements that may become unavailable. That means that if they don't come to you, you go to them. It was once perfectly viable to live across the country from your kids, and say, have them spend summers with you, but it may no longer be possible. I realize this will be enormously painful and disruptive to families, but if you are the resource for people very far away over the longer term, you need to find a way to be closer to one another, or accept that you may not be able to take on that role.

4. If you live in an extreme climate, likely to become more extreme with climate change, but you are not particularly well adapted to it.

   Unless we check global warming in some way — which at this point seems unlikely, if highly desirable — many places are going to be uninhabitable for many of the people who presently live there. Some may become literally uninhabitable over time, but what we're more likely to see is that small populations, extremely well adapted and attuned to their environment, become native to any places that are even marginally inhabitable. The question is, are you one of these people?

   If you live in a very hot, dry place and are an expert desert farmer, gifted at retaining and using every drop of water, comfortable living without lots of air-conditioning and happy to live on the food that grows there, well, great, you and your descendents will probably do very well there. But if you are fond of long showers, keep the a/c on six months a year and think that hamburgers are a right, you might want to think about somewhere else. Moreover, if you need income from the sale of your house, you might want to think about it sooner rather than later, because there will probably come a point at which the number of people who want to live in your desert declines dramatically, and it will be even tougher to sell than it is now.

Now even if some places do become uninhabitable, they probably won't do so immediately — you might well be able to live out your life where you are. But remember that it will probably become gradually and increasingly harder — the summers will be worse, the storms will be stronger, the ice pack will be smaller. Are you prepared to be that adaptable?

5. If you live among people with lousy values.

I'm on the record saying that most of us can probably get along in most places with at least some people. I don't think everyone in your town has to be like you, or that ecovillages are the only way to find community — and I put my money where my mouth is and live in a place where I am very different from my neighbors. That said, there are places you might not want to live in. And even if you can find some small community in a larger culture of rotten values, you may find that it wears you down.

Thus if your neighborhood is chronically ridden with violence and crime, one good idea is to fight it — but maybe you'd be better off somewhere else. If you bought in a gated community full of self-centered rich jerks, and now you regret it because they are pissed about your garden, living elsewhere might be nicer.

If you belong to a minority community, you might want to live where people like folks like you, or at least tolerate them, rather than a place that is hostile to them. If you rely on a religious community, you might want to live where the cultural values reflect your own.

Personally, I've always had a lot of luck finding allies wherever I went, even if we didn't share faith or experience. But there are root values we did have in common — integrity, kindness, a desire for community.

6. If you don't think your children (I mean the children in your family, even if they aren't your own) have a future where you are.

Now this is somewhat speculative, and may partly contradict what I said above — you may, for example, simply not be ready to leave a place, even if you don't think it will be sustainable in the long term. But it is worth thinking about the larger consequences of committing to a place that may not have a future. If your children have to leave to get work, or because home isn't safe or is underwater, are you prepared to part with them? Are you prepared for your family to be parted in circumstances that might not be conducive to cross-country travel? More importantly, if you have land or something you hope to pass down to your kids, are you prepared not to be able to do so? Is it an asset that they will be able to do without? Again, you can't know all this for sure, but it is worth thinking about.

7. If you plan to move anyway.

    That is, if you have a family place or somewhere you have always planned to return to, if you can, now is probably the best time. It takes time to build soil. It takes time to get to know people. It takes time to see fruit trees come to maturity. If you were planning on going anyway after a few more years of earning, now might be the right time. That said, I'd be awfully cautious about buying, and only recommend this *if you can leave* — either by selling your current place or if you've been renting. But building roots is important.

8. If you aren't prepared to live where you are the way its culture demands.

    As we get poorer and travel and transit become bigger issues, living in the country is going to change a lot— instead of living an essentially suburban life, commuting to faraway activities and relying on trucked-in supplies, you may have to shop less frequently and stay home in the country most of the time, making your own entertainment. Are you prepared to do that? Urban dwellers may have to make do in tougher conditions as infrastructure degrades. My own analogy is this — if you'd be OK living in the worst neighborhood in your city the way most of the people there live now, you'll probably be fine. But if you've been affluent and comfortable and might not be forever, be sure you can afford the city and like the life. I believe strongly that city, suburb (most of them) and country all have a future — but the differences between them are likely to become starker. If you aren't prepared to deal with those differences, consider moving.

9. If you live in an outer suburban housing development, particularly a fairly new one.

This is the one exception I make to the question of whether the suburbs are viable. Generally speaking, I think a lot of suburbs will do fine and others will adapt in different ways — some may become more like small cities, others more country-like. But the ones I think have the least hope of surviving are the larger developments that were built in the "drive 'til you buy" model of the last few years, when lower-income families had to move farther and farther away from urban or suburban job centers. If your suburb was built on a cornfield forty miles from your job, think seriously about how you will get along in an energy-constrained world or one where energy is much more costly. Do you really think anyone is going to run public transport out there? Is there topsoil? Is it a place worth maintaining and farming? Are there neighbors? Are there going to be? If you are already in a half-finished development, you really might want to get out before it's really finished.

10. If you are native to another place.

By native, I mean that many of us have a strong sense of place, and a strong sense of belonging to a place. My husband once went on a job interview at UIL Champagne-Urbana. He recalls looking across the land and seeing the horizon and thinking, "Oh, there's the ocean." But of course, there was no ocean there. His misperception lasted only a second but revealed something about his ability to live in that place — he comes from people who live on hilly land around water and know the flat horizon as the space of the sea. It is possible that he could have adapted to the flat open land of the Midwest and learned to love it, but it is also true that you should respect your sense of place if you can. I know people who have never fully adapted to their place, in the sense of being truly native to it — desert-born people who could never breathe comfortably in the humid air of the Southeast, warm-climate people who found the cold of northern winters unbearable, city folk who find the country abnormally empty and silent, water folk who can't imagine life away from a boat.

Not everyone is tied to a place — some people can live anywhere, others in a wide range of places. Some people can take their sense of place with them wherever they go, and find a new home. But some people can't. And it is simply the case that your body, and parts of your soul, are shaped by your experience. A college friend of mine once spoke of people who grew up by the sea as sharing "water thinking" and noted that she, who had lived in Hawaii, and I, who had lived in Coastal Massachusetts, had that in common in our way of viewing the world. More mundanely, people who grow up in hot climates develop more sweat glands and a better ability to cool themselves than people who grow up in cold ones — our physiology is shaped by our place.

And our native knowledge of our place is valuable — in fact, it may be the most powerful tool we have. Now some of us will have to leave our native places, to journey again as people so often have. But if we can stay where we are, knowing our flora and fauna, knowing what grows where and how things smell when the seasons change and how to heal or feed or tend with what is native there is absolutely valuable — as is the ability to adapt that knowledge as our places change. So if there is a place where you feel at home, and no other constraints bind you, perhaps you will want to go there, and be there, and help other people be there.

Again, all of these examples will have exceptions. No one, especially not me, is saying "Move now!" And some people who probably should leave will not be able to for reasons of family or obligation, or underwater housing or job commitments. But do think about all your choices.

IV. City, country, suburb — where to live

What if you don't have a place, or are definitely going to move, or you fit into one of the "shouldn't stay" categories above? What kind of place should you move to? Should you race to the country for land? Move to a walkable urban community? Choose a suburban house near your sister and nieces? All of those could be good options, depending on you and your circumstances. I'd argue that many, perhaps even most, cities, suburbs and countrysides have a future of some sort.

What's important, though, is that in every case, those futures are very different in ways they aren't right now. That is, right now the differences between the three places are easily overcome. It is perfectly possible, through miracles of cars, delivery trucks and online retailers, for city and country dwellers to have very similar frames of reference. One may live in an apartment, the other in an old farmhouse, but they can vacation in each other's neighborhoods, go see the same films, hear the same music, wear the same clothes, eat much the same diet, etc. Now they may have different priorities, and there are distinctions, but the differences are comparatively small, and easily overcome if that's one agenda.

We are about to enter a period in which the differences in way of life between urban, rural and suburban are going to be magnified dramatically. It will no longer be possible, for example, for city dwellers to have a "country place" far away, or for people to move out to the country and keep the amenities of suburban life. So the question becomes, How do you want to live?

There has been a lot of lively debate about the merits of suburb, country, city — much of it, I think, far too polarized. For example, the powerful impact of James Kunstler and the (otherwise excellent) film *The End of Suburbia* have effectively led a lot of people to dismiss the suburbs. And yet many suburbs have approximately the same population density as large nineteenth-century towns that supported considerable infrastructure. In many cases, because of the ridiculous zoning laws, there is no such infrastructure today, but large suburban houses and garages are appropriately sized to create it — interstitial businesses will spring up rapidly as people can no longer afford to shop, and zoning laws will be overthrown.

Let me be clear, I agree entirely with Kunstler that suburbia was a tremendous misallocation of resources — I think the project of the suburbs was deeply flawed. Where I disagree is in the idea that we now should— in fact must — abandon them. I think we must not, simply because industrial agriculture is increasingly disconnected from producing real food for real people. As more and more Americans get poorer and are priced out of food by rising energy prices, we will absolutely require suburbia to keep fed — that arable land, much of it superb farmland, has to be brought back into production. And since we won't be commuting from the cities, we'll be living in the houses. Yes, it would absolutely have been better if we'd designed and built better houses — but that doesn't make suburbia uninhabitable.

The same thing is true with cities — cities of one million inhabitants or so have existed for a very, very long time. I have my doubts about whether cities of eight to ten million will be sustainable in a world with high transport costs, but I also have no doubt that most cities, which were established for reasons — because they sit in useful or valuable places — will continue to be cities, even if their infrastructure changes and their population drops in the longer term. Manhattan and Chicago do have a future — but it is important to be able to live within the kind of future they do have, and within the limitations of urban centers.

The countryside suffers most from transportation costs, a small tax base and the lack of jobs. It is reasonable to believe that high energy prices may eventually mean that deliveries cease to be made to rural stores, that rural towns may find themselves unable to pay for schools or snowplows in winter, and that job losses will reverberate more severely here. And for those who live in the countryside and have enjoyed the advantages of city jobs and suburban amenities, this is likely to be a rough transition — we saw how people began to struggle in 2008 when gas prices skyrocketed. But that doesn't mean we will abandon the countryside — that's where the food comes from, and that alone creates tremendous incentives to keep some lines of connection open.

In short, I think it is important to talk about how to live in the suburbs, the city or the country in a low-energy future. I think that's more productive than extended screeds against one model or another.

Country

The countryside may suffer first and deepest from the shortage of fuels and loss of services. There are (and I am overgeneralizing here) two broad groups of people living in the country right now. The first is made up of the rural poor and working class: farmers, homesteaders and country people and those who want to be country people, that is, people with ties either to land or other people in rural areas. The other group are exurban commuters who may have hobby farms or keep horses (not all people with hobby farms and horses fall into this category, obviously) or who built McMansions out in the pretty countryside when gas was cheap, but who have no particular tie to the area, and strong ties to suburban-style amenities. They have either gotten these amenities by encouraging rural towns to use their growing tax base of exurban commuters to provide them, or by driving to where they are available.

Now the harrowing process of energy costs, high unemployment and low salaries are likely to drive a lot of Group #2, the exurban middle class, back toward population centers. Some will stay and become part of Group #1, or find some other way to do well in the rural areas, but most of them will probably pick up and move in the coming few years, dropping tax bases, leaving a lot of empty housing and otherwise emptying a large part of the rural landscape. This change is likely to have two big effects. The first is that the exurban middle class (who often moved out as far as they did because they couldn't afford good housing nearer population centers) will be competing with poorer urban residents for housing — that is, they are likely to displace lower-income people from cities and out into the countryside in a process of gentrification. The second is that the tax and service base of rural areas is likely to collapse. Many of these areas were pressed into making changes that won't be sustainable — bussing pupils to large multi-town district schools, for example, is simply going to be too expensive.

On the other hand, Group #1 probably won't move, and shouldn't. They are (not universally, but often) lower in income than the departing exurbanites, but they are also better adapted to their place. The thing that makes it possible for most of the rural working class to get along where they do is that land prices are (often, the ethanol boom has changed this in some areas of the US) comparatively cheap — and they are going to become more so, for a while at least. In many ways this may be good — some of the buyers for the foreclosed McMansions are likely to be extended families, people who were already living together by necessity in trailers, and who now can live together in a four-bedroom house. Universally my rural neighbors are extremely handy, and if they can't afford the foreclosure, would be happy to help build an addition onto their trailer from the scavenged pieces of the McMansions as well. The un-gentrification of rural areas may actually have some benefits. The same is true as absentee property owners of rural land sell or rent their holdings — some of these may be purchased, others simply reclaimed if left unused long enough.

The other thing that Group #1 often has are family ties — social connections that mean that Grandma takes care of the baby while they do their crappy low-wage jobs, and then they take care of Grandma, rather than putting her in a home. These ties are going to become increasingly valuable. Yes, the cost of gas is going to be troublesome, but rising prices for food, firewood and fiber will partially offset this, and in general, these places haven't even begun seriously economizing. Yes, it is presently illegal to put eight people in your pickup flatbed and drive to the Walmart for morning shift. How much enforcement do we expect there to be when the rural police can barely afford gas? I'm guessing, not much. Rural dwellers are suffering now because of high food and energy prices, but they have barely begun to use mitigation strategies — in most rural areas, the jobs are all in one or two locations, as are the supermarkets. It will not be hard to put together large carpools and taxi services. The problem is that, as yet, no one has figured out that this is a permanent situation, so the adaptation process has not begun.

The same goes with growing food — yes, many rural dwellers don't grow gardens. But they are often not very far removed from people who did, and they probably hunt and are often very resourceful. Living in the formal economy, it is often very hard to do more than just get by — living in the informal economy can actually be much easier in rural areas, where there are natural resources to build upon (or exploit).

My expectation is that many of those displaced from cities will be recent immigrants, many not very far removed from agricultural livelihoods. There are likely to be some difficulties with this transition, and some hostility on both ends, but in the end I suspect that many rural dwellers will find that they have a considerable amount in common with their new Mexican or Somali or Hmong neighbors. I anticipate some trouble here — and some surprising alliances.

What will not be possible is for rural dwellers to live the way they do now — families will have to do subsistence work and most may have to go back to one-earner status because they can no longer afford transport costs, which should be possible as property values begin to fall. The shift will be difficult and painful and particularly hard on the elderly, but it will be possible in many cases. That is not to say pleasant, or that many people won't be ground up and spat out in the process, but it will be possible.

Living in rural areas will mean being comfortable with a new degree of isolation — you won't be taking the kids to soccer practice and swimming lessons, because you may not be able to afford them. Many of the amenities that once made exurban towns seem like suburbia in the country will disappear. You will have to get along with the neighbors — you are going to need to work together to truck your produce into the city. You will have to be very comfortable with fixing things yourself, making do and adapting to shortages. Meeting your own needs becomes more important when every trip to the city is begrudged, and won't be repeated for a month or more.

The nature of shopping changes — every expenditure of precious cash is resented (in the county my great-great-grandfather lived in in Maine, there was the story that the only cash money in the whole county was a gold piece brought home by a neighbor from his service in the Civil War), and barter and growing/hunting/foraging your own become more and more essential. Because shopping changes, eating practices will have to change too. Do you drink a lot of milk, or eat a lot of meat? Well, I hope you plan to milk each morning and butcher your own — or have good relationships with someone who will, because you will not be buying fresh milk and meat regularly.

That's not to say that rural towns won't have resources. For example, exurban McMansions will make great home business sites, and rural areas have been known to produce great local culture — many small rural towns had opera houses and theaters, recitation and music groups, and the blues and Appalachian folk music grew up largely in rural areas where nearly everyone made music. As the urban poor move outward they will bring urban cultures into rural areas, and the cultures will blend and merge in creative (and probably sometimes destructive) ways. Rural towns once had thriving cultures — it is not impossible to imagine them having them again, or continuing to have them in many cases. But they will be small cultures. It will be necessary to derive one's pleasures from intense, deep knowledge of a narrow place rather than broad, shallow knowledge. That is, we will have to find culture and diversity in new ways. But while we can imagine having culture, we should assume virtually no *services* in rural areas — we will be on our own for protection, trash disposal, regulation of pollutants, etc. What people don't band together to do won't get done.

Access to markets will be intermittent — when you can afford the trip, rather than when you necessarily want to go. Employment may be intermittent and seasonal as well. It may also be strenuous. Eventually new market lines will be built in many places, and some places may die for lack of them. But while the transition from the habit of being able to transport quickly may be painful, it is worth remembering that rural life has existed for centuries. Anyone who has ever seen a man in a poor country walking for days bringing his flock of sheep to market, or a truck full of farmers heading down a mountain on market day, all crammed together, knows that it is perfectly possible to overcome scarcity of fuel — but setting up systems to do so is hard. Ultimately, the ability to adapt and make do will be a fundamental requirement to rural living.

City

But that's true of urban dwellers as well. Cities will certainly continue to be centers of trade, but as prices for urban infrastructure rise, money, which becomes less available and less important for rural dwellers, becomes harder to come by and more essential for urbanites. Perhaps the defining characteristic of successful urban dwellers is the same one that defines rural dwellers — the ability to adapt. But the adaptive abilities required are different. While rural dwellers may need subsistence skills, urban dwellers may need the ability to recognize commercial opportunities and fill them, to rapidly shift from one business to another — first importing goods, then auctioning repossessed items, then being the middleman with local farmers. The informal economy is likely to be just as important for urban dwellers as for rural ones, but instead of the subsistence economy subsidizing job loss, scavenging, black market activities and meeting newly opened needs and taking advantage of short-notice opportunities are likely to be among the biggest sources of jobs in cities. Economic flexibility will probably be key.

While urban centers are likely to be the last places actual shortages hit, the high cost of urban living — even slum living — is likely to effectively cut many people out of marketplaces. And there is far less space for further consolidation in urban housing — but there is some, and consolidation there will be, both because urban owners will only be able to keep their condos and homes by bringing in other people, and because density is profitable. Slum housing is among the most profitable house per square foot in the world, ironically.

Living well in cities will probably involve the ability to live in quite small spaces, and to tolerate infrastructure breakdowns with reasonable good cheer. These won't happen as often as they will in the countryside, but when the sewer lines break or the gas goes off or the electricity goes out, the consequences are likely to be considerably more acute. While country dwellers may find that many services simply disappear — no one to plow the road, no police anymore — intermittency is likely to be a characteristic of urban life.

The ability to work with others and self-regulate well is also likely to be absolutely essential. Urban population densities bring the threat that fairly commonsense responses to breakdown could lead to disaster — for example, if the water stops flowing, it only makes sense to begin bringing human manure out of the buildings, but everyone must do this in a way that avoids water contamination and that handles the wastes wisely, or disease spreads and the city stinks. If the gas goes out, the temptation to use a small burner to cook becomes almost intolerable — but the need to regulate these and train people in safety is acute, since a single fire can take out a whole apartment building — or neighborhood.

One of the questions worth asking is whether you will like urban life as it is lived by the poor — because that is probably the reality for most of us, no matter where we live. For those who are living comfortably in cities, this may be a very rude awakening. And for those whose experience of urban poverty is primarily of the graduate student or actor/waitress kind, a similar, if not quite as acute, shock awaits.

Job losses are rising in the financial centers and in tourism and tourism-tied industries, and will rise further. People won't be able to borrow money to go to college, so professors will be laid off. Those who aren't comfortably well-off themselves but rely on the disposable income of the middle and upper middle classes may also suffer as that class becomes less wealthy. If you presently enjoy all the benefits of urban life with extended trips into the countryside to reconnect with nature, ask yourself how you will like doing without these — in August, during a heat wave. If you have depended on air-conditioning to keep cool and heat to keep warm, think about what happens when the infrastructure fails, or when you simply can't pay the bills. If you love your job, ask yourself whether you will love the work you are going to be able to get. Generally speaking, I would say that if you would be reasonably comfortable living in the poorest and worst neighborhood in your city now, you'll be fine in the city. Many urban poor already experience most of the dangers of post-peak life — health complications, insufficient access to food, energy shut-offs, indifferent responses from the wealthy, an inability to rely on the police.

The two worries most articulated about urban life are security and food. Both of these are real worries — but they apply to everyone else on the paradigm too. Rural areas that don't produce all they eat risk not getting imports because it isn't worth bringing in supplies to the outer margins of the supply lines. Rural areas that have poor alliances between neighbors are likely to experience rising crime rates, as poverty provides greater incentives for crime and violence. There is generally more crime in urban areas, but there are also more people — alliances are remarkably powerful in this regard. Again, urban dwellers may be broadly divided into two groups — the kind who politely try not to know their neighbors and who never make eye contact, and those who have strong community ties. Many urban dwellers in poor neighborhoods have been dealing with precisely the same things we are facing for decades — inadequate security, poor police presence or reason to fear the police themselves, high crime rates — and often community groups are able to minimize these problems. The successful will be those who are prepared to work together in deep ways, and to prioritize the welfare of the whole community.

As for food, it is far more likely that you will go hungry because you can't afford to buy food than because there is none in the stores. Shortages are a possibility, but again, cities are cities for a reason — they are often at the hub of rail, water or other supply lines. Some cities, particularly those with acute water shortages, may simply end up with a comparatively small population by necessity. But for the rest, the food will come in, usually. The question is, will you be able to buy it? My own feeling is that cities will have to produce a large portion of their produce and probably meat — the end of refrigerated shipping is coming for most of us. While grains will probably be shipped out by train, things that have to be kept cold, that now come from irrigated farmlands far away, are probably going to slip out of the reach of many people. Fortunately, urban farming is possible — Hong Kong, for example, produces a large portion of its meat and vegetables within the city limits. For the driest cities — LA, Las Vegas, Phoenix-Tucson — this may not be possible, and that may be their undoing (they won't go away, but the populations of these cities may contract dramatically). Not coincidentally, these are also tremendously hot places, and without air-conditioning, urban dwellings may be nearly intolerable.

But it is completely possible to imagine even Manhattan or San Francisco or Chicago or Toronto producing quite a lot of its own meat and produce, and certainly Cleveland and Atlanta and Ottawa will be able to do so. It will be done in vacant lots and rooftops, on stoops and balconies in containers, in tiny backyards and by the reclamation of public space. Food, including livestock, will have to go wherever there is room.

Anyone who plans to stay in a city really must take some responsibility for their own food systems in a commitment to produce as much as possible within city limits. The great difficulty for cold climate cities will be heat — if utilities become intermittent or too expensive, it will be very cold, and there are fewer options for heating in densely populated areas. But cold won't generally kill you — it will be merely unpleasant, and in worst-case scenarios the heat island effect and the sheer proximity of neighbors will probably keep most people alive as they wait for spring.

And thus we are back to this question of what kind of person you are. There are those entrepreneurial spirits who will take any job, do any work, turn anything into gold, and will always be able to buy food. And then there are those that simply can't. It is worth knowing thyself. Again, the merits of strong family and community ties come up — a great deal can be accomplished by self-help groups working together. Food supplies can be bought collectively, slum conditions overcome, community gardens reclaimed from the city, security provided, soup kitchens opened. But one must work together, and be prepared to adapt. Where to live may depend on how you want to work with people.

Both urban and rural life will require community ties. In rural places things simply won't happen without them; in urban ones they will be required to restrain one's self-interest for the greater good. My own observation is that most people tend to prefer one kind of these regulations to another — they chafe, for example, at the idea that someone could restrict their right to do as they want on their property, no matter how stupid or dangerous, or they chafe at the idea that others might be doing things they consider unwise in the privacy of their own homes when they are not there to observe and stop them. It is useful, I think, to decide which sort of person you are, and thus, where you will be happy — out in the country where you can get drunk and shoot deer through the unopened windows of your trailer or in the city where you can get drunk and lecture a passerby on the evils of jaywalking or public urination.

Suburbs

Then again, many of us prefer a middle ground — and suburbia, of course, is supposed to be precisely that. Whether the 'burbs are the best or the worst of both worlds depends on your perspective and probably on the kind of suburb you are living in. Many suburbs near where I live actually have long histories as towns with meaningful economies, and now simply have more housing in them. It is not at all improbable to imagine much, say, of suburban Boston reconstituting itself as towns, changing its restrictive zoning to allow the transformation of garages into shops and spare bedrooms into rental housing.

The great advantage of suburbia is that it is often both reasonably close to some kind of employment and has land attached to it that can still produce a substantial part of one's needs. Most suburban lots won't enable any kind of self-sufficiency, but most suburbanites could meet a surprising portion of their needs, though not enough to obviate the need for supplemental income. While rural dwellers may have little or no cash to pay the property taxes and urban dwellers may not have enough cash to buy food, suburbanites will struggle on both ends — their houses cost them a great deal initially and they generally won't have large enough surpluses for sale. Successful suburban dwelling may require more flexibility than either urban or rural life, because in most cases it will involve maintaining an income while also minimizing costs so that people can keep their houses.

On the other hand, this may actually be possible. If people are willing to consolidate housing and bring extended families (biological or chosen) together, keeping a roof over one's head should be more manageable. Meanwhile, there will probably be several empty lots across the road, and a few foreclosed buildings to take down and scavenge. We have essentially been filling suburbia with a large chunk of our wealth — it is no longer worth what we thought it was, of course, but that doesn't mean that boards and reclaimed insulation, copper piping or shingles have no value. That wealth will probably keep a surprisingly large number of people going, while they also grow gardens and commute, crammed together, into population centers.

The transition from nuclear to extended family is unlikely to be easy — and less easy on middle-class suburbanites than on either the rural or urban poor, who already require social ties to keep their lives going. The distances between suburban families will also be a problem as people begin to negotiate — which set of parents do you live near or with? Who moves? Whose house goes on the block and who keeps theirs? In many cases, this process will be shaped by events rather than intent, but I suspect it will go better if intent is involved, if the conversations required for it to happen begin sooner rather than later.

The anomie of suburbia is legendary, and probably wildly overstated. Some neighborhoods are better at ties than other, but it is true that these ties are generally recreational rather than practical. That is, neighborhoods are having barbecues and commercial parties (cooking equipment, sex toys and lingerie being the most popular), playdates and PTA meetings, not organizing for survival. That is true elsewhere, but suburbia has tended to have fewer self-help groups (by which I mean practical, not emotional) than cities or the country. That will have to change for suburbia to be successful.

And this, I think, may be the root shift that has to occur in suburbia — what must finally change is the perception of what constitutes "a good life." The suburbs were the good life for millions of Americans and Canadians — and what may ultimately hurt us most is what Kunstler calls "the psychology of previous investment." It was our inability to let go of what we expected a particular life to be that cost us. I think that Kunstler and others are right when they say that this is particularly acute for suburban dwellers. Zoning regulations, for example, will have to be overturned to allow people to survive in many suburbs — and that is likely to be contentious, simply because disaster never hits everyone equally.

But the psychology of previous investment has another side — it may prevent us from abandoning the suburbs, but the sheer psychological weight of our investment in them may ultimately enable us to make the shift. That is, people are attached to their place, to the idea of their place, and may find ways to make that space mean something else in order to keep it. The question of whether the suburbs are the best or worst of both worlds will depend, finally, on whether our attachment to our previous investment is to the physical place or to the very idea of suburbia. If it is to the place, to the actual land and soil beneath our feet, and if we can become attached to our actual houses and stop moving so much and settle in one place, it is possible that suburbia could thrive in many regions. If it turns out that what we wanted was Eden without the snakes, suburbia will fall apart.

Suburbia is so tied up with children and family life that I feel I should say something about that. The suburban model of childhood will simply have to come to an end. Many more children will probably be home-schooled, more locally organized schools will emerge and many more children will probably be put to work sooner helping out at home. The child-centered model will probably disintegrate, replaced by a family-centered model in which children are expected to pitch in and listen and are not always treated like visiting heads of state to be deferred to and offered the best. For those who moved to the suburbs for their children, the loss of that way of life, and with it the hopes of giving their children the best they could, will be painful. For the children involved, who have been under tremendous psychological pressure due to their place at the center of their parents' universes, there may actually be a measure of relief.

Suburbanites will always be more at risk in the general economy than those who are closer to economic centers, and will always be more at risk in terms of food security than those who can meet their entire dietary needs. But most suburbs offer enormous potential to allow people to live with one foot in the formal economy and another in the informal economy (or both feet in the informal, but in different branches thereof). Dmitry Orlov observes that most post-collapse Soviet gardens were very small — smaller than the average suburban lot. Now grains will keep coming in — but except for the very outermost suburbs, the lines between city and suburb are fairly strong. Even if public transport doesn't exist, there are enough people, a large enough market, to justify moving food and fuel and goods out to many suburbs. Houses are large enough for suburban dwellers to stockpile, just as rural people do — both the produce of their gardens and food bought on infrequent trips to supply centers by shared vehicle.

Suburban dwellers will probably need a wider balance of skills than either their city or country counterparts — they will simultaneously need the skills to minimize dependence on the public economy and the ability to function well there. They will need to be able to grow their own, fix their own and make do, and also to run businesses or find work when old sources dry up. And like everyone else, they will require strong community ties to keep back the forces of collapse, and to create a local economy and culture worth having.

On the other hand, while rural dwellers may struggle to get their pigs or their fruit to market in an era of reduced transportation, suburban-ites who can produce moderate surpluses will have hungry and relatively proximate markets at hand. I recall someone telling me about their cous-ins who became "dill millionaires" growing dill on an eighth-of-an-acre suburban lot outside of Moscow, simply bringing their herbs into the city. For those in the areas around cities, the old system whereby subur-banites shuttled in to work in city businesses may continue — and the commuters may be bringing in eggs and apples to sell to coworkers. Or the jobs themselves may disappear, and the eggs and apples become the point of the trip.

In short, I don't think it is easy to generalize about where the best place to live is. In all cases, flexibility, adaptability, self-sufficiency and practicality will matter a lot. And no choice is inherently bad — it depends on what we are prepared for, what skills we want to emphasize, what balance we hope to find. It is easier, of course, to generalize about one choice or another, but to do so is ultimately less productive.

Profile 2

Bruce and Kathy, western Massachusetts:
The open house

When you walk into Bruce and Kathy Harrison's home, you instinctively feel like you've come into a place anyone could call home. There's a warmth and friendliness that pervades the house in a small village in a rural community in Massachusetts, and it speaks volumes. Bruce and Kathy and their children, too, are the sort of people you could settle in with and talk to for hours over a cup of tea, even if you've just met. And that's just what Eric and I did when we visited on a cold day in November.

This sense of comfort and hominess is important, because for decades, Bruce and Kathy opened their home to hundreds of foster children. Besides their seven children, adopted and biological, and four grandchildren, the house has been a short- and long-term home to many children who needed, more than anything, to feel a place could be home. They were Massachusetts Foster Parents of the Year once, and Kathy is the author of two wonderful books about their experience. Their home really is their castle — not a fortified one with barriers around it but a welcoming space integrated into their community and open to the world.

Bruce is retired and Kathy is a writer. Her book *Just In Case: How to Be Self-Sufficient When the Unexpected Happens* is a modern bible for people who have no idea where to begin with basic preparations for more difficult times. And Kathy lives what she preaches — her home is a model of preparedness, but nothing could be further from the stereotypical bunker.

Their home backs onto a river, and the flat land that spreads back toward it is home to their garden and bee yards (Bruce took up beekeeping), alongside the playset and kids' toys in the yards. When we visited, they had two of their children at home, Phoebe, six, and Karen, fifteen, and one of Kathy's foster daughters had returned to stay as well. My kids were thrilled to be welcomed into the house and the younger ones set off as a troop to play and explore while we enjoyed Kathy's wonderful cooking.

Every corner of the house is put to good use — there is toilet paper stored in one bedroom closet, and grains and beans in another. Kathy knows that, in tough times, she might see quite a number of people flock to her home for a secure place, whether needy kids or extended family, and she's really ready. She's been building up her supplies gradually over the years.

The garden was put to bed for the winter, but the raspberry bushes and the garden beds showed signs of abundant harvests — signs that you could see reproduced on her kitchen shelves. There was wine being made and jars of jams. We ate the most delicious pickles, into which she'd thrown all the last of the garden produce.

Kathy's tiny town is home to a surprising number of actively engaged people, and they've organized a number of events — preparedness isn't just personal, it is collective. The day we visited, Karen and Kathy's foster daughter were out getting ready for an annual event held at their church just a few houses over. Neighbors had donated items they wanted to get rid of, and everyone would gather later for food and a chance to take something home — everything free. The two teenage girls spent the whole afternoon setting up and getting ready for the event. Another friend dropped in, neighbors called and one got a sense of a community working together.

We stopped to see the community sewing space built into the same church and ran into members of their local preparedness group. Kathy talked about her share in a dairy CSA, and the way she works with neighbors who house the pigs that they collectively butcher.

Kathy and Bruce are preparing for a world in which their two youngest daughters, both of whom have disabilities, may need their support because larger social supports aren't available — and they recently had Kathy's son and daughter-in-law move in as well. In each case, they make room — as they have been for decades — to work together and build a better life.

Five

Staying warm and keeping cool

I. Thinking about heating and cooling

OUR FIRST WORRY WHEN WE IMAGINE LIVING WITH LESS is probably basic issues of health and comfort, and high on the list are keeping warm and cool. Some of us are already struggling to deal with these issues, thanks to the increasing number of violent heat waves and struggles to pay the electric or heating bills.

Before we go to the question of how exactly to remain as comfortable as possible, it's important to go back to the question of what we actually need and how we are thinking about this, because it has at least as deep an effect on how we approach this as the actual method we use.

We all know that people have lived in very cold and very hot places in the world for most of human history, and most of them still have no central heating or air-conditioning. We all know that no one, not even the richest folks, had those things until the last century or so. So any discussion of heating or cooling has to begin from the recognition that our sense that we "have to" have certain temperatures, barring a few comparatively rare medical conditions, is, in fact, cultural rather than physiological. Human beings would not have survived in northern climates living in houses (or caves for that matter) heated only by an open fire for thousands of years if they couldn't tolerate temperatures below 65 degrees inside.

I realize this probably won't make me anyone's best friend, but the truth is that except for the ill, the very elderly and the very underweight, you can regulate your body temperature in a house that is quite cold — in fact, you evolved to live that way. If you dress very warmly, in layers, and move around a lot and have enough blankets, you will be fine — period. If you have an infant, the best strategy is to keep them against your body all the time — and they will be just fine. That does not mean you will always be happy and comfortable about temperature, however.

What is true about living with minimal heat is that people lived very differently — they slept with another person and spent their days together in warm spots or moving around and being active. They often slept a lot more in the winter and spent a lot of time when they were not active in bed.

The same is true of extremely high temperatures — while the world is manifestly warmer than it once was, it is also true that human beings have lived in very, very hot places for much of their history and handled the temperature extremes. Again they lived differently — activity ceased in the heat of the day, life moved more into the nighttimes, people spent more time in and near water. For example, in some parts of Southeast Asia, a shower (a bucket with holes in it to sluice yourself with) is a basic part of hospitality — you are greeted with the questions, "Have you eaten?" and "Have you showered?"

It is true that most of us are physiologically better adapted to one kind of temperature than another — if you are from a hot place and move to a cold one, you will feel the cold more, and vice versa. People raised in warm places actually do have more sweat glands, for example, than people from cold climates. That said, our bodies can also adapt individually — someone who spends a lot of time working outdoors in a hot climate will build sweat glands, and someone who doesn't overheat their house and goes out a lot will acclimate to colder and colder temperatures.

The process of acclimation and adapting our lives is probably the most basic thing we can do to deal with heat and cold. And up until now, we've been using tools (central heating and cooling) that prevent acclimation — that is, we spend half our day in air-conditioning, so our bodies don't adapt to the heat. Everyone who has ever worked outside on a bitterly cold day knows how hot even a lightly heated house feels when you go in.

Now the odds are good our bosses probably won't let us take a siesta during the heat of the day, or give us the winter off to hibernate, and that we can't totally change our lives to adapt to temperature. But we can change some aspects of our lifestyles, and our ways of thinking to adapt to the weather, and can work on acclimation.

One of the things that rising energy costs change is our relationship to central heating or cooling. When energy is cheap and widely available and perceived as having no major environmental consequences, we can afford to keep the whole house at a comfortable temperature whether we need it or not. When costs go up and impact matters, central heating and cooling don't work very well — the house temperature goes up above your comfort level or down below it, and localized heating or cooling starts to have the advantage.

Why? Well, we tend to think of heating or cooling as "keeping the house" at some temperature, but localized heating or cooling simply doesn't work that way. Over by my woodstove there's a spot that is often nearly 80 degrees — it feels great if I've been sitting at the computer in my chilly office, but it's far too hot to sit there all the time, although my mom, who is always cold, makes it her headquarters when she visits. Out a bit farther the temperature is optimal, and that's where everyone reads or hangs out. Farther still it gets cooler, and the sleeping spaces (where we are warmed by heavy blankets and body heat) are the coolest of all. Elderly people or those who have been ill or new babies can have the spot next to the fire and be warm — this has a long tradition. Those who need it less can have periods of warmth for quiet work, and less heat when they are up and moving.

The same is true of cooling — if you truly need air-conditioning, localizing it to the most urgent spot — perhaps the bedroom or living room — gives you comfortable sleep or a place to congregate and do your work. This is less costly than trying to cool a whole house, but it also gets you adequate cooling in a localized space. If you don't use a/c, it may be enough to move your bedroom to the shady north side of the house where the cross breeze comes, or put your mattress on the floor for summer, or sleep outside on the hottest nights.

The most localized heating and cooling of all is the heating or cooling of your body — this could be as simple as dressing warmly, wearing a hat indoors, holding a cup of tea or coffee or even hot water, using a hot water bottle in bed or on the back of your chair, or putting your feet on a hot brick or other heated substance. Last year my office, far away from the heat sources, hovered in the low 50s to high 40s, and I wrote this book that way, rather cozily actually, with my fingerless gloves, my tea, my hot bricks and a bathrobe over my clothes. For cooling, soaking a bandana or freezing it and putting it under your hat or over your hair, drinking copiously and sticking your feet in cool water are good strategies — it isn't always necessary to cool your environment, just your body.

The people who most need to be wary of both extreme heat and extreme cold are the elderly, disabled, ill or very young. They should have the protected spot — but that doesn't mean the entire house needs to be a protected spot. It is also important to note that the victims of extreme temperatures generally live alone — it might be more accurate to say they die, not simply from heat or cold, but from isolation and lack of support to handle the temperature extremes. So as we talk about this stuff, both for winter and summer, start thinking about your community and neighborhood. Are there people who are potentially vulnerable? Well, now would be the time to get to know them, start checking on them occasionally, build a relationship so that no one in your neighborhood dies from lack of other people's support. We all have some responsibility to keep one another alive.

II. How not to freeze

Despite the fact that I believe people should use a lot less energy, I am not proposing here that people in cold climates go cold turkey on supplemental heating. This is about how to survive if you find yourself without heating fuel in a cold climate. Why do you need to know this? Because it happens, and more often than you think.

How could it happen? Well, you could live in a place that requires minimal supplemental heat, and have a sudden, unusual cold snap, as much of Florida did in 2009. Or you could rely on electric lines that are down, and find yourself without a furnace. You could find you can't pay your utility bill, and despite legal obstacles to shutting people off during winter, find yourself, as some people have, without heat.

You could rely on propane and oil and simply have no money to fill your tank, as others do. Existing gas lines could fail or be disrupted. Or your furnace could break in winter, and you could not be able to get a repairman for several days. The reality is that heating can fail for many reasons in both the short and the long term, and people end up cold.

It is important to remember, however, that cold can kill you — but barring total lack of shelter or certain medical conditions, most of us NEED NOT die of heat or cold. The truth is that most such deaths do not have to happen — so we need to make the information that allows people to survive cold and heat much more widely available, or we will have more deaths and more suffering.

This information is also necessary because fear of cold, particularly, may lead us to do things that make us *less* able to survive in the long run — burning wood or other sources unsafely and causing fires, or misusing gas and propane heaters, burning toxic substances like pressure-treated wood or any burning with inadequate ventilation, etc.

Or it might lead us to prioritize short-term comfort over long-term survival, deforesting the northern US to keep warm for a few winters and leaving our kids with an eroded, polluted, warmer world, or burning coal in personal stoves on a large scale. Our fear of heat and cold, and our mistaken impression that we'll die if we let things get colder, can lead us to actually die — or make ourselves sick, or the world less habitable for the next generation.

The first thing you need is shelter — homelessness is deadly in the winter. Find some — this is why you need community so badly. This means that if you lose your house, you and yours still need a place to live. If you don't have family, you need friends or roommates or some way of finding a place to live, whether couch surfing or using existing safety nets, including shelters. Many people live in vehicles, and while this is not at all ideal, it is better than no shelter at all. And if you are lucky enough to keep your house, I hope you'll be the one opening the doors to others — because it could be you next time.

Even the most hideously insulated houses in the US (and there are some truly appalling houses out there — the older parts of mine not wholly excluded) are far better in many cases than the shelters people survived in for millennia. I know I keep harping on this, but badly insulated is a relative thing — yes, more insulation would be good, and contacting your congressperson to get more funding (especially including *GRANTS* for low-income families) for insulation is essential — but it is worth remembering that the Lapps routinely dealt with minus 50+ temperatures in tents made of one layer of reindeer skin and heated only by body heat. It is worth recalling that when people began living in the US, winter temperatures were considerably colder than they are now, and windows were made of oilskin over holes in the walls, and houses were heated by a central fire pit. Human beings can manifestly live without central heating. I know you don't think you can, but you can. It is in your genes.

Let us imagine you are now living in a very cold place and cannot buy heating fuel, or it isn't available, and you are facing a long, cold winter. Assume that social support programs are overwhelmed or unavailable (these should be your first resort). What do you do?

The first thing you do is feed yourself and your family well. This may seem secondary, but it isn't. If you have a choice between inadequate heat and enough food for your family, dump the heat and buy more food. There's an ongoing crisis in the US of families whose food budget gets consumed by winter heating — their children lose weight and get sick from the cold, because they aren't getting enough calories and can't maintain their body temperature. Food — and good healthy food — is essential. If you are going to live with little or no heat, put what money you have toward food.

Next is heat yourself — this seems obvious, but I'm continually surprised by people who skip this step, or don't go about it thoroughly. You should be wearing warm clothing — and lots of it, in layers. If you are going to be going in and out of different temperature spaces, you want layered breathable fabrics if possible. Good clothing is far cheaper than heating your house — the same goes for blankets. Think lots of layers, insulation of extremities: multiple layers of warm socks, hats indoors, fingerless gloves, pulse warmers, leg warmers (yeah, yeah, I know it isn't the '80s, but they still have their place, especially if you wear skirts in the winter a lot — and personally, I find skirts over heavy tights or leggings warmer than pants). If you have the skill set, you can make warm woolen things — and if you can't afford yarn, get old wool sweaters from Goodwill and unravel them and use them for yarn.

Layer your clothes — long johns under T-shirts under turtlenecks under flannel shirts, and throw a bathrobe over it (at our house, bathrobes aren't just for bed) if no one is going to see you anyway. For children, blanket sleepers are your friend. You can get them to very large sizes these days. My kids sleep in bedrooms that have no direct heating, only ambient from the wood heat downstairs, and are comfortable wearing long johns and socks with blanket sleepers over them. You could put sweatpants and sweatshirts over the blanket sleepers, if necessary. And the kids can stay in the sleepers all day long if you don't have to go out.

OK, once you've got so many clothes on you look like the Michelin Man, you have to deal with retaining heat — that's where the calories and hot beverages come in. That means you need some capacity to warm food. This means either keeping some traditional energy source (gas, electric, propane, oil) or burning some fuel that you can afford in a way that will warm your tea and your hands as well. Sterno or a kerosene stove, or even a hot burning candle (there are multi-wick emergency candles) will work, but these are short-term solutions. What you probably want is a rocket stove, a super-efficient homemade stove — plenty of information on the Internet! Remember to use these outside unless you know they are safe indoors!

Once you have a stove, you can probably heat enough water for hot water bottles, or warm up a hot stone or some grains or beans in a bag, and either put these near your body (with a layer or two of cloth to prevent accidental burning — be careful with this when using it with children) or in your bed to warm it. Elderly people and those who can't move much to keep warm will probably need a regular supply of hot water bottles, tea and other warming items to keep comfortable, or a warm body — a cat or several cats, a dog or a human — to snuggle up to.

It is very important to understand hypothermia — most of the people who die of cold, besides the homeless, are elderly or disabled. Hypothermia muddles your thinking — you can even start feeling warm and strip off your clothes. So it is important to move around, eat regularly, be checked on — more people in your house represent a significant safety net. In addition, more people mean significantly more warmth. Animals also have a role here — the proverbial "three dog night" is not just a band.

The next thing you need is a warm place to sleep — if you mostly keep moving when you get cold at home you'll be fine, but at night, when you are lying down, you need to be warmer. Again, good blankets aren't always cheap, but they are cheaper than heating oil. Check out Goodwill, thrift shops, yard sales. You will need a lot of them. Space blankets are also a good insulator, layered between other blankets. Wear a hat while sleeping, plus warm pajamas and long johns. Down comforters are ideal — and even better are down sleeping bags designed for winter camping.

Again, other people are a huge help, so sleep with someone. We live in a weird culture where sharing a bed implies sexuality in a way it does not in most cultures. My four children sleep together in a bed (they have four beds, they just always end up together piled up like puppies in a heap). We make jokes about children sharing a bed and think of this as a sign of poverty, but it is in fact about warmth, love and comfort. Very few people in the world sleep in their own rooms, in their own space, with no one. So find someone to sleep with — even if it is a pet.

If it is very cold, you can further insulate your sleeping area by making it smaller and tighter. One option is the classic four-poster bed — build a frame around your bed, then hang heavy, warm curtains on all four sides and over the top. Your body heat will warm the space around you. Or set up a tent in your house and sleep in there (kids think this is cool). Do NOT sleep in a tent in a room with a heating stove of any kind, and don't sleep in a tent you don't know how to get out of easily — that's a major fire hazard, and remember what I said about not doing short-term things that will kill you. If you go the four-poster route, you'll want to wash the bedding regularly if you have allergies.

You can also insulate rooms inexpensively by using heavy cloth for tapestries, plastic or bubble wrap over windows, window quilts — basically, you should think in terms of living in as small a space as possible. Again, think, "What did my ancestors do in the winter?" They mostly hung out together in the warmest spot. That spot will be warmer if you are all there together, and do any cooking there if you have an indoor-safe stove. Be mindful of ventilation, however — it is better to be colder and alive than warm and dead. I strongly recommend that everyone have a battery-charged smoke and CO detector in any room they will have any kind of heater in, and that you either acquire solar battery chargers and rechargeable batteries and/or long-life smoke detector batteries.

What else can you do? Spend some time if you can in a warmer public place — go to the library, visit friends, go shopping. There will probably be warming shelters in cold times — don't be ashamed to go to one. A short period feeling comfortable makes a big difference. Keep up everyone's immune system by exercising, getting fresh air, eating well and taking care of yourself — the cold is quite tolerable when you are healthy, but tough when you are sick.

III. How to keep cool

Just as it is possible to live without supplemental heat in a very cold climate, most people can live in the worst hot weather without cooling — but not without water. Without adequate water, you may well die. This is a major concern because in many places hot weather and increased air conditioner usage lead to power outages that may affect water access, and heat waves also often come during drought periods. This is why you should store water, have a good filter system and work with your community to have backup water systems — because dehydration kills, and most heat mitigation strategies involve water.

How do you know if you are drinking enough? Well, if it is really hot, you should pretty much always have water around. If you are working hard in hot weather, you should be drinking pretty constantly — and some of what you drink should have a little bit of sugar or fruit juice in it (assuming you aren't already eating things that do). Rehydration.org has information on making oral rehydration syrups and the best things to drink when you are dehydrated. Everyone needs this information, not just people in hot places — but don't get dehydrated to begin with if at all possible. Your urine should be light colored, not dark. If it is dark, get drinking. Make sure that babies nurse often — and do choose to nurse if at all possible. In a crisis, if safe water isn't available, breast milk can save lives!

Next, dress for the weather (it is astonishing how much of our clothing is designed for indoors even in hot weather — T-shirts have non-breathing polyester in them or are otherwise unsuitable). There are essentially two theories of how to dress for hot weather. The first is to wear something roughly like the Indian salwar kameez — loose-fitting, light-colored cotton clothing that covers your whole body and keeps the sun off. Add a natural fiber hat that breathes (remember, covering your head will make you hotter if you don't choose breathable materials) and you are set. The other possible model for dressing is to wear as little as possible — this will depend on where you live, how much time you spend in the sun and a host of other factors. I personally think the former has a lot of advantages, but there are many people who prefer to minimize clothing altogether. Remember risks of skin cancer in your planning.

Once you are dressed we come back to how to handle extreme heat, and the answer is, with lots and lots of water. If you don't have to sit in a board meeting, you might be able to sit in a pool — even a kiddie pool can do a lot. If you don't have that much water, how about a pan of water to put your feet in? Soak a bandana and put it over your head or around your neck. Take a shower. If the power isn't on or you can't, fill a bucket and pour (or dip) it over your head, or take a sponge bath.

Get outside in the shade — and if you don't have shade, make some. If you live somewhere hot and have the luxury of owning, you need trees, lots of them. Plant trees that will shade your house and minimize your cooling costs and need for air-conditioning. Vines can provide quick shade over your windows — you can plant them in containers and trellis them up over windows if you don't have dirt. The more green stuff around you, the cooler you will be. Urban dwellers with flat roofs might look into green roofs, in which your roof is covered with growing plants that help reduce heating and cooling costs.

Use awnings, blinds and shade screens to keep sun from warming the house. Open windows at night and close them during the day. If your heat is dry, hang wet laundry or sheets up in the house to lower the temperature (this will make things worse in humid climates). Swamp coolers use less electricity than a/c, but again, are only suitable for very dry climates. Just as insulation is the key to minimizing heat usage, it is also the key to cooling — just make sure you do it well and keep good air quality and ventilation in mind.

Stay outside as much as you can. If outside has a breeze and the air quality isn't too horrible, sleep there. This is what people did before air conditioning — they slept outside. City folks slept on balconies (make sure they are safe and this is legal), others got out in their backyards. Certainly do all cooking outside, or if you must cook inside, cook everything that needs heating the night before or early in the morning. Part of our problem is that we are such an indoor people — both for acclimation and comfort, we need to recognize that life can be moved outside to the porch or the yard when weather requires.

Once, farm families had screened summer kitchens or outdoor cooking areas designed for dealing with summer and keeping the heat out of the house. A simple screen house could provide eating and sleeping shaded areas, with food prepared on a nearby fire pit, earth oven, grill or sun oven (or better yet, a combination). Others might move a wood cookstove outside, or get fancier with some permanent structure.

If you have the luxury, you can shift your work times — get up very early, stay up late and sleep or rest or work quietly during the hottest periods. Get a headlamp so you can do chores outside at night. Don't exercise much during the worst weather, if you can avoid it (many people have no choice).

Now we come to the fly in the ointment — air quality. While most of us can deal with pure heat, many people simply can't tolerate the air outside during the hottest weather. People who are ill or vulnerable to air quality (and while we vary in sensitivity, poor air quality affects everyone) or who have to do strenuous work are screwed.

If there is power in the area as a whole, you can often make it to an air-conditioned cooling shelter — so make use of these if you need them and they are available. If nothing else has power, your local hospital may still have a generator and might allow someone with severe health issues to sit in their lobby. If there is no a/c around, go near water — even a small lake will have slightly better air quality over it, as well as cooler temperatures. You can also soak a bandana, piece of muslin or cheesecloth and tie it over your mouth and nose to reduce pollutants and cool the air going into your lungs. If you have to work outside, move slowly, take it easy, and again, drink.

If you have a serious health problem that means that the air quality and temperatures in your area are intolerable to you during routine summer weather, or the routine summer weather projected to be normal in the coming decades, you may have to think about relocation. The statement that no one needs to die from cold is not quite true for heat —as long as we continue to pollute the air as heavily as we do now, there are going to be people who suffer badly from that pollution. If your life depends on adequate heating or cooling or air cleaning being provided by grid systems, I really don't like saying this, but you would be smart to seriously consider living in a place where you are in less danger.

IV. Making our buildings work better

Most of us heat our home one of three ways: with traditional furnaces using natural gas, electricity or oil. Natural gas is the most common, then electric, while oil is extremely common in some rural areas of the Northeast and very rare everywhere else. Almost all cooling is electric.

All of these come with the potential for rapid, prohibitive price rises in the coming years (and are already prohibitive for some people), and all are potentially vulnerable to supply disruptions too. Oil is the most vulnerable, but gas and electricity may also be subject to supply constraints and systemic problems. We already have problems with brownouts and blackouts during peak demand periods for electricity in summer, and other heating and cooling resources may also experience difficulties.

So what options do you have? Basically two: you can rely on less (or in some places, no) heat or cooling, by increasing your insulation, or you can use some other energy source to generate the resources you need to heat and cool yourself, your immediate area and part of your home. Again, I emphasize that most of us should not be thinking of heating a whole American super-sized house, but instead living in smaller spaces with less heat and cooling. Period.

First, insulation. The Affordable Comfort Institute has been working to find ways to retrofit American homes along the Passivhaus lines — those are European homes developed to use 90 percent less heating and cooling energy than the average conventional home. ACI has developed retrofitting programs, but these are prohibitively expensive for most private homes. The least expensive version looks to add rigid board insulation to existing inside walls, but they are still putting their materials together and this is a job to be worked on carefully, as ventilation, outgassing and mold are all concerns.

For most of us, using vastly less heating energy is going to be less about getting the same warmth with less energy and more about learning to adapt to different models of heating and cooling. Still, there's a great deal that good, careful insulation and design can do. Much of it is outside the scope of this book, but there are resources in the bibliography that can guide you through them. If you can afford to do a major reinsulation, this is a wise place to put extra money.

A lot of people don't have any extra money, however. Without grants for weatherization for the poor and lower middle class on a huge scale, most people won't make major retrofits, simply because the cost is utterly prohibitive — for most low-income people, coming up with $4K to heat your house is simply more feasible than $10K to retrofit it. There are grants and reinsulation programs out there, but they fall vastly short of the need, particularly in places where oil heat is the norm, as in the rural Northeast, where millions of homes would need to be reinsulated very quickly to handle a major oil shock.

Reinsulating, taking full advantage of solar gain, warming yourself — all these are important issues. There are lots of inexpensive ways to minimize heat loss as well, such as window pop-ins (rigid foam-board insulation cut to the size of your window and covered and then slipped into the window at night to cut heat loss).

Ordinary, simple things like caulking, putting plastic or bubble wrap over windows, replacing windows, hanging draperies and insulated curtains, shutting off unused portions of the house, insulating pipes and banking a house with hay or even snow can make a significant difference in your indoor temperature. Shades, awnings, vines and deciduous trees can cool in summer. Consider shutters that shut or wall hangings that hang over unused doors. Even if we can't afford a major retrofit, all of us can insulate.

At some point, however, most of us will also want some supplemental heating and cooling. Here are your options:

1. **Electric space heaters.**
   Newer ones are much, much more efficient than older ones — don't waste money on an old used one if you've got a choice.

   Pro: Cheap to buy; can provide localized heat when the furnace doesn't work — as long as the power is on and widely available (most places don't permit electric shutoffs in the coldest months).

   Con: Vulnerable to grid failure; won't help you during intermittent power outages; mandatory no-shut-off laws may be overturned;

can bring about grid failure if enough people add them to winter electric loads; expensive; dangerous — can cause fires.

2. **Propane heaters.**

   Note: MAKE SURE THESE ARE PROPERLY INSTALLED — every year people die of CO poisoning using these improperly in a power outage. You must own a usable CO detector to use one of these safely.

   Pro: Cheap; can be installed through walls; propane is cheaper than oil; can be used during electrical failures.

   Con: Not much cheaper than oil; vulnerable to supply constraints; delivery issues; dangerous if not properly installed; must be used very carefully.

3. **Kerosene heaters.**

   Note: There are two kinds of these — cooking stoves, often used by the Amish as summer stoves, and heating stoves. Both will create ambient heat; the heaters are more efficient, but one you can cook on has advantages.

   Pro: Cheaper than oil; don't have electric ignition so can be used during power outages; not terribly popular so not hard to find; can cook on some of them.

   Con: Not a terribly clean fuel; dangerous if not properly installed; smelly; ventilation must be good.

4. **Geothermal heat pumps.**

   These are good choices for a lot of areas, particularly if you have a lot of local geothermal energy. The technology seems to be improving rapidly, too, so do your research.

   Pro: Uses a cheap source to both heat and cool; uses much less energy than heating and cooling with electricity directly; low-carbon. Not such a big energy draw that they aren't solar system compatible.

   Con: Requires electricity to operate; some use more power than others; may not regulate temperatures as much as you like.

5. **Woodstoves.**

   Note: I am *only* talking here of fairly new, airtight stoves. Don't use anything but a newer UL stove — period, unless you are desperately poor and have absolute no other choice. The pollutants and the efficiency issues are so great that you simply shouldn't use a very old stove, unless the choice is to freeze. Don't buy old heating stoves (cookstoves are a slightly different issue). Buy the tightest, most efficient one you can, and the smallest one appropriate to your space, and burn only seasoned hard wood if possible.

If you are going to buy a stove and need to heat and cook, a cookstove is a lot more versatile, and new ones are only slightly less efficient than a wood heating stove. You also can cook, in a more limited way, on almost all heating stoves.

Pro: Technically carbon neutral, depending on how you get your fuel; abundant, renewable fuel in many rural very cold places; output (ashes) can be used to fertilize garden and keep soil healthy; extremely cheap fuel if you have a woodlot; can cut wood in national forests with a permit, use waste wood, or downed trees; many with baskets and adaptors can burn multiple fuels including corn, pellets and coal, giving you the greatest possible adaptability.

Con: Pricey if you have to buy one; legal issues in some areas, a lot less carbon neutral if firewood has to be moved around; can lead to deforestation; has particulate emissions issues that can cause health problems; expensive if you rely on purchased wood; you have to have a place to put it; some areas are not good for a lot of woodstoves due to air quality issues.

6. **Corn stoves.**
I gather that these are experiencing a big boom in sales and are back-ordered in many areas — just fyi.

Pro: Uses fuel that some low-forest areas of the Midwest have a lot of; at least it doesn't make ethanol; fuel can be cheap; possibility of growing your own and being even cheaper; low emissions; legal in many cities; cheaper than comparable woodstoves; might be sustainable … but would require massive changes in agricultural practice to make it so.

Con: Most corn is grown with artificial nitrogen so heavy global warming and soil impact; increasingly expensive; uses human food for fuel, on a large scale would increase food prices dramatically, added to ethanol and heavy meat consumption could be an absolute disaster; require electricity.

7. **Pellet stoves.**

Pro: Uses a waste product of the construction industry; can be stored; low emission; possibilities for cities; no stovepipe.

Con: Backorders; pellets use a glue that may be toxic when breathed; pellet supply issues already exist; construction industry in the toilet so its by-products will rise in price and decrease in availability; requires electricity to run; relies on delivery from distant places.

Both corn and pellet stoves require electricity to operate the fans that warm the house.

8. **Coal stoves.**

OK, using these will be freakin' apocalyptic for the planet if we do it on any scale. My worst nightmare is that the Northeast responds to freezing temperatures and high heating fuel prices by looking for the cheapest option and discovering coal stoves. That said, however, I mention them because if you are poor and have no choice, this may be your best option. I do recommend people who get them consider trying to get ones that can burn both coal and wood, so that you can convert to the somewhat better, renewable option later. And may G-d have mercy on my soul for mentioning this.

Pro: Cheap. Cheaper than any of the above options. While coal is rising in price, it still may remain cheap for some time, particularly in coal-producing areas. The stoves are cheap too.

Con: Are you kidding? This is the single worst way to create heat ever.

9. **Natural gas stoves.**

These are also comparatively inexpensive and more available than corn or pellet stoves.

Pro: Cheap; uses less natural gas than a furnace; easy to install; comparatively clean burning?

Con: Subject to all the disadvantages of natural gas. Gas is cheap at present, but may or may not remain so in the future.

10. **Wood masonry stove.**

These are amazing — everyone should have one. Except, of course, that they cost a bazillion dollars and can collapse your floors. Still, if you can build one in or retrofit to add one and have the money, these are ideal.

Pro: Uses minimal wood; produces gradual heat; very clean burning; beautiful; can be made with bread ovens and warming benches — probably the ideal solution to all our problems, if only we could afford one.

Con: Heating even a small house costs $10K plus — bigger ones in the range of $20K to infinity; prohibitive for many — require floor reinforcements if added to an existing house in some cases.

11. **Rocket mass heaters.**

These deserve much, much more attention; see dirtcheapbuilder.com/rostforcobbu.html

Pro: Cheap, with all the advantages of the above. These are probably the best option we've got.

Con: A major DIY project; big; require a lot of skill to build and set up.

12. **Passive solar heaters.**

Pat Murphy at the Community Solution is rather dismissive (based on extensive research) of most passive solar designs or retrofits, saying that they don't actually do what they say they do. Still these are worth exploring. I'm not going to list pros and cons, because the options are so varied and each project has its own issues — do your research before you invest in major projects. Again, check out the bibliography for resources.

So what's the best choice? The best choice is to change your thinking, get used to winter, deal with the cold, adapt your house and yourself as best you can, and use the absolute minimum amount of heat from the cleanest source you possibly can. There is no perfect option — and we're not going to get to one in the US without a massive commitment to retrofitting our dwellings. Sometimes people will have to do the best they can — but most of us can do rather better than we do at minimizing our heat use and expectations, and thinking about our neighbors and the future as well as ourselves when we make our choices. We need to plan now for a long term with less energy — and as difficult as that is, we need to do so carefully and wisely.

Six

The basics of daily life

Ten basic rules to making real Adapting in Place change

1. Buy a lot less stuff.

So much of what's out there focuses on replacing one consumer need with a marginally less toxic or awful one. This is a lousy way to make substantial reductions in your energy usage. What makes a huge difference is reducing consumer spending radically — that is, cutting back on everything from lumber to socks. When you do buy things, buy used if possible. This is really hard for most people, but the reality is that all those dollars operate like votes — they say "make another one, and make more packaging for it, and run the factory a little longer." Not buying stuff is one of the most powerful tools we've got.

2. Structure your life so that it is easier to be green than not.

Most of us have a limited amount of self-discipline — we are a little lazy. So if there's a choice between a mile-and-a-half walk or just hopping in the car, we find that despite our best intentions, we just don't get going in time to walk. Well, the harder you make all that stuff for yourself, the better. So disconnect the appliances you don't want to use, and put them up on a high shelf so it is easier to do without. Don't have a car, or don't have a second car, so that if you want to go to the library you have to walk, bike or take the bus.

3. Take a Sabbath or a no-use day and enforce it.

Try and establish at least one day a week in which you don't drive, don't turn on the computer and don't shop. The value of this is that it gives you the gift of what we all say we want anyway, time with family and friends, quiet time, etc. It also prevents us from constantly powering things up. Turn stuff off — start with one day, try and add more if you can. What's amazing about this is how much of a pleasure it becomes — but it is hard to get over the idea that we have to be connected all the time.

4. Pick the low-hanging fruit.

You are probably wasting energy in some really obvious ways. For example, not putting your TV and other devices on a powerstrip allows them to continue drawing power when you aren't using them. Eliminating this "phantom load" is a pretty easy step. Or perhaps you don't meal plan so you've been running out to the store two or three times a week. But it isn't really hard to shift to only going once, while you're doing other errands. You've been meaning to stop your junk mail, and you don't really like it, but you haven't gotten around to it. Get around to it.

5. Do things that are just as easy with human power with human power.

Got a little postage stamp of a lawn? Well, get a push mower. By the time you change your oil and get the thing out of the garage, you will have used more of your own energy than it takes to run a good push mower over that bit of lawn (if you've never used a new light one, don't assume it will be too hard). Want to start baking your own bread, but assume you need a bread machine? Get a book that shows no-knead recipes that rise overnight — you can have better bread for breakfast with less effort. We tend to assume that labor-saving devices save labor — we assume it so strongly that we often don't check, and it turns out, they don't always.

6. Eat appropriately to your place and season.

What grows well there? What's in season? What's local? What's in your backyard? No one should eat as much meat as the typical American does, and often recommendations on diet focus on less or none at all.

This is important, but the kind of meat matters too — what grows well naturally near you? Did you know that meat, eggs and milk are seasonal as well? What is ready now? What can you get inexpensively? Can you preserve some of what is abundant now for the time when it won't be? Local diets are really local — the food you'd eat in Nebraska and the food you'd eat in coastal Maine are not the same, and shouldn't be.

7. If it is the end that matters — change your means.

Consider household heating — most of us want to be warm enough to be comfortable at home. There are lots of ways to accomplish this, including wearing more clothes, putting on a hat, heating a rice bag or hot water bottle and placing it strategically, using space heaters or radiant heaters, adapting to cooler temperatures early in the season, not heating the whole house, etc. Focus on achieving your goal (being comfortable) and on finding new ways to do it, like focusing on heating yourself rather than the entire house. You want to have tea or coffee available all day? OK, try a thermos instead of running the coffee pot all morning. Need enough light to read by? What about an LED book light? You want the kids to look like their friends? How about finding a nice consignment shop, or organizing a clothing swap with friends? Sometimes we mix up ends and means, and assume that the means are the point — that what we care about isn't being warm, but what the ambient temperature is.

8. Go at the big hogs.

Your biggest energy costs are probably heating, cooling, refrigeration, transport and your meat consumption. So when you try and figure out how to make an impact, focus on those issues. Find that carpool. Try the bus. Make more vegetarian meals. Replace your fridge with a smaller model. Reinsulate. Run the a/c only when it is above 82 in the house.

9. Cut things in half.

Nobody enjoys giving things up, so consider halving them instead. Use half as much detergent, shampoo, conditioner — those measures on the bottles are meant to sell things. Spend half as much on movies and treats. Wash towels and sheets half as often. Try and walk or bike half the time. Try and waste only half the food you have been. Remember, things don't have to be 100 percent — and often, the impact of doing something half the time includes recognizing that we could do it even less.

10. We do like things to be easy, but not everything we like is easy.

It is important that people not feel befuddled and overwhelmed by the idea of reducing energy usage, and it is possible to get people involved by the creative, fun and engaging elements. Even if it never is as simple as rolling off a log, people are engaged by complex things when they derive a sense of artfulness, accomplishment and pleasure from them. That is, you can get people to try and navigate a local diet, even if that's more complex than "don't eat X," if you can convince them that really local diets taste better and offer opportunities for creative expression. It may not be easy to figure out how to make your own, mend your own or do without things — but if people get to be pleased and proud that they learned something new or accomplished something difficult, they may do it anyway. Making the hard stuff interesting goes a long way toward making people forget that it can be hard.

All of us, in an extended crisis, are going to need to be able to meet some basic needs, needs we discussed in Chapter 4: Triaging your situation. You will want to be able to supplement natural light. You will want to be able to wash clothes and your body and handle toileting issues. You will want to make dinner. Everyone will be happier if these very basic issues are resolved.

I will say little here about the basics of food and water, because I've written several books about them — there is an extensive discussion of non-electric ways of getting water out of the ground and many chapters on preserving and storing food in *Independence Days,* which I won't rehash — but don't forget those things in your planning. For the purposes of this book, let's start with light.

Lighting

Now you could go to bed when it gets dark and get up when it gets light, but most of us will want to have some supplemental light for reading and working. One of the funny things about generating light is that most of the seemingly lower-impact models are actually higher-impact — that is, the petroleum-based candles you buy at the store are probably of greater impact than simply running a compact flourescent lightbulb, at least by some estimations (it depends on whether you include the grid infrastructure in your calculation). So is your kerosene lamp. Even beeswax candles may be bigger impact, depending on where you are getting them from. That's because electricity isn't a bad way to generate light — and solar lighting systems have a lot of merits. I'm particularly fond of outdoor solar lighting — it is cheap and sturdy and can be kept outside during the day and brought in and placed in vases to light rooms at night.

That said, plastic and battery-based things do break. I find that my best solutions are a mix of all of these — candles and kerosene lamps, solar lanterns and rechargeable batteries. Again, using less can get you pretty far — turning off the lights, using good lamps where you need them rather than lighting up the whole room.

Remember that our adaptations need to have two functions —they have to meet your needs in a crisis and must also allow you to live the kind of life you want even when you aren't in crisis. Presuming that most of us want our light sources to be ethical ones, and to provide the most for the least, that means sorting out some options. So let's talk options.

Actually, let's first talk about not setting your house, child, cat or ferret on fire. Many of these solutions involve open or slightly enclosed flames. If you are going to use them, use them very carefully. Have a good smoke detector and extra batteries around, keep fire extinguishers and know how to use them, and never leave them unattended where kids or pets could get at them. If you have children or pets, stable candles with solid bases are better than tall candles with narrow candlesticks, and hurricanes or other lamps in containers or wall sconces are safer than the table, where the kids can reach or the dog can bump into things while hoping someone will drop something for him to snack on. I have several wall sconces with hurricane glasses that I found at a yard sale. Mirrored sconces will nearly double the amount of light in a room as a side benefit.

If you really desperately needed light, and wanted to be outside, you could make rushlights or flaming torches — dip cattails in oil or set a stick on fire. You almost certainly do not want to do this in your house, just in case you were wondering. Nor is it the most carbon-efficient option or terrifically convenient (although flaming torches have their place in driving monsters out of the local ruined castle, I suppose).

You could also burn olive oil, in a homemade lamp, with a wick made from a shoelace (cotton only, pull off the plastic ends). This is not cheap, but it is clean burning. It won't give tons of light, but if you have olives where you live, you can make a simple lamp. There's even a variation that uses a Mason jar; see motherearthnews.com/Do-It-Yourself/Make-Olive-Oil-Lamp.aspx.

The next possibility is candles. Most candles are petroleum-based, and some have lead wicks, which are not good to breathe, so be careful when buying cheap candles. I think scented candles are generally disgusting, and they can cause problems for people with allergies or scent sensitivities, so I avoid those as well (is there anyone who thinks those Yankee candle stores actually smell *good*?!?!). Soy, beeswax and bayberry candles are much nicer and better for you. Tallow candles don't smell so hot when burning, and you really can't buy them, but you could make them out of leftover animal fats. If you plan to use candles, think about where they will come from — get to know your local beekeeper, plant some bayberry bushes if you've got sandy soil, or get your own hive and candle molds.

Kerosene is not environmentally sound, really, but lamp oil does store well, and kerosene lamps can provide a good backup lighting source. Make sure you know how to use them, and how to trim wicks and clean them. Lamp oil stores pretty much indefinitely, but make sure you keep it in a fireproof container. These oils are by-products of coal production, so not likely to run entirely out, but also not really environmentally cool.

You can get lights that will run on propane or natural gas — try lehmans.com. These are used by the Amish and if, for example, you have a natural gas well or use propane for other things, are another possibility. Again, they aren't necessarily a huge improvement over grid electric (depending on how your electric is generated and unless you have onsite natural gas), but they may allow you to escape from your reliance on it.

Flashlights, battery-powered lamps, booklights and headlamps make a lot of sense when combined with rechargeable batteries and solar-powered battery chargers. Set these in your window, have several sets of each battery type to rotate, and these can give excellent light for extended periods. Headlamps are especially nice for a host of purposes — going out to the barn with stuff in your hands, washing dishes, etc. Book lights clip to your book and allow you to read with tiny quantities of light. Rechargeable batteries are also a great mix with LED night-lights for kids.

If you are going to get flashlights, get at least one serious, heavy-duty, police-officer style flashlight, or a floodlight type. The reason is that sooner or later you are bound to have to help track the dog through the woods, find out what's making that noise under the house or otherwise do something with a light with *power* — little flashlights are adequate for most jobs, but once in a while, these are useful. They are also an excellent security device — most people prowling about will stop, blinded, when you shine one on them, and many pesty critters will run away.

Hand-crank flashlights are good, too, but usually not super powerful. Plus you might have something to do with your time besides crank — get a good one if you get one and make sure you can charge it for a good long time. I have several but also recommend having a few battery-powered ones, although the crank type is great for kids. Although they're not at all sustainable, for emergency and travel bags and such, I also see the value of chemical lightsticks for little kids, who need something to be secure but are not necessarily able to use a flashlight yet.

Solar lights are also great — and the kind designed for gardens are very cheap these days. Buy a bunch, plant them outside, then simply stick one in a bucket of sand or a vase in rooms where you need light. Unlike many of the other options here, they are quite pleasant to read by. I also have a couple of solar lanterns, which are very nice, especially when children and pets are about. They are easy to carry about with you, as are the outdoor lights, if you keep buckets about. Plus, the outdoor types can be used, well, outdoor.

You can, of course, put in a solar, wind or microhydro system and use it to power lights and a few other things. A small system that can run your computer, your lights and your CD player won't be too expensive, if a couple of thousand dollars is "not too expensive" for you. I generally only recommend this, however, for people who either aren't grid tied to begin with or who have done most of their other preps — because it is perfectly possible to run those things on rechargeable batteries for much lower cost.

The most important thing you can do about alternate lighting is change your attitude toward it — that is, instead of assuming that everyone needs their own lighted room, you can all congregate together. One person can read aloud near the light, or perhaps everyone can do something like handwork that only needs low-light conditions, to conserve energy. This is pleasurable as well — sitting together, enjoying the evening when work is done, reading, singing, talking and working is the stuff of which memories are made.

Laundry

First, I should say that I do a lot of laundry — as do most people with a bunch of kids. My eldest is disabled and not fully toilet trained. At least one of my kids still wets the bed (this is the sort of thing your kids can legitimately sue you for if you publish books about it, so we'll leave it at that). At any given time at least one or two of our foster children are usually in cloth diapers.

Furthermore, we live on a farm. If there is something gross you can get on your clothes, we've got it. Simon was carrying eggs in his shirt pocket and forgot they were there? Got that one. Goat gave birth on my lap? Got it. Mud? Muck? Manure? You name it, we've got it. We also use cloth rather than disposable products for almost everything (we use some disposable pull-ups with my eldest) — so we make a lot of laundry. Even furthermore, we live in a climate with a distinct season known as "mud season," where your laundry freezes on the line half the year, and we have every mineral known to man in our water — it is so hard you have to hit it with a hammer.

I say this not to be competitive about who has the most laundry, but to point out to people who say "but I have kids ... but we have diapers ... but it gets cold/humid/rainy here ... but I have hard water..." that you can deal with all of those things and still use energy efficiently while washing. Seriously, it is totally doable. It just takes a shift in perspective, and a little practice.

Maybe you'll think I'm insane when I tell you that I love hanging laundry out, but I really do. I go outside and watch the world — I love the quiet, the birds, waving to my neighbors as they go by. I find hanging laundry a meditation, a pleasure — it's stopped being a chore. I will

not say the same about washing or folding or putting laundry away —
but I do think it is worth mentioning that the part of this that probably
sounds hardest to most people is the part that feels easiest to me.

But first, the washing. Until I had a child in my late twenties, I never
owned a washing machine. For more than a decade of my adult life, I
brought my laundry to the Laundromat for washing — usually either in
one of those little carts or by carrying it. In the interim, I washed underwear, socks and some larger items by hand in the bathroom sink. Were
my husband and I childless, I would probably still choose this method,
rather than purchasing a private washer — it just doesn't seem necessary. If
I lived in an area where private washers were the norm and Laundromats
distant, I'd probably try and barter with a neighbor to share a washer
once or twice a week. While households with kids may need their washer
nearly every day, households made up primarily of adults simply don't,
and it doesn't make a lot of sense to have one in every house.

Or I might make do with a combination of sink washing and a pressure hand washer. I used one — it is simple to use, inexpensive and gets
the clothes quite clean. It isn't made for families with lots of laundry, but
it would work great for a single adult or a couple that doesn't get dirty
that often.

The best way to reduce your laundry energy use is to do less. This is
one of those obvious things that we sometimes don't think about. So the
first strategy we use is to try and minimize the number of items getting
washed, and thus the loads per week. That means we:

1. Take a careful look at our clothes to see if they can be worn again
   (this is my job, since my kids and husband tend to think that everything can be worn again, no matter how revolting).
2. Change into play clothes when wearing dress clothing. Put on smocks
   or aprons or previously dirtied clothes when doing especially vile jobs.
3. Lower standards. Now I'm sort of a slob, so I probably shouldn't
   lower my standards any further, but in some households this would
   be viable — change sheets and towels less often, for example.

But even though we do all that, I do have kids and we do get dirty, so
we do have a washing machine. When the one that came with the house

died last year, we considered shifting to a James Hand Washer and doing all our laundry by hand — for about thirty seconds. Then I purchased the most energy-efficient front loader in our price range (not that high). I wish in retrospect that I'd purchased the front loader sooner — the difference in electrical, water and detergent usage is dramatic. For me, the single most important appliance in my home is the washer — it is the one that gives me the most freed-up time and ease, for the lowest price.

We do virtually everything on "quick wash" with cold water, with the exception of one pile I keep for "exceptionally filthy" things, which I do a load of once every week or two on "regular" with warm water and a little vinegar added to the rinse. As you can probably imagine, given the kind of things I wash, it has to be pretty disgusting to make it to this pile. But even with hard water, we find we are able to get most clothes clean with a quick wash in cold water.

We use a couple of brands of eco-friendly detergent. I used to make my own laundry soap, but I haven't since getting the front loader, since I called the manufacturer and they told me that they don't recommend any homemade soap, because of the problem of over-sudsing. I've since read accounts of mixtures that can be used in front loaders, but haven't yet tried them.

We use a little less detergent than is recommended — if you had softer water, you could presumably use less still. We don't use fabric softener. Once in a great while I do use a capful of bleach on some particularly recalcitrant stains — usually I soak them beforehand, rather than adding bleach to the wash water. Remember, the less you put in your laundry, the less often you have to shop, the lower the cost, the lower the resource use....

As deeply as I love my washer, I think there's really little point to a dryer for most people. Generally, I think using coal-fired electricity to do something the air will do for you for free is overpriced and wasteful. Gas dryers are better, but these are still fossil fuels we are using — and the sun and the wind or your winter heat source will do this without using fossil fuels.

There are a few exceptions to the rule that using a dryer is wasteful — I think it is unreasonably onerous to ask people who have no vehicle and are reliant on Laundromats to carry wet laundry back to their apartments to dry. And every once in a great while, you can't get something to dry without a dryer — we had that happen one June, when it rained twenty-six days out of thirty. My husband took several loads of our laundry to the Laundromat one day, simply because I couldn't keep up with the quantity, given the time required to get it dry. But that's only happened once in ten years (and we get nearly sixty inches of rain a year). I have also used a dryer while traveling, when we wouldn't have been able to wait for clothes to dry.

How do we dry our clothes all year-round? Well, first of all, I've got two clotheslines. The first is one of those spinning circular ones, the second, a regular line that goes around the margins of our front porch. The advantage of having it there is that the porch roof provides some cover, so that I don't have to go racing outside every time a sprinkle of rain hits — it won't protect them from a downpour, but it does reduce the number of times I have to worry about it.

It takes me about seven minutes to hang a load of laundry — less if it is big things like sheets and towels, more for socks and underwear. I try and mix things up when I can, so that I never have to pin too many little things. I hang small stuff like socks and undies together — I can often get three small items on one clothespin.

For people with disabilities, who have trouble standing or raising their arms up long enough to hang laundry, you can hang the wet laundry on hangers while seated using clothespins (thanks to Pat Meadows for this tip!), then just hang the hangers on the clothesline. This also works indoors on a shower curtain bar.

I hang laundry out about nine months of the year consistently, plus during warm spells in the winter. The reason I persist in the winter, when clothes may take several days to dry, is because winter laundry smells better than anything in the world. You can buy detergents to give you a fake-springtime smell, but honestly, the best-smelling laundry is the stuff that comes cold off the line. I don't know why this is, but it is a wonderful scent.

When it is extremely cold, rainy or humid, I move clothes indoors. I have a freestanding clothes dryer — not one of the cheap ones that your grandmother put in her tub (or my grandmother did, anyhow), but a heavy-duty laundry rack that can dry more than one load of laundry at a time. It won't collapse under the weight of wet laundry, but folds down and fits in a space in a corner.

We heat with wood, so we often set up our dryer near the stove — if you have radiators or floor vents, they're good too. You can also use the shower curtain as a laundry rack, directly or by using the hanger method mentioned above. If I can keep up with my laundry through a New York winter with no dryer, odds are most of you can do so as well.

What about the "crunchy" texture of the laundry? Honestly, while we noticed it at first, we don't notice or mind at all anymore. One possible answer if you just can't bear it is to run things through the dryer for five minutes with a damp towel to soften them — that's still better than running an entire load. But honestly, just accepting that it takes a little time to adapt is probably better. No one in my household even notices it anymore. Shaking the clothes out, adding vinegar to the rinse and wearing them will add a little natural softness.

What about the time involved in hanging laundry? Well, you do need enough clothes for a load of laundry to take a day or day and half to dry. You should plan on keeping up with it. But hanging a load of laundry really isn't that time-consuming. Remember, if you use the dryer, you have to pay for the dryer, the dryer sheets, the repairs and the electricity it uses, and calculate that into the time equation as well.

What about dry cleaning? We dry clean once a year — my husband and I are fortunate enough to be able to wear serious dress clothes infrequently (his suits at funerals and the high holidays, mine for the occasional professional event). Otherwise we try to avoid dry-clean-only clothing, air out dry-clean stuff if it needs it, spot clean and try not to get it dirty. For those who have to dress up more often, we find that most natural fiber clothing can be washed safely by hand. If you do dry clean, find a low-toxicity dry cleaner, since the chemicals used are really nasty and bad for you. Even at our low-toxicity cleaner, we hang the clothes outside to air for twenty-four hours afterward.

How about ironing? I admit, Simon, my eight-year-old, once took a developmental test when he was about four. Afterward the person giving it came out to talk to me, saying that he had done extremely well on the picture-word ID segment — in fact, he'd missed only one word, "ironing board." I blushed and admitted that there was a good chance he'd never seen one. We're not much for ironing here. I do have an iron and an ironing board, and use it occasionally for sewing projects and when I absolutely have to iron something, but generally I find that choosing clothes that don't wrinkle much and hanging things out on a windy day will make my wardrobe look fairly crisp without it.

As with dry cleaning, those with serious professional jobs may need to iron more, and the best you can do is only iron what you need to — if you are ironing your underwear, you are probably not making the best possible use of your energy.

How does all of this actually stack up from a profit and loss standpoint? If you use it a lot, replacing an old top loader washer with a front loader will save you 70 or 80 kWh per month and seven to fifteen dollars, depending on your electric budget. Not buying a washer at all and sharing with a neighbor or using the Laundromat will save you still more. Reducing detergent could save as little as a dollar a month if you do laundry infrequently anyway, or as much as eight dollars. Giving up the dryer could save you twenty dollars a month or more, and a much larger number of kWh. Even reducing their use will make a difference.

Using a front loader is no more time-consuming, if you use the quick wash cycle, than running a top loader, so the time is the same. Hanging laundry takes two to five more minutes per load than using a dryer. Using less detergent, no fabric softener and no dryer sheets saves you time and money — less shopping. Less dry cleaning saves you pick-up and drop-off, not to mention chemical exposure. Less ironing saves you time and electricity.

Potty time

OK, time to discuss with perfect strangers stuff you normally do behind closed doors. Because hygiene is so tremendously important to survival, this is another one of those "everyone needs to know their options and have a plan" things. While living with no or little fossil fuels won't kill you, a whole lot of the potential health consequences of inadequate hand washing, unsafe human manure handling and other things will. It is easy to get caught up in other stuff and forget how important this is.

So, toileting. If you have some water, and the sewers/septic aren't backed up, you can keep flushing with a bucket occasionally (and I do mean occasionally). But in a long-term crisis your septic or water treatment plants may stop operating and you may want that water for something else, particularly if you have to laboriously haul it by hand from somewhere. Composting human manures is tough in tightly packed urban areas, but is one of the best environmental choices in many places.

Now everyone with a garden can use their urine to fertilize it. This is safe — to be paranoid, you shouldn't harvest from the plants for a week (or until after a rainstorm), but this is actually almost certainly over-paranoia. Don't do it if you have tularemia — though if you do, you have much bigger problems than where to put your urine. Dilute the urine one part pee to ten parts water (you can use one-to-seven if you drink a lot, but just in case, if your urine is very concentrated, more dilution is better) and pour it over a plant you love. In fact, IMHO, it would be crazy not to do this — free nitrogen in a world where fertilizer is increasingly expensive.

Poop is a bigger deal, and needs to be properly composted at fairly high temperatures. If you live in an urban place and have limited space, this will have to be a neighborhood affair, since you can't do it too near water, and you must do it safely. Since the whole neighborhood's health will depend on it (do you really need me to make a list of the diseases you can get from not finding an appropriate and safe way to deal with human wastes in an extended emergency — let's just say it would be very long and have very unpleasant things on it). The bible on this subject is John Jenkins' wonderful *Humanure Handbook,* a very important book that is available as a free download. If you can afford it, though, I'd buy a copy directly from him, as thanks for a serious service to humanity.

The basis of humanure composting is pretty simple — you poop and pee in a bucket, add some carbonaceous material and compost it carefully in a large pile that heats up enough to kill all pathogens. You then have something that is not a health risk, but an asset. This is important, and the world as a whole is going to have to deal with this concept if we are all to continue living. You are not advised to use it on your vegetable garden, but it can be used for trees and ornamental plantings.

For very short-term problems, those in very urban places can use plastic bags over buckets and dispose of their poop that way, but this creates methane in landfills and warms the planet. You can also go out in the woods and bury (more than four inches deep) your wastes, or dig an outhouse. But if you've got any decent space at all for composting, these options are less good — and less pleasant in bad weather — than a simple composting toilet.

Make sure you have hand-washing facilities in an emergency — hand sanitizer (alcohol-based, not antibacterial) is OK if water is really restricted, but what you want is water and soap. Store soap or learn to make it, and teach everyone in your house to wash their hands properly every single time, especially before they eat. In ancient times, those religions (among them Judaism and Islam) that insisted upon washing before eating had much lower death rates than those that didn't (of course, if we actually regress to ancient times, we'll go back to burning those who don't get diseases for being witches, so it would be nicer all round if everyone would consider hand-washing a sacrament).

The next problem is toilet paper. Several people have told me it was worth its weight in gold during a crisis, so you need an option there, then. One option is to use waste paper but don't flush it (most systems can't handle anything but tp), and dispose of it by burning. But eventually you will run out of old phone books and Danielle Steel novels, and be confronted with a deep and urgent question — what can I do besides wiping my ass with the works of Dickens?

The answer to this is cloth toilet paper — the reusable tp. This is especially accessible for pee — if you don't want to wash poopy cloth (although those of us dealing with diapers might have a lower freak-out level than others), use it for pee only (for them that use anything when peeing). But if you need it for poop, segregate it from the rest of the laundry and wash it well, maybe with a tiny bit of hydrogen peroxide or bleach, and dry in the sun to kill germs. I realize this is a tough idea for a lot of people, but let's be honest — many people wipe their butts with cloth wipes now. It really isn't that big a deal.

The kitchen

My kitchen is old-fashioned. I'm not talking about the wooden cabinets, the open shelving of grains and stored foods, the home-canned jams or the lack of a refrigerator in my main cooking space. I'm talking about the electric stove and the fridge itself. That is, these appliances are archaic residues of a life in which energy was cheap and abundant and our whole lifestyle was created around that abundance. These energy-sucking appliances may have a place in our future or they may not, but they are fundamentally a product of a day when energy-sucking appliances with five-to-ten-year lifespans could be made, replaced and disposed of. Those days are as over as the days of the Crimean War, and my kitchen has a growingly retro look to it — and I bet yours does too.

As it becomes more and more necessary to reduce our usage of fossil fuels and as more and more people want to live an environmentally sound lifestyle, perhaps we'll change our kitchens and find we don't need as many energy-sucking appliances as we thought we did. For example, my family does quite well without a conventional fridge. We do have a freezer because we sell meat from our farm, but we don't have a plug-in fridge. Instead, during the warm weather when the freezer is less full, we rotate old soda bottles full of water and freeze them to provide ice for an icebox (our old fridge, only unplugged). In the winter food goes out on a sheltered enclosed porch for natural refrigeration. Done this way, our refrigeration and freezing uses one sixth of the energy it used to — because fridges are big energy consumers in most households.

Would this work for everyone? Nope, but for more people than you'd think. We've also managed to get along without a number of other common appliances. The fact is that most of us don't need all those fancy things.

But here's a question — if we do get over the big psychological hump that tells us we desperately need a house full of appliances (or if we get to the rapidly approaching moment when we can't afford to run them), what do we do with these houses, built for a world of cheap energy and accessible appliances? What do we do with the appliances?

Getting to the point of not needing appliances can be hard if you have a cheap-energy house. The truth is that the appliances themselves often create their own necessity. For example, consider the vacuum cleaner — the classic example of an appliance that actually creates more problems than it solves. In *The Overworked American* Juliet Schor observes that vacuum cleaners saved women exactly zero minutes per day on cleaning floors — in fact, peak floor cleaning time was hit in the 1980s, when vacuums had made it to virtually every house.

With vacuums came the possibility of wall-to-wall carpeting and new, higher standards of floor cleanliness. If you have one of those houses filled with wall-to-wall, it really does seem impossible to get by with a manual carpet cleaner. Ripping out the carpet and replacing it with something else is vastly more expensive than leaving the nylon in place and vacuuming it. So when we say we need our vacuums, in some senses, we're right — it is damned hard to turn a cheap-energy house into a low-energy house sometimes.

So while a bunch of us pedants point out that we technically could live without things, I understand the perspective that answers, "Umm … no way." When someone asks you whether you can live without your stove cooktop, which came with your house and which comes with an energy infrastructure that pipes right out of the wall, you have to go looking to change your mind. It takes time and research and thought — things we don't often devote to our kitchens — to figure out how to get a kitchen that actually meets twenty-first-century realities. The solar oven is a mature technology and a wonderful thing — but people can be forgiven for not knowing they exist, or how to get a hold of one, or being uncomfortable with people telling them to cook one way in the summer and another entirely in the winter.

If we ever finally get to the point where we actually want (or have) to live without all this stuff, what will we even do with the old infrastructure? In a perfect world, we'd all have the money and not need to worry about waste, so we could pull it out and remake our kitchen in the image of the non-electric fantasy in our head. In truth, however, by the time most of us get to that point we'll have either less money or less time to worry about how the dishwasher goes with the masonry stove. Waste not, want not, and no environmentalist wants to haul those appliances to the dump. So how do you turn the twentieth-century, cheap-oil, retro kitchen into one that meets modern, low-energy needs?

Now you can sell your appliances to someone else, or if they are completely unsalvageable, send them to the dump. But I'm going to assume that you want to do something else with them.

Fortunately, my side job as design consultant at the fine magazine *Better Homesteads* gives me every qualification to offer suggestions for how to make use of those old appliances, now that you've shaken off the past and moved on to the low-energy future. So here are some suggestions for post-electric uses for common appliances.

Dryer: We actually bought one of these about eight years ago, because my husband's grandmother insisted. And it was used, mostly by her, until her death, and once in a great while by me, until we started seriously cutting our energy usage. Now it is sitting in my laundry room, waiting to be pulled out and put in the garage as permanent storage for apples or potatoes (pulling it out involves removing the washer and some other stuff, and I'm a slug). With a small piece of metal over the dryer vent, it will be rodent proof, provide a nice surface to set things on, and a measure of insulation on the coldest nights. Other possible uses: manual compost tumbler (would require a bit of adaptation, but I bet there are some handy folks out there with ideas).

Washer: I have heard several people mention the possibility of hooking a regular washing machine up to a bicycle to power it, and the wonderful book *The Human-Powered Home* has plans for doing so. In the meantime, I have one of those small, no-power washers that can handle a couple of shirts or small load of diapers, and I do some laundry with the soak-and-hang method described in *The Plain Reader* — in winter we get the water out by putting it in the tub and letting the barefoot kids dance on top of it like they are stomping grapes (yes, we wash their feet first). If I couldn't bicycle power my washer, I might still fill and hand agitate it to wash wool for spinning. I once met a small farmer who used his to wash large quantities of greens for sale. But I'm leaning toward the bicycle method, if I can find a set of plans that are moron-proof enough for me.

Electric/gas stove and oven: If you already have a flat-top cookstove, you've got a perfect counter, and it isn't worth messing with. For gas ranges, a piece of sheet metal or thick butcher block cut to fit would probably serve the same purpose if the stove stops working. Most of us home cooks and gardeners never have enough counter space, so I'd keep the stovetop for that. We have two electric stoves in our house — one was for the grandparents, and since we're not using that kitchen, we've unplugged it. The oven, it turns out, makes a large, superb breadbox — it is airtight enough to keep baked goods remarkably fresh for a good long time. So we use it for that.

Dishwasher: Now there is a case to be made for not getting over the dishwasher. People who hand wash generally use more water than a dishwasher will — and in water-scarce areas, this is a real virtue. Of course, they also use more electricity, since hand washers can usually use cold water. Depending on where you live, it might be better to use the dishwasher to save water, or hand wash to save electricity — for me, electricity is by far the bigger concern. So what to do with the dishwasher? Like the oven, the odds are you can't take it out without creating an unsightly mess.

Well, you could do what we used to do with it — use it to hide the dirty dishes. Most dishwashers are right next to the sink, and they work fine as mess concealment, even when you haven't run them. Or you could use the racks as storage for clean dishes, freeing up your cabinet to hold food or your collection of canning jars. Or, use it to store the canning jars.

Refrigerator: Right now we use our fridge about seven months a year as an icebox. Because we still have a freezer, what we do is freeze several large jugs of water and ice packs and simply rotate them in the fridge. I put the jugs in, and when they are wholly melted, take them out and replace them with other ones and put the melted ones back in the freezer. This keeps us with a functional refrigerator, maybe not quite as cold as a regular fridge but cold enough that you can feel it if you open the door. Keeps food just fine. The other five months a year we don't bother with this because we have natural refrigeration outside on an enclosed porch.

One possibility is simply to convert your fridge to an icebox, particularly if you were thinking of keeping a freezer. They also make decent storage for jars and tools — those bins and things would work very well. The most creative use I've seen for an old fridge or, even better, a chest freezer, is to dig a big hole in the ground, bury it, and use it as a root cellar.

Freezer: This is the next appliance we're going to look into — the problem is that we do sell meat off the farm, and customers want it frozen. And there are some foods we like to store in there — greens, for example, are better frozen than dehydrated. But they are better still sea-son-extended and fresh, and we're planning on putting up a hoophouse in order to achieve that, so we may yet be able to lose the freezer.

Old freezers make great root cellars, either buried, as above, or sim-ply set in a place that stays cold over winter. The other possibility is that if you need a fridge, you could turn your chest freezer into one. There are plans all over the Web for converting chest freezers into low-energy fridges, and they work quite well. My own take on this is that if I have to have one device (and I manifestly do not) I'd rather have the freezer, which effectively also gives me refrigeration.

Microwave: This is a point of some pride to me — I am probably not the first person ever to come up with this idea, but as far as I can find, I might be, and I am a little proud of it. I turn black microwaves into solar ovens. Now depending on your perspective, microwaves are either great energy-saving tools or nutrient destroyers. I'm kind of agnostic on this subject — I've read some research for, some against, and I occasion-ally use the microwave we inherited from Eric's grandmother to warm something up — once in a great while my kind mother-in-law brings us take-out Thai. But if you don't want a microwave, or run into a cheapie old one at a yard sale, my best use for it is to hack the cord off, make a set of reflectors out of tinfoil and cardboard, cover up the vents, and point the thing at the sun. It won't heat up as well as a commercial oven, or even the best of the homemade ones, but it is perfectly adequate for heating water, cooking beans and rice, etc.

Vacuum Cleaner: OK, you got me. I have no idea what to do with this when you don't need it anymore.

I recently got a copy of this year's *Old Farmer's Almanac* and it had a discussion of future technological advances that we can expect any day now in our houses. My favorite was a toilet that, umm, measures your output and tests it for health problems, then discusses the results with you. Ignoring the larger question of who in the Holy Name of George Washington Carver would ever want such a thing, all I can say is that they clearly have no idea what the new hot appliance trends of the twenty-first century really are: composting toilets, hand pumps in the kitchen and the hot new appliance — the wood cookstove ;-). That other stuff is just so last century!

Dances with wood

Perhaps the single most visible symbol of the difference between my life and ordinary American lives is my wood cookstove. So much of what we do to conserve energy is invisible — we don't go places, we don't use things, we don't buy stuff. And the rest often looks fairly ordinary — lots of people have clotheslines, lots of people have gardens, and not necessarily for the same reasons I do. But my wood cookstove, well, that's something rather different, something not found in the kitchens of most houses. Everyone who comes into my home stops dead and wants to know how it works.

Why choose a cookstove? We have both a cookstove and a heating stove, although they only run simultaneously on *very* unusually cold days or when we have guests enough to need to heat the whole house. During much of the year, the cookstove is our primary heat source, particularly in the early spring and late autumn, when the worst of winter's cold abates but it is still chilly enough to need a little heat. Since wood smoke pollutes, we try not to use it when it isn't truly necessary. But I do always look forward to the first fire.

If you are trying to decide whether to buy a cookstove or a conventional heating stove, it is worth considering your priorities. Do you already live in a climate where you can use a solar oven or outdoor masonry oven most of the time (i.e., somewhere sunny, fairly dry and warm)? Then you probably don't need a cookstove. Do you have trees on your property or lots of sustainably harvested and carefully managed forest in the area, so that wood makes sense at all?

Do you cook much? Can or preserve? If you live alone and rarely cook, I would go for the more efficient wood-heating stove — remember, you can cook on one of those as well, you can put a pot of soup on top and even get or make a sheet metal oven to go on top of it that will allow you to bake. It isn't as precise, easy to control or as large a surface, but it can be done. On the other hand, if you live in a large household, preserve a lot and cook from scratch most of the time, a big flat hot surface and oven going all the time might be a huge blessing. Also, where does your cooking energy come from? If you are cooking now with coal-powered electric, replacing that stove with a cookstove might make sense.

Also think about the costs and impacts of the wood you are using. If you live in a forested area, or can manage your own woodlot or track how wood is harvested locally, wood might make sense. In an area without a lot of woodland, where wood has to be trucked long distances, another fuel would be wiser. Many woodstoves can be adapted to use pellets or corn, but I'm not aware of a pellet/corn basket that would fit the smaller firebox of a cookstove — although such a thing may well exist.

How often are you prepared to tend things? A cookstove necessarily has a smaller firebox than most woodstoves, simply because a lot of the space available is used for the oven, so while some stoves can be banked and kept going overnight, many cookstoves can't be. Certainly when you are cooking, if you need precise temperatures, you'll find that you need to be around, to feed the stove more often and keep an eye on things — it isn't quite like setting the oven to 350 and walking away. It probably doesn't require as much attention as you assume it does, however.

Are you prepared to learn how to keep your chimneys clean, prevent fires, cut wood, etc? There's a basic skill set required by any kind of wood heating, though again, it probably isn't as hard as you think it is.

Finally, how worried are you about having a source of heat and cooking power that doesn't require electricity or natural gas? Since we have regular power outages in our rural neighborhood anyway, it is just commonsense not to depend on the electric lines to make dinner. If you use your woodstove only rarely, during power outages, you probably would be better off getting a less expensive conventional woodstove, rather than a cookstove.

If you pressed me, though, to say which of the above was the major factor for me in choosing a cookstove, I would have to admit my choice wasn't logical. I just wanted one, and now that I have it, I find that I love it.

Some of the things I do to cut my energy use and live more sustainably are fine, but I don't feel passionately about them. But the cookstove is one of my favorite things in the world (milking goats and hanging laundry also fall in that category). I love tending it — I actually love the regular interruptions to my work to go tend it when I'm the only adult in the house. I love the dance of adjusting temperatures and cooking, and the huge expanse of hot surface that entices me to start just one more pot. I love canning on it in the fall and the combined smell of the wood and applesauce. I love the way I feel it helps me cook better — the way things taste when they come out of it, and the way its enticingly hot oven and surface encourage me to cook, and cook creatively.

What is it like to use it? In the mornings, whoever is up first lights the stove — we don't usually keep it going overnight, even though we can, simply because if it is cold enough to need a stove going overnight, we usually prefer the heating stove with its larger firebox and longer burn. Sometimes we take a scoop of embers from the other stove, or if it isn't as cold, we play match games with our junk mail and the newspapers friends save for us and the kindling that my kids collect all autumn. It takes about five minutes to get the stove lit and make sure it is going, and another twenty minutes of hanging about doing other things while checking periodically on the stove and gradually getting it up to a proper burn before we can load it up and go about our business. This work is entirely compatible with the rest of the things we do — getting breakfast, filling the kettle, sterilizing the milking equipment, doing dishes, getting the boys dressed in the morning, so much so that the stove itself doesn't actually seem to take up much time — it is all just morning routine.

Once we're up and running, I immediately put the kettle on the hob, and when it starts to boil, I'll pour my first cup of tea and move it over to the cooler part of the stove. Since we often bake bread in the morning that we've set to rise overnight, many mornings the first project is to get the oven hot enough to bake bread, which is good anyway, since a short, hot burn will keep creosote from forming on the stove. Meanwhile, the bread is put on for a final rise in the warming oven above the stove — a nice toasty spot that sends it bounding right up. If you are in the market for a stove, the enclosed warming oven is a wonderful place to make yogurt, raise bread and dry mittens, or even dry pieces of wood for the next day's fire that have been iced over or had snow melt on them outside.

Meanwhile, I will probably put something on to simmer on the stove — it could be a pot of soup or stew or some applesauce, the kind of warm, hearty food that one craves in the cold weather. Lunch will be ready when I want it, rather like a giant Crock-Pot. The stove is good for multiple purposes — the kids come there to get dressed, I come to warm my hands and refill the teacup after typing in a cool office. We can take the grate off and toast marshmallows or grill vegetables. We don't have a reservoir for hot water, my one regret about my stove, but occasionally we take a big stock bucket and bathe the kids in front of the stove anyway, just for fun, heating the water on the top of the stove. If the power goes out, we hang our solar shower bags up on hooks behind the stove to get them hot for a bedtime shower.

Once the stove is going, and if there's not much food to tend, I usually visit it once every hour. It doesn't have to be done that often, once every two or more hours would be sufficient, but I find that it helps me avoid getting engrossed in work or homeschooling and forgetting about the stove entirely. Plus the break — getting up, bringing in some wood or poking up the stove and adding wood — is pleasant. I fill my teacup again, fill the kettle and check on my simmering thing then too.

Lunch and dinner somehow seem easier with the cookstove — it is so simple to put something on to cook when I'm tending the stove anyway. The structure and discipline of dancing with wood bring food along with them. And the rich smells of meals that come out of the woodstove oven seem to make things even more delicious. We eat in the dining room, basking in the warmth of the cookstove.

This reminds me that where you put the stove, and the shape of your house, will also affect your decision about having a stove. You could put your cookstove in the garage or somewhere away from the kitchen, I suppose, but that will likely create a good bit of hassle for you — carrying food that is bound to be spilled sometimes, running back and forth for things. So if the kitchen — or a room right off of it — isn't a place you want to be, having a cookstove might not be for you. We have a good-sized older kitchen with room for the stove, and right off of it is the dining room where most of our homeschooling is done. The stove concentrates us in the kitchen and dining room, which is lovely — it makes our public space more public and collective. We are all together, often working on different projects.

A big cooking project, with things in the oven and on the stove, requires more attention, a familiarity with the vagaries of our draft and the best strategies for heating things quickly. Learning to use a cookstove does take some practice, and will probably involve a few mistakes as you master the idiosyncrasies of your particular stove. I think I burned things once or twice, and underestimated the time for something at least as often, but it was a surprisingly short learning curve, and you shouldn't be intimidated by it. It wasn't nearly as hard as I expected it to be, and the learning was a lot more fun.

You'll want a plentiful supply of potholders and wooden utensils, since these don't transmit heat, and cast iron cookware is the nicest and easiest to use on the stove — but since I like wood and cast iron better anyway, that's no hardship for us. Other than a few basic fireplace tools and a tight metal can for storing ashes, that's really all you need.

During the daytime we all gravitate to the stove, to tend it, to enjoy the enticing smells and to be warmed by it. The kids pull their chairs in for story time. At night, it warms the bedrooms — that is, we put bricks into the oven to get hot, then carry them upstairs, wrapped in flannel, and put them into the children's beds to radiate warmth to the sheets, and then gradually to warm up the children's feet as they cool down. We also heat water in hot water bottles and rice bags to warm the beds. Since we do not really heat the upstairs — we all prefer sleeping in a colder room with plenty of blankets — this means the pleasure of getting into a cozy, warm bed without the fire risk of an electric blanket.

If we do keep the stove going overnight, there's an art to banking it — it takes a little time and practice again. In the autumn and spring we let it go out after dinner, while Eric and I sit and talk about our day, basking in the residual warmth. When it drops into real cold, we fill it up before bed, and then just let it go out — because it is cast iron and tight, the stove will still be quite warm to the touch most mornings, even hours after going out, still radiating heat into the kitchen.

All of it, to me, feels like a dance — occasionally clumsy or awkward, but often delicate and oddly liberating, despite the structures it imposes on my day. It seems odd that one of the secondary loves of my life (after the husband, kids and other family, of course) is green, squat, named Stanley and often too hot to touch, but so it is.

Seven

Getting around

I. The car without a future

MOST OF US ARE SO USED TO OUR CAR-DEPENDENT LIFESTYLE that we don't think about it much — in fact, despite the fact that cars are one of the most dangerous things in the world, we see our use of them as very safe. We worry more about BPA in our cans than we do about the cars that are the leading cause of death in children. What would happen, though, if we started to recognize the true price of cars and the public health costs they come with? In an honest assessment, most of us would, I think, have to realize that everyone having a personal vehicle simply can't be part of a healthy future.

It is hard to de-normalize cars from our systems of thought — to change from viewing them as normal and necessary to dangerous, vehicles to be used only when absolutely necessary, and then while car-sharing or otherwise minimizing per-person emissions. And yet, from what other resource would we tolerate the deaths, maimings, asthma and planetary consequences? What dangerous item would we allow ourselves to be so dependent upon? Shaking the car habit is hard — even coming to see it as a bad habit is hard — but it starts with how we view the issue.

Even before NASA released its study demonstrating that road transport was the single largest driver in economic terms of anthropogenic global warming, we knew that our current transportation paradigm, which prioritizes personal vehicles, was a major detriment to public well-being.

Worldwide, we can attribute 1.2 million deaths per year and forty million injuries significant enough to merit a visit to the doctor to auto-related accidents. There are forty thousand car-related deaths in the US alone every year. The disability claims alone from car-related loss of work and permanent injury come in the hundreds of millions of dollars (all data from the NTSB). Motor vehicle accidents remain the leading cause of death in children.

We also know that motor vehicles affect the public health in other respects. Besides the role of particulate emissions and pollution from road traffic in rates of asthma and lung disease and a host of other health problems, motor vehicle ownership is associated with obesity and a reduction in exercise. In just one study in Colombia (where there is a meaningful population that doesn't own cars), household motor vehicle ownership was shown to be significantly correlated with obesity.

Up until now, the focus has been on reducing the severity of the inevitable car crashes — on booster and car seats for children, safety belt use, new technologies for those who can afford newer vehicles. But while the impact of these changes has been significantly lower per capita deaths, a growing population and the increases in car ownership and trips taken mean that the difference between 1975, before any of these safety measures were instituted, and 2008 was minute. All of those gains are being lost as more and more cars hit the road.

A significant move toward a society with reduced auto-related mortality, illness and disability would involve getting people to get rid of their cars, reduce overall trips taken and travel shorter distances — i.e., the famous "lifestyle changes" that are so central to almost any major health issue.

Like all lifestyle changes, this requires both conversations with those affected and public policy changes — but a surprising amount can be done even if public policy is slow in catching up. Most of us are implicated in the car culture ourselves, my family not excepted. Living in a rural house with a lot of young children, there just aren't many places we can get to by foot or bike. There are at least as many factors preventing people from getting rid of their cars or substantially reducing their mileage as there are stopping them from making other lifestyle changes involving diet and exercise. And yet, one way we could significantly reduce illness and mortality would be to reduce car usage and ownership.

While giving up all vehicles may not be viable, many households could dramatically reduce the number of trips they make weekly, by carpooling for at least some activities or consolidating errands. Most households could incorporate more use of public transportation, bicycles or "shank's mare" (walking). Car use is an acquired behavior, and while most of us like to think all our trips are necessary, research suggests otherwise. My own experience is that we were able to reduce our driving annually by more than half without any cost to our quality of life.

I am a participant in the Riot for Austerity, a program that encourages people to reduce their resource use to one tenth of the American average. We had people in fourteen nations and in every possible life situation attempt to reduce their car usage, and nearly everyone — no matter what their personal situation, no matter where they lived, whether they were able-bodied or had children, no matter how long they commuted — was able to reduce vehicle usage by 25–50 percent without any major structural changes; and this is in the absence of public policy changes like more public transportation. Many were able to reduce their usage further still, but at a minimum, most people should be able to make significant reductions — one study found that more than 25 percent of all trips were discretionary.

If cars were seen not as a necessity and a status symbol but as a public health threat, we could begin to make significant inroads into their reduction — and to lowering the greenhouse gasses they emit. Even beginning to speak as though cars are a significant threat to public health and car-related pollution, disability and death are not just inevitable outcomes of a lifestyle we can't seriously reconsider begins to open up a conversation that we are simply not having yet.

II. Why I don't worry that much about personal transportation

Oil powers 97 percent of the world's personal transportation. Now that's a concerning sort of a figure if you are worried about oil supplies and prices, and we've all seen gas prices go wild in the last few years. All of us have felt the pinch in our purse, and anyone who remembers the 1970s oil shocks knows that we can experience a sudden, radical shift in our ability to get around. Why aren't I more worried about this?

I do have concerns about how high energy prices or supply constraints might affect the commercial trucking industry and commercial aviation — that we may not be able to get supplies trucked in or go and visit faraway family easily. Those, I think, are real and legitimate concerns. At the same time, I'm not that worried about personal transport — I think we'll probably mostly manage to get around.

The reason this isn't a major concern for me is because I've seen what happens in the Global South when gas is comparatively unaffordable — we radically reduce trips and no one travels alone.

When we talk about mileage, we tend to think about miles per gallon and imagine that what we need is a more efficient car, and of course, if you can afford such a thing, that can be a good choice. Truly, however, the central issue is MILES PER GALLON PER PERSON — when two people who would normally be traveling in two separate cars get into the same vehicle, you functionally take one of them off the road and double your mileage.

During the extraordinarily record gas prices of 2007, there was a great deal of talk about how to respond — news stories about people selling their houses in outer suburbia to move closer to their jobs or about the move toward newer and better hybrids. There were virtually no news stories, however, about the cheapest, easiest-to-implement response — upping the number of passengers in existing vehicles and reduce the number of trips people take.

That's because most of us imagine that our personal commuting habits are just that — personal. We don't want to leave ten minutes earlier, go five miles out of our way to pick someone else up or have to share the radio in the morning. We imagine it has to be all or nothing, so if on Wednesdays we have to stop at the store, we assume that precludes us sharing rides. In most of the world, however, where gas isn't cheap, transport is collective. It isn't perfectly convenient, and everyone has to make accommodations to one another — when you put nine people in a VW bus, everyone has to work around one another. At the same time, this is a model that can operate anywhere — we can share transportation. We can do it formally, as some of the unemployed make jobs moving people around, or we can do it between ourselves, talking to our neighbors about how to combine resources and at least some of our trips.

It is unlikely that most of us will entirely run out of gas in the near term — what is more likely is that we're never going to know how much gas, food, electricity, heat and other costs will take out of our pocket book in any given year. We are likely to face wild, volatile fluctuations in price — as we've already seen. We are likely to see economic declines that make us less able to afford gas. What we probably won't see is a complete end to driving — but we're going to do less and combine more, and it will be less convenient but also less dangerous, less polluting, less serious.

One of the things we can do is begin this collaborative and shared transportation model now — asking your neighbor if they need a ride, dropping the kids off together, making that effort to reduce trips, asking others if they will give you a lift. Like all sharing, it can be difficult to initiate, but those of us who depend on cars will have to begin here.

There are a lot of ways to reduce your vehicle usage. The ones we hear about most involve buying an expensive new hybrid car — but most of us aren't able to afford that. There is nothing wrong with a higher-mileage vehicle, but a lower-mileage life may be a better place to start. Our family of six (sometimes more) finds that we're able to get by with about sixty gallons of gas per person per year — a big difference from the five hundred the average American uses.

We do this by a combination of fuel efficiency (until we added foster children to our lives, we used a small car, sometimes with three car and booster seats abreast), combining trips, planning activities for our children so that all four could participate at once, picking and choosing our outings and reducing temptation by not everyone always having a car.

We found that we didn't need two cars for the period when I was working from home, but had a tough time getting along with only one — one or two days a week, we really needed a second vehicle, so we took the next step: we bartered with friends to share a car. They too had a work-from-home parent and didn't really need a second car every day, so the four of us shared three vehicles. Later on, we were able to reduce our needs to one car, but this gradual process was very helpful. We have considered sharing a single vehicle but with our large and fluctuating brood of foster children, we haven't quite pulled that off yet. Still, we often loan out our large van to others who need to transport a crowd or move something big — not everyone needs a large vehicle if some of us can share.

We use biking lightly, because our oldest son's disabilities and the size of our family make it hard for us all to bike much of anywhere. We do walk and push a stroller a few miles to the library or playground at times, but mostly we make our fun and our lives around our home so as to minimize trips. Those who live near public transportation or have more walkable and bikeable households can make different choices.

What concerns me about transportation is longer-distance transport by air and the shipping of goods. To reduce our oil dependency, we need to be able to get more of what we need near home and bring our families together as much as possible. Neither of these things is easy, nor are they always going to be possible. But when thinking about transportation, I think it makes sense to recognize that personal transport is comparatively simple to deal with — and we have to focus on strong extended families and local economies, as well as reducing our individual time in cars.

In this regard, it makes a lot of sense to concentrate not on the means of transport but on the ends desired — can we get more things made and built in our communities? Can we stockpile some essential resources in our homes or at the community level to reduce our dependency on distant transport? Can we use technologies that are comparatively less intensive to keep close to people we love? Can we think about ways to come together in proximity? Can we anticipate the needs we will have in a less transport-rich future? These seem to be the central questions that we face — not so much miles per gallon in our vehicles, but getting out of the vehicles themselves and altering the circumstances that drive us toward requiring them.

III. How To ride a bike

Note: I didn't write this part of the book, I stole, er, borrowed it from Aaron Newton, my frequent partner-in-crime. While I do ride a bike some of the time, I don't have Aaron's depth of experience, so these are his words, not mine.

> *"i used to fantasize about living in a healthier place,*
> *one where i could ride my bike, for example. then,*
> *one day, i started riding my bike. now, without having*
> *fled or escaped to anywhere, i live in a place where*
> *i can ride my bike."*
>
> — heretic fig

In 2007 I gave up my car commute and started biking. Yes I burn less carbon, yes I use less oil and yes I'm in better shape, but the reason I've stuck with it is that riding to work is so much fun. I'm going to go over some bike basics for those of you thinking about spending less time in your car. By the way you'll save quite a bit of money if you're able to give up your car.

I started at my local bike shop (LBS). I had done my own research online and thought I knew what I needed but I turned out to be wrong. My LBS owner helped me put together a great setup tailored to my commute. I mostly ride a Trek 7.6 hybrid. I strongly suggest that if you're interested in a bicycle as your main means of transportation you should get to know the people at your LBS. Their knowledge is very valuable.

But there are some things you can consider before talking to someone locally about what might work best for you.

Riding positions. Bicycle geometry is a somewhat complicated topic. Your needs will vary depending on the size and shape of your body, the distance you plan to ride on a regular basis and what you plan to carry. For instance my commuter cycle has a straight bar like a mountain bike. This means I ride in an upright position. I see cars and they see me. I usually only ride 10 miles or so at a time so this position doesn't get too tiresome. On longer trips it does. I switch to a road bike with drop bars and a geometric configuration that is better suited to longer distances.

Lights. I have two headlights and two taillights. All are capable of producing a stream of light or a flashing light. I have two of each because I never want to leave home after dark and find out the batteries are dead on my only headlight. Plus two lights are brighter than one. I have rechargeable batteries and check them regularly. You might think you'll only be riding during the day but inevitably you'll end up out after dark or caught in a rain shower. Lights will help you ride more safely.

A helmet. Of course in terms of safety you'll want to wear a helmet. I've gotten so used to leaving the house with a helmet that I often grab it even when I'm planning to take my car. Of course I don't actually wear it when I'm driving. ;-) Helmet = Good.

Tires. I have 700 X 38 tires on my commuter cycle. They are wide enough to be stable if I have to leave a paved surface but they are made for traveling quickly over pavement. You can also get 27" tires with all sorts of tread types from smooth to very stubbly for off-road biking. Somewhere in between you're likely to find a tire that's right for where you plan to ride. There are lots of options. Ask your LBS people.

A way to carry stuff. I have a friend who is fond of saying, "Cycling is just recreation unless you can carry stuff." This is key because if you're riding to work or to school or to go shopping, you're going to need a way to take stuff with you and back again. Rear- and front-mounted racks can carry bags for goods or people. My commuter cycle has a rack that is compatible with my two-year-old daughter's bike carrier and also with the pair of saddlebags called panniers. In them I carry my lunch, a change of clothes and anything else I need. For bigger stuff or bigger people I switch to my xtracycle. It can carry up to 200 lbs with a child on it and still have room for groceries.

Security. I have several bike locks. I keep one on my bike at all times. You never know when you're going to want to stop and you'll need to be able to leave your bike safely by itself.

A tube replacement kit. This also stays with me on all rides. With precautions, tube punctures can be minimized, but every once in a while I have a flat. A spare tube, the tools to install it and a way to inflate the tube have me up and running again in no time. To prevent flats consider a tire liner.

Toe clips or clipless pedals. Using these will help you better leverage the full power of your legs. It helps me get to work and back faster. They aren't for everyone and they take some getting used to but for many people this will help you get around easier and faster.

A water bottle cage. Stay hydrated.

Fenders and rain gear. By hydrated I meant on the inside not the outside. If you are going to ride in the rain (and everyone will eventually;-), I suggest fenders and waterproof clothes.

A computer. OK this isn't necessary, but I admit I like to see how fast I'm going, how far I've ridden and to track my progress as a cyclist.

Extras. There are plenty of add-ons that you might find very useful for your bike setup. I have bar ends with built-in rearview mirrors on my commuter. The bar ends are a great way to change hand positions during longer rides and seem to help me get better leverage on hills. I seldom flip out the rearview mirrors, but I do use them occasionally, especially in more urban environments. You might find that a bell for alerting pedestrians or special seat make your ride more enjoyable.

Again depending on where and how often you plan to ride and what you need to carry with you, your particular bicycle needs will vary. That's why I recommend visiting your local bike shop to help get you started. For most of us, using a bicycle for many of our daily trips really is possible, and I urge people to give it a try. You might wind up addicted like me.

Profile 3

Risa and Pattiebuff: Doing it over again

Pattiebuff, fifty-eight, and Risa, sixty-one, met in 1976. They had both lived and worked on small farms as well as in cities, and on the whole they preferred farms. Pattiebuff had taught in a farm school, and Risa had spent a year on a communal farm with Hutterites. The "back to the land" movement was in full swing, and among their heroes were Wendell Berry, Carla Emery, John Seymour and Ruth Stout.

They had little money of their own but had built up a store of goodwill among friends and family, so they issued handmade bonds for twenty dollars, each with a face value of twenty-five dollars, to be redeemed over time. In this way they raised twenty thousand dollars to put down for land of their own.

They settled on twelve unimproved acres in a narrow valley in Oregon's Coast Range, adding to their skills by reading, asking questions and trial and error. Soon they were living from their garden and woodlot, and by seasonal labor. Pattiebuff taught in her one-room schoolhouse while Risa worked half of each year in forestry.

Besides the schoolhouse, they built a house and a small barn using post-and-beam construction, out of rough lumber and found materials. They lived off-grid with twelve-volt lighting and learned to use a wood cookstove that they had been given.

Risa dug an outhouse in the woods by the schoolhouse. They piped water in from a spring to a pitcher pump in the schoolhouse and another in the kitchen of the main house. Their shower was a five-gallon bucket with a showerhead attached to a spigot at the bottom. Perishable foods kept cold most of the year in the springhouse, and in high summer they ran a propane refrigerator.

In the 1980s, when local forestry went through a recession, they moved to the suburbs and Risa worked in a print shop while Pattiebuff kept the house place and homeschooled. Later, Pattiebuff worked in the city library, and Risa studied and worked at the local university.

They missed the big woods, but raised apples and pears, ducks and a large garden on their quarter-acre lot, and continued to heat with wood. The family was outdoors so much they were called the "rubber boot people." After some years, observing a deterioration of social and economic conditions in their surroundings, they decided to try again to live out of town and commute to their city jobs.

In 1993, wistfully driving through an area of seemingly unaffordable hobby farms, they discovered a rundown house on a little over an acre with a "for sale" sign — and blue tarps covering the entire roof. "Ah," they said. "Where there are so many tarps there must be a relatively low asking price."

This was the case, and they relocated there, thirteen miles beyond the city limits, bringing the ducks, the shop, the garden tools, the packets of seeds and a will to make up for lost time. Doubling payments whenever possible, they secured the title in thirteen years.

A small seasonal creek runs diagonally through the property, challenging any and all land-use plans but providing a high water table for the wells and for the luxuriant thicket of blackberries that grows along its banks. The creek bed is covered with thousands of stones, so they have named the little place Stony Run Farm.

The house and the small barn, handbuilt of good materials but old and prone to dry rot, have proved adaptable to a variety of "independence days" schemes. The land, described by surveyors in 1855 as "good enough soil but very rocky and poorly drained," slopes slightly north and needs all the help it can get.

Empty-nesters, Pattiebuff and Risa have time now to "return to their roots," especially as Risa has recently retired. They have added a cold room for vegetable and dry food storage, a "wine cellar," a potting shed, a grow tunnel, a chicken run, duck pens, a solar water heater, a woodshed, ducks, chickens, geese, a bummer lamb, twenty-five fruit trees and twenty-one slightly raised no-till garden beds. They have a flourishing grape arbor and hope soon to add kiwis and hops.

Risa cuts and brings in firewood and Pattiebuff splits and stacks it. They both garden, mostly vegetables; and Risa "puts by" the root crops, beans, dehydrated fruits and vegetables, saves seeds and apples for each winter and cans whatever is left over. Pattiebuff manages the poultry and plans to breed rare Ancona ducks. Risa owns a scythe and threatens to raise barley on the "other side of the creek." Nothing has come of that yet; she's slowing down!

Asked what would be the first piece of advice she'd offer to young homesteaders starting out, Risa says, "Well, the best decision we made back in the Seventies was to do without TV. That has pretty much made time for living the good life." She chuckles, and adds, "Of course, chickens put on about as good a show as you'll ever hope to watch."

Eight

Growing

I. Do I have to grow food?

B ECAUSE OF THE ENORMOUS IMPACT OF AGRICULTURE ON CLIMATE CHANGE, pick up any book about "green" solutions and you'll find the suggestion that you grow a vegetable garden. Bang into the "we can't go on as we are" end of the environmental movement (mine) and you'll see the general assumption that growing food is part of any process of adaptation to lower resource use.

This often then morphs into the assumption that all of us should be able to grow all or a vast majority of our food — that sustainability means the country life for everyone. You might think that because I do produce most of my own food, and because I wrote a book advocating for millions of additional farmers, I might fall into this category. In fact, I don't. At least in the short term, I think those farmers will mostly be amateurs, farming very small plots indeed, often land they don't own, rather than full-time professionals.

I think there will be no substitute for being involved with your food and your food system, and I think that for many people, food growing provides a measure of security not available even through sustainable purchasing from local farmers. But I don't believe that means that all of us are going, as the song goes, to "Get behind the mule in the morning and plow." Indeed, I think the majority of local food production will probably occur on small scales in urban and suburban areas, by people who either owned their land before the present crisis or who do not own land. The "move to the country and buy land" model is unlikely to dominate the future because of the economic costs.

Many people rightly point out that both the US and Canada are food exporters with no shortages of food, so it seems strange to imagine that growing gardens could be important. It is easy not to realize that most hunger doesn't occur because of a shortage of food — it occurs because people can't afford to buy it. Most world hunger takes place in areas where markets are full of food — and where many people go hungry because they cannot purchase any.

This is an easy one to miss — learning about peak oil and climate change, many people become fixated on the idea of transportation or other system disruptions that cut food supplies. And this is possible — indeed, when food and gas costs rose to their highest point in 2008, end-of-supply-line regions like Alaskan Native villages found themselves struggling to get supplies in. But the vast majority of the world's hungry live in places with sufficient food blighted by fluctuating or high food prices. It is credible, then, to assume that, at least in the shorter term, our collective crisis is likely to play out as it has in the past — with more and more people unable to keep food on the table.

Just as the most likely reason for any of my readers to have to live without heat or utilities is because growing poverty makes it impossible for them to pay utility bills and they get shut off or become homeless, the most likely reason for anyone reading this to encounter a food crisis is because of growing poverty. This is obviously the pattern in the United States. We are seeing a steady rise in hunger — how much is hard to establish. We know that food stamps are at their highest level of use ever — that one in seven American households, and one in four American children, now rely on them.

That doesn't tell the whole story — food stamps are a fairly good measure of food insecurity, in which people don't know whether there will always be food or not, but not of hunger. Statistics on hunger are hard to collect. We know that it is rising rapidly, that food pantries in many regions are seeing tripling and quadrupling of demand. We know the situations are direr, and more acute. But again, this can't tell the whole story — there are families in crisis who do not receive food stamps, and demand at food pantries or soup kitchens isn't a good measure since at many of these, people go away with needs unmet. Many agencies don't track information about demand or recipients, because they either lack the capacity or are afraid of driving recipients away.

The rise of hunger in the US in the last few years is astonishing — and it is occurring in times of food surplus, when grain and other yields are at record levels. There are no shortages in the US, and yet people are going hungry. Americans spend less on food than almost any other national population in the world, so hunger in the US often doesn't make sense to people — why aren't we at least buying food?

The answer is that food is generally a somewhat fungible expense for people, unlike other costs like housing, medications and transportation. Consider a working-poor single parent household with a job. They live in one area, and the job is forty-five minutes away by car in an area with no public transportation. The job has no standard shifts, like much low-paying employment, which makes it nearly impossible to provide stable childcare — if you have to be at work at 4 am one day and until 10 pm the next this is next to impossible.

The largest fixed expenses are transportation and housing — usually a car loan and disproportionately high rent or mortgage payments. It would be easy to say that people should abandon their car and get a job somewhere else, but this is often not viable. It would be easy to say they should move to a lower-cost area, but they are often pinned down by family obligations, employment or even the inability to produce first month's and last month's rent. Incomes are often unstable, and depend on whether overtime is offered or not. Most low-paying jobs have no benefits, so a single illness or a sudden expense like a car breakdown is enough to force families to move into the few areas of their lives that are fungible — and food is the big fungible expense.

Now some of my readers will point out that the poor often make poor choices — this is absolutely true. The rich do too — but they are not penalized for their inability to cook or their decision to buy a luxury item before they realized there would be no overtime that month. Moreover, I think it is safe to say that as more of us become poor, more of us will make some bad choices too. Many of us have already, and now we may pay a high price for it. In fact, in the case of the poor, those paying the biggest price are generally those who have no choices at all — children.

I think it is fair to say, building on current patterns, that we can expect hunger and food insecurity to increase even among people in net-food-exporting nations that would never have thought they too could be hungry. We can say this because it has been happening, and quite dramatically. Those most immediately affected will be people who have always lived closest to the margins of food insecurity, or who were already food insecure — the rural, urban and suburban (there are now more poor people living in the suburbs than in cities in the US) poor and working class.

These people will not, generally speaking, be "getting land" — credit has already tightened dramatically for low-income people, and they already rely heavily on the informal economy, including community networks and existing family and social structures, for support. Most of the US poor can't afford a mortgage, they can't afford first and last month's rent or security to move, they can't move away from their sister who watches the kids while they work third shift, they can't move to a new city where they don't know anyone who can help translate, they can't afford to move to a place where there are no bus lines.... Some may be pushed into rural areas because of the lower cost of living, and a few will choose to relocate there, but most have fairly limited mobility and won't be buying land to grow all their food anytime soon.

If the US were to shift its focus from bailing out the financial community to providing for the basic needs of the most vulnerable, and if programs like food stamps and unemployment benefit extensions could continue expanding indefinitely, we would still see real and serious hunger here. The odds are, however, that these changes won't happen. Most American state unemployment funds are functionally bankrupt, relying on federal subsidies to keep them paying out. States are already slashing aid to education, social welfare programs and support programs for children, the elderly and the disabled.

The question becomes, How much can and will the federal government do? It is certainly in their interest to stop food riots from occurring — but we've seen the way American attitudes toward the poor pit them against one another, and naturalize a hatred and fear of the poor. For there to be riots, large numbers of hungry Americans would have to achieve some kind of solidarity. If we view the present as an experiment in how many people can go hungry or food insecure before anyone recognizes a fundamental social failure, the answer seems to be "a lot."

All of which leads to the conclusion that the people who are most likely to be hit by hunger in the near term, the people most in need of more food and better nutrition, will be people least able to go out and buy land and move to the country. This pretty much supports what I've been saying for many years, that "we most need to grow food where people already are." For rural dwellers, many of whom are land rich but poor in most other respects (although not all own land), the answer is a new way of viewing the land they own. After decades of farming not paying, it may start to — not well, but enough to keep people off the margins. Rural communities should be able to build new economies around kinds of farming that will be needed.

We're often dismissive, however, of suburban and urban agriculture. How can someone's window box, community garden plot, rooftop garden or thirty-by-twenty-foot backyard really make a difference? But in fact we know that in much of the world, urban and suburban food growing makes an enormous difference in food security. For people in cities and the suburbs, the answer is not "get land" but "make the best possible use of what you have." The aggregate of urban and suburban systems that integrate food production into local systems is potentially substantial. No, they will not entirely feed themselves, but for now at least, that's not what's required — what's required is that we make a critical difference in household food security, and city and suburban gardens can do that.

How do we know? Because growing food has been doing this very thing for poor people for a very long time. Among poor and landless households in Lusaka, the capital of Zambia, households that garden, usually on land they do not own and often by squatting, are substantially better nourished by every measure, while also producing more food per acre and using water more sparingly than farmers in the surrounding countryside. In Moscow during the collapse of the Soviet Union, 65 percent of economically struggling households grew food. A UN report on urban agriculture in Kampala, Uganda, found that children in families that grew food crops were as healthy as far wealthier families.

Fifty percent of produce grown in China in the early 1990s was grown within cities. In much of sub-Saharan Africa, up to 20 percent of all calories consumed are produced in cities. In 1981, Hong Kong had five million people and 1,060 square kilometers and was using 10 percent of that land to produce 45 percent of the fresh vegetables, 15 percent of the pigs and 68 percent of the chickens eaten in the city, according to Isabel Wade's essay "Fertile Cities." In 2002, the city had grown to 6.3 million people and had seen much of its good land developed (for example, between 1981 and 2000, all rice farming, even on the outer islands, ceased), but the remainder was still producing 33 percent of the produce, 14 percent of the pigs, 36 percent of the chickens and farming 20 percent of the fish consumed within the city. The animals were raised for the most part on 160,000 *tons* of food waste being recycled every year into meat and egg production.

We know that small-scale gardening can make a critical difference for the poor, be they chronically poor or newly becoming poor. The difference is not that it magically provides all food, but that it provides access to high-value, high-protein and high-nutrition foodstuffs that are expensive or hard to access in rural and urban "food deserts." Small gardens allow poor people to turn low-cost resources like seeds into high-cost items like healthy food. They also allow people to turn food wastes into high-quality protein, if combined with small-scale animal husbandry. Because gardening can often be done almost entirely outside the cash economy, it is particularly valuable for those with minimal or tied-up cash incomes, who have little financial leeway.

Just as importantly, community gardens and other local food production exercises have political implications as well — they tie communities together in ways that other activities don't. In a fascinating study, SUNY Albany Professor Donna Armstrong finds that:

> The most commonly expressed reasons for participating in gardens were access to fresh foods, to enjoy nature, and health benefits. Gardens in low-income neighborhoods (46 percent) were four times as likely as non low-income gardens to lead to other issues in the neighborhood being addressed; reportedly due to organizing facilitated through the community gardens.

This mirrors what urban dwellers in places as diverse as Zimbabwe, Russia and China report — that the value of gardening is that it is never a wholly private activity, but one with profound communal, political and social implications.

It would be easy to trivialize the impact of small gardens in suburbs and cities — but their aggregate is enormous. As Michael W. Hamm and Monique Baron write in a case study, the entire produce needs of residents of New Jersey could be met by large numbers of small household gardens or by new acreage brought into production, but given the high level of development, the small household garden model might be more feasible.

There may come a time when we face immediate, pressing and absolute shortages of food, but we aren't there yet, and it doesn't seem to be the most pressing reality for most of us. What's more likely is that we will struggle to pay for food, be pressed into purchasing it at unaffordable prices due to lack of good access and be forced to take money out of our food budgets to meet other needs. What's most likely is that hunger will begin for many of us (has begun for many of us) as a slow grind, wearing us down, and as safety net after safety net begins to slip, we will find ourselves more and more in need of our gardens — and every other mechanism we have to support ourselves.

Do you have to grow food? No, and some people never will, from lack of ability or because they are doing other, equally important work. But for most of us, the world is no respecter of persons of importance. I would say you do not have to grow food as long as you have faith that you yourself will never become poor — will never lose your job, never struggle to make ends meet, never fall through the increasingly shaky safety nets. But that is, of course, precisely the most likely thing to happen to all of us in the near term of our ecological crisis. Most of us fear that outcome, often fear it so much that we deny it could happen to us — and thus deny ourselves a chance to learn useful lessons from the 85 percent of the world population who has already navigated this territory before us, who have already shown us the deep urgency of growing what we can.

II. Putting me in my place

But what about those of us who do have some land? Is it worth asking what we can do, how we fit into this picture? I think so. The first thing you need to know about my farm is that it is huge. I mean absolutely enormous by world standards. The vast majority of the world's farms — more than 80 percent — are very small farms, less than two hectares (about five acres), and they produce the majority of the world's food. With twenty-seven acres, my farm is gargantuan.

I suspect most folks in most of the Global North will find that a little surprising. The term "farm" in the US tends to be applied most often to very large operations. We have a strong internal sense that small-scale agriculture is particularly unsuited to growing staples. Most small farms in the US concentrate on smaller or specialty markets — the fact that the majority of the world's rice, for example, is grown on farms of less than five acres would probably startle most people.

If you take out my nineteen acres of woodland, the proportions get closer, but that nineteen acres represents an indescribable wealth for the nearly a billion small producers who live in areas that are seriously deforested and who struggle to get firewood, building materials and other forest products readily available to me. Moreover, although we preserve and protect our woodlands and wetlands, we also derive both household and economic benefit from them — from the wood we burn to the mushrooms we harvest to the food we forage and the wetland plants I specialize in growing.

In US terms, of course, I have a very small farm. Very small farms in the US are defined as less than fifty acres, and I'd need another 973 acres to make it to "large." Very small farms have been increasing in numbers over the last few years, but slightly larger small- to mid-sized American farms are disappearing as the trend toward larger- and larger-scale production increases. While there are more farms under fifty acres than there were twenty years ago, those farms still produce a tiny fraction of the food consumed in the US. Moreover, as the above link shows, the growth of very small farms has in some ways concealed the continuing consolidation of agriculture, the elimination of the once-vast agricultural middle that until recently fed the nation.

There is a tendency to dismiss very small-scale agriculture in the US as not serious. And if "serious" is defined as producing primary calorie crops — those staple grains and roots that are the basis of our diets — there's a case to be made. Most very small farmers deal in small markets where a lot of attention can make their high-value, labor-intensive crops stand out. They find that it is simply not economically viable to produce staples — we found that during the period we ran our CSA. We can and did grow grinding corn, potatoes and sweet potatoes, as well as smaller quantities of other staples. But we also realized pretty quickly that a population accustomed to paying six dollars a pound for organic tomatoes won't pay that for potatoes or cornmeal.

So like most small farmers, we found ourselves pushed toward high-value crops. We were also shaped by our choice of farm, because of the amount and kind of land. If we take "serious" to mean "feeds the most people, cars and livestock the most grain," very small farms in the US are not very serious. On the other hand, if we're talking about the value of crops produced per acre, and about what crops are not generally produced on large-scale farms because of realities of centralization and shipping, then smaller farms become very important indeed. Moreover, the world example should show us that small farms can play a substantive role in producing our primary calories. Half the rice in India, for example, is grown on small farms.

When we purchased our farm, we considered large parcels. While our goal was to reduce fossil-fueled inputs, we didn't reject the tractor for that reason — I consider agricultural production to be one of the better uses of oil, and wouldn't have had any problem using one. But what kept me from getting one was watching other farmers — barring those who could afford the best equipment, most spent many long days tinkering with their tractors. Most of them liked the work, but I don't, and neither does Eric. We had doubts about our ability to do good maintenance, and our patience for dealing with the frustration.

We considered draft animals more seriously — I am not a horsey person, but I do love draft horses, their calm, quiet size appeals to me deeply and I have fond childhood memories of holding reins behind a family member. I like oxen too, and have friends who would have taught me the tricks of using either. But at the time I had a nursing fifteen-month-old and was pregnant with my second son.

Almost thirty years ago, Judith Brown wrote a short essay, "Notes on the Division of Labor by Sex," in which she pointed out something that should have been blindingly obvious, had not historians and anthropologists largely ignored women's work — that whether or not communities or households can rely upon women to do the work of providing depends "on the compatibility of this pursuit with the demands of child care." Since pregnancy and nursing could easily last four years per child in most societies (the worldwide average age of weaning is four even now), the work women do must be compatible with the realities of child rearing.

That is, the work must be safe enough that you can take babies with you and do it while carrying one on your back or front, and be easily interrupted to meet children's needs, and not place small, mobile children in danger or not require your whole attention. Working with draft horses or oxen meets none of these requirements. So to make good use of the horses would have been Eric's business, and Eric does not love draft animals as I do.

Because I am the primary farmer on our farm, and we were facing at least three more years of pregnancy and my nursing (it turned out to be six more, actually), we chose a smaller farm. My being the chief of agricultural operations here (to put it pretentiously) puts me largely in sync with most of the world — the majority of the farmers in the world are women.

This is one of the reasons the world's farms, despite enormous efforts to expand, consolidate and mechanize them, are mostly small, and probably always will be. Just like me, the vast majority of agrarian women in the world must do their farm work with their babies on their backs and their children or grandchildren interrupting them to ask questions. To get bigger, a farm must be able to support two farmers — one to do the local work, to manage those animals kept close to the house and tend the household garden and those fields that can be handled with a hoe or a digging stick, and one to do the work with draft animals or tractors and other dangerous tools, farther away from the home, while the home-farmer stands guard and watches the children.

But just like my family, most farm families in the US and in the world do not live entirely on their farm income any longer. Indeed, as Peter Rosset writes in *Food is Different*, the whole world effectively benefits from the fact that even when it isn't economically remunerative, farmers essentially subsidize their agricultural production with off-farm labor. This is one common ground that ties me to much larger farms — all of us have trouble making ends meet without non-farm labor. Big or small, most of the world's farmers rely on additional outside work performed by themselves or by family members.

Farmers drive trucks and substitute teach in the winter, or one partner in a farming household works full-time off-farm for things like health insurance and a stable income. In the Global South, it is common to send daughters to the factories in some countries, or sons to the US to work construction or do other labor and send back money to keep the family farm afloat. Rosset documents that farming truly is a way of life, rather than simply a job, because even when the off-farm work is more remunerative than the farm work *and* the farmers have the opportunity to give up farming altogether, they often persist in agricultural pursuits, while working longer and harder outside in order to support the practice of feeding others.

For a long time in American history, it was possible for a small-to-mid-sized farm to support two adults working full-time on the land at agricultural pursuits, broadly and not always accurately divided into "housewifery and husbandry." That is, you could divide agricultural production into field-scale agriculture done with draft animals, usually by a man (although women certainly worked in the fields more often than they are credited with), and home-scale agriculture — dairying, poultry keeping, gardening, small-field crop tending — along with childcare, usually done by a woman.

This is why we developed the assumption that a farmer is a man, and his adjunct is "the farmer's wife." In a society, if such a society could ever exist, that gave full credit to women and housewifery, this tragedy of labeling might be less unfortunate. But the difficulty of the "farmer's wife" assumption is that it erases primary women from agriculture — millions and millions of them. Indeed, we can see this erasure particularly in Africa, where for more than half a century development dollars in agriculture have overwhelmingly gone to the men who often own the land — but don't farm it. More than 80 percent of African farmers are women, and it is only in the last two decades that efforts to address agricultural difficulties in many African countries have even fully recognized who was doing the farming.

More directly, in my life, the farmer's wife syndrome erases me —
even though I'm the primary farmer. Don't get me wrong — on a farm,
everyone farms in some measure, and Eric and I are full partners —
but the reality is that the farm is driven by my efforts. Yet almost every
month someone comes to the farm to make a delivery or a purchase and
immediately assumes that Eric is the person to talk to. Eric is extremely
good at fending this off — I remember how appreciative I felt when our
real estate agent, taking us around to view these farms, assumed that I
would be more interested in the house and Eric would take charge of
viewing the barn. Instead, Eric very calmly observed that he was going
to take Eli to look at the house, leaving me to evaluate the barn, as I was
better qualified than he. The agent looked stunned, but gamely turned
back to me. Some variation on this scene gets played out regularly here.

The other way that we are more rather than less like the world norm
is in the quality of our farmland. Frankly, ours is dreadful, and I say that
fondly — I love my terrible soil. Indeed, most of the places we could
afford that wouldn't have involved a forty-five-minute or longer commute for Eric were pretty awful in some way — either the house was a
wreck, or the barns were, or the soil was, or occasionally all of the above.

This too is typical of the world scene. The trend toward agricultural
consolidation has not just shaped America. All over the world, much of
the best land has been shifted to export crops and larger farms, while
more and more of the 2.5 billion pastoralists — very small farmers, fish-
erpeople and the remaining hunter-gatherers — have been pushed onto
ever more marginal land and water.

In our case, we weren't pushed — we wanted our land, it was the best
of an imperfect lot of choices. We knew that we'd be dependent on Eric's
faculty job, and didn't want to substitute small inputs on the farm for
large ones spent in gas. We knew of people to carpool with in this area.
Moreover, I didn't really want to devote myself full-time to making the
house habitable, or trying to prop up a collapsing barn. This place had a
decent house, although one that needed work, and several functionalish
outbuildings. It had a size and scale within my capacities and our reality.

Its vast disadvantage was that the topsoil had been strip-mined —
quite literally, the place was a sod farm for decades — and most of the
never-deep topsoil had been cut up and sent to people who couldn't wait

for grass to grow (it still grew grass fairly well). But it had ample water, and soil for vegetables, I reasoned, could be built.

And we did build it — it was a long, deeply labor-intensive process, but we managed to make it work, with almost no fossil fuel inputs, using only hand labor. The vast majority of it was done by a woman laboring under the constraints of traditional women's work — toddlers, babies, pregnancies and all. In the end we created a CSA that had twenty-two members and provided a huge basket of vegetables to each one twenty weeks a year.

It took us a while to figure out that what we needed most was more livestock. As David Montgomery, author of the superb *Dirt: The Erosion of Civilizations*, observes, land is rapidly exhausted of topsoil if the organic material is not replaced. And it is hard to produce enough organic material entirely using vegetable means. We were enthusiastic replacers with all we had — but we raised only poultry for the first five years.

We raised a lot of pastured poultry — turkeys, chickens and ducks — but the pasturing meant that half the manure was going back to our grasslands — good for them, but not for the garden. The remaining half, their night droppings, mixed with bedding, were not enough. We got manures from neighbors, from the alpaca farmers, the horse people and a nearby dairy farm, but we needed more, and more directly.

Both our predecessors, in stripping the soil, and us in our failure to replace the organic material as quickly as needed, were following an American tradition, if an appalling one. Disregard of soil, the idea that you can always move on to better land — many agricultural observers have deplored the way that American farmers misuse and deplete their ground, and been astonished by the fact that, particularly in the South, they did not manure their fields.

George Washington wrote to Alexander Hamilton, "It must be obvious to every man who considers the agriculture of this country, how miserably defective we are in the management of our lands.... A few more years of increased sterility will drive the Inhabitants of the Atlantic States westward for support; whereas if they were taught how to improve the old, instead of going in pursuit of new and productive soils, they would make these acres which now scarcely yield them anything, turn out beneficial to themselves." He was prescient, Washington. But some of us stayed — my ancestors among them, staying in place in the cold, rocky Northeast, and I think some of that remains in my blood, the desire to take the imperfect land and claim it and make it all it can be. This project, whether by necessity or choice, will be a central work for all of us in country and in cities all over the world.

We did not move fast enough initially in soil restoration, but we have improved since, adding more livestock to our land. We have taken up the project, partly from necessity, since we cannot afford the best land, but also partly from desire to restore marginal land to productivity. We have shuttered our CSA, I think for good — I loved doing it, but I know that the river bottomland below us will always produce better, faster vegetables than we will, with less cost to the soil. We will always be ten days later to market with our tomatoes and our sweet corn. So it is enough to me that we begin from our subsistence, and produce those things only for our family, some friends and the food pantry.

And in that, too, there is a real resemblance to the world's average farm. The average farmer and small agricultural producer feeds themselves first, and only then sells extra produce or high-value items for cash. This model of prioritizing subsistence production over maximum cash production was the norm even in the Global North for most of human history, before it was replaced here by the idea that even farmers should produce food only for cash, and then purchase their meals at the same supermarkets everyone else shops at.

We, like everyone, have our cash crops, but they are for the most part overages — our priority is always getting our own food from our own land. We are not doctrinaire about this — I have grown small grains, but don't grow much of them. Instead, we grow lots of potatoes and sweet potatoes and substitute these for some of our grains, while buying our other staples sustainably from small producers in bulk. There are some crops I don't grow — because I save seed, I grow only one crop of sweet corn, and we happily devour the stuff from the farmstand in the valley. I eat their tomatoes for a couple of weeks before mine are ripe. I get peaches from a farmer down the hill in a warmer place than mine. We are hardly perfectly consistent.

And yet we produce all the milk we drink and many of our other dairy products (we still buy ice cream occasionally, and butter locally) and all our eggs. We raise most of our meat and vegetables, about half our fruit and about a third of our staple foods. We do this not only during the growing season but by preserving our food for winter and using season extension, also through winter.

Meanwhile, the crops we specialize in are ones that our land does best, or that we can do better than others. Pastured poultry, goat, lamb and eggs. Healthy livestock, raised for small-scale production. Herbs and salad greens for the off-season. Seeds we save. Native wetland plants for land restoration. Garden plants for other people's gardens. Medicinal plants and dried herbs, produced in small, high-quality batches. We are also able to experiment with other crops — tree crops for winter feed; unusual fruits for making jams, juices and syrups; and new fiber crops.

We can experiment with fertility improvement and soil building. We can do whatever we want within the real constraints of the land we have, the people and time we have, the tools we are willing to use, the money we have and the realities of agriculture. As my son Simon once wrote on a homemade pencil sign for our farm, "Glenings [sp. actually Gleanings] Farm: Flora, Fauna and Food." That's pretty much what we do.

I put myself in place here not to make any grand point. It is not that my farm magically duplicates the realities of small farms in the Global South — it doesn't. It isn't that my farm is just like the big farms only smaller — it isn't. And yet, I like to think it is not only pretense that ties me both to larger and smaller farmers, because they too are bound by the realities that bind me — that the land and the life shape and control things in ways hard to explain to someone who has never done it. When I began to farm, I do not think I fully realized how much it would shape my life, or how much, in picking a place, a piece of land, I had determined my own future, the kind of farmer I would be.

All of us can grow something, even though most of us will never own a farm — but still, each of us will have to place ourselves in the context of our land and place and future, our biology, ecology and desire.

III. Developing a vernacular

At first glance, swept yards, derived from Africa, at one time traditional in the South and now mostly the province of a few, aging African-American Southerners, and cottage gardens, invented in Britain under the feudal system and now evolved into the trendy "flower garden style," mostly a mix of abundant plants and mulched paths as seen in any supermarket magazine, have nothing to do with one another.

But look past the obvious and the two have a great deal in common indeed. Both emerged from the need to make good use of a comparatively small piece of land for a family with subsistence needs. Both responded to climate and culture and evolved over time in keeping with their climate and the needs of the people that grew them. Both allowed for a substantial variety of activities and plant life in a small space. Both made use of what was available, valuable and abundant, offering a sense of plenty and abundance to people whose income was often deficient. Both responded to inadequate housing by transforming outdoor spaces into living spaces. And perhaps most importantly, both took pragmatic traditions and made them respond to two equally important needs — the need for food and medicine and subsistence from one's garden, but also the need for beauty, peace and respite, a place to express one's artfulness.

In his superb history *African-American Gardens and Yards in the Rural South*, Richard Westmacott tracks the origin of the swept yard back to West Africa, and explores how it changed over centuries, from slave yard to a now-dying way of life. Instead of attempting to grow grass or other ground covers in the hot summers, often on red clay, rural Southerners would sweep and tamp down that clay until it baked hard as a rock, reducing dust tracking and making the space suitable for yard work. Houses, hot during the day, were abandoned and people moved outside to shaded yards where they could cook, eat, butcher animals and do the washing and other heavy work in the shade of trees.

The gardens, a separate but often connected space, contain the crops — and the areas for pigs, chickens and other livestock. The yard was separate from the garden, often marked by an enclosure, and was originally marked by medicinal herbs and dooryard plants.

A yard swept bare of plant life may not sound very pretty, but in reality, it made wise use of what there was — it allowed housekeepers to manage the clay and dirt, while transforming the dooryard into the "outdoor rooms" that ornamental garden books like to praise but rarely actually succeed in creating.

It wasn't an empty space — containers and marginal areas were planted with trees and shrubs, where water could be focused. Recycled materials and scavenged ones made a remarkably creative yard full of planters made from abandoned materials, themselves artful. Moreover, there is, in the photos in Westmacott, a seamlessness to the transition space between yard, garden, livestock and field. Indeed, although I refer to this as an African-American tradition, it was so successful that before the advent of warm-weather grasses, the swept yard was the norm in much of the rural South in both white and black households.

Most interesting to me is how the swept yard made space for both ornamental and food gardening. Westmacott observes that traditional African-American yards were often a riot of flowers and plants — but not organized as most white gardens were. First of all, the emphasis was on vigorous and abundant production and self-seeders. Flowering plants, instead of being organized by color and form, were interspersed with one another, with a preference for bright colors. Until recently, few shrubs were involved — because of the high cost of woody plants, most woodies were food producers rather than purely ornamental plantings. Medicinal herbs would have been mixed in with flowers grown for scent and beauty. Because of the high cost of plants, annuals and seed-grown plants were preferred and were shared widely. In this sense, the vernacular traditions of the rural South sound very much like the cottage garden.

In contrast to the swept yard, at least superficially, the cottage garden is booming. Googling "cottage garden" got me a bazillion entries. The problem is that all of them are hopelessly watered down — very few have anything to do with the cottage garden as it existed before it was taken over by the affluent, who had no reason to grow anything but flowers. Yes, they are very beautiful — but their original beauty lay in the way they combined aesthetics and subsistence, and the subsistence has been erased.

The history of the cottage garden has as much to do with bees and pigs and vegetables as it does with wisteria and foxgloves. Its recasting as an intentionally informal style to be propagated by comparatively affluent ornamental gardeners obscures the fact that it grew up among people just as poor as many of the rural African-Americans who preserved the swept yard.

Christopher Lloyd's and Richard Bird's *The Cottage Garden* offers a concise history and at least tries to draw us back to the mixed-use garden with a heavy emphasis on food plants and herbs. The authors observe that, in the eighteenth century, John Claudius Loudon attempted to help cottagers with reduced land access (a result of the destructive enclosure laws) to use cottage-style gardening to feed a family of five on six hundred square yards of garden.

Pigs, chickens and bees were essential to this project. Lloyd and Bird track back the ornamental elements of the kitchen garden to the Elizabethan dooryard and the herbs that grew there. As in the African-American yards in the South, medicinal and other functional herbs predominated at first, but they too had ornamental value, and it was hard to tell if the tall spires of hollyhock were central because of their medicinal or aesthetic qualities.

Despite the radical differences in climate and culture, the presumptions of the cottage garden were much the same as the African-American yard — that much had to be gotten out of a small space, that one needed a place to live and work outside when the weather permitted, that ornament and utility were not incompatible, and that the best plants were abundant self-seeders or easily grown annuals. The cottage garden had the additional virtue of using vertical space well — which some African-American gardens did too, particularly with scavenged articles as trellises. The ubiquitous cottage garden image, of course, is of a cottage covered with ivy or wisteria.

As the British cottage garden was adopted by more affluent people and moved away from the real cottages of low-income farmers and workers, it changed into what we see today — a garden style, more heavily invested in perennials, with more shrubs and almost no emphasis on plant utility. The romanticization of the cottage in both gardens and literature worked to the detriment of the actual cottager — now that people admired them and longed to live in them, they became harder for most working people to afford. In *Sense and Sensibility*, Jane Austen's romantic Willoughby threatens in jest to tear down his estate and replace it with a cottage. But the cottage of the romantic imagination was relieved of its subsistence functions.

The beauty of the cottage garden was in many ways its success, and thus its downfall — while beauty was always part of the project, always intertwined with utility, the garden's very success at being lovely made it ripe for the erasure of its utility. But it is possible to come back to the cottage garden and the swept yard as proximate spaces that extend the kitchen and the household outwards, bringing us outside into a riot of color and forms that are both beautiful and useful. There is still a place for the herb garden, and the cottage garden and the traditional African-American yard remind us to value plants that may be both ornamental and useful, that are vigorous and energetic.

In my wet climate, the cottage garden model makes a lot of sense. I may have twenty-seven acres, but I also have a yard — a space outside my kitchen door that I have gradually been converting to herbs, flowers, vegetables and fruiting trees. Looking at the cottage garden model, I can think of ways of better integrating aesthetics and practicality.

The reality is that a shift to subsistence in a densely populated world will require us to draw upon all of the things we have learned about how to meet our needs — for both food and beauty — in smaller spaces. There are thousands of traditions to draw upon from all over the world, and all of them have things we can take and make use of. If we look back upon our collective history, we will find that the answers to how we will feed ourselves — and our souls — are contained in part in stories from our past.

IV. 25 things you might want to consider growing

There are a million gardening books out there to tell you how to grow perfect tomatoes and lettuces. And that's important — in my house, salsa is a food group. For those of us attempting to grow a large portion of our calories ourselves, however, tomatoes and lettuce are not sufficient — we need to either get the most calories or the best possible nutrition out of our kitchen gardens and landscaping. So I've compiled a list of plants, both annual and perennial, that I think are an important addition to many home gardens.

1. **Buckwheat.** Buckwheat is the perfect multipurpose plant. Many of you have probably used it as a green manure, taking advantage of its remarkable capacity to shade out weeds and produce lots of green material to enrich the soil. But it is also one of the easiest grains to grow in the garden — simply let it mature and harvest the seed, and the leaves make a delicious and highly nutritious salad or cooking

green. Although it won't be quite as good at soil building if you do it this way, buckwheat can be used as a triple-purpose crop — plant a few beds with it, harvest the greens steadily (but lightly) for salad (it is particularly good during the heat of summer since it has a lightly nutty taste not too far off lettuce and will grow in hot weather), cook some of the mature greens, harvest the seeds, then cut the plants back to about an inch, leaving the plant material on the ground. The buckwheat will then grow back up again and you can harvest young salad greens and cut it back again for green manure.

2. **Sweet potatoes.** Think this is a southern crop? Not for me. I grow "Porto Rico" sweet potatoes in upstate New York. Garden writer Laura Simon grows them in cool, windy Nantucket. I've met people who grow them in Ontario and North Dakota. Sweet potatoes have quite a range if started indoors, and more northerners should grow them. They are enormously nutritious, unutterably delicious and store extremely well (some of my sweets last more than a year). They do need light, sandy soil and good drainage, so I grow them mostly in raised beds with heavily amended soil — my own heavy wet clay won't do.

3. **Blueberries.** If there was ever an ornamental edible, this is it. A prettier shrub than privet or most common privacy hedge plants, it produces berries and turns as flaming red as any burning bush in the autumn. I have no idea why more people don't landscape with blueberries. Add to that the fact that they have more antioxidants than most other foods and, unlike other good-for-you crops, will be eaten by the bucketful by kids. They do need acidic soil, but there are blueberries for all climates. They are definitely worth replacing your shrubs with if you can.

4. **Amaranth** — I've grown amaranth before, but my first year growing "Golden Giant" and "Orange" was fascinating. In two five-by-four-feet beds, I harvested 11.2 and 13.9 pounds of amaranth seed respectively. The plants are stunningly beautiful — nine feet tall, bright honey gold or deep orange, with green variegated leaves. The leaves are also a good vegetable cooked with garlic and sautéed or done Southern style. Amaranth is an easy grain crop to harvest and use, is delicious, can be popped like popcorn and makes wonderful

cereal. Despite its adaptation to the Southwest (where it routinely yields extremely well with minimal water), it tolerated my wet, humid climate just fine. My chickens love it too.

5. **Chickpeas.** Unlike most beans, which must be planted after the last frost, chickpeas are highly nutritious and extremely frost tolerant. Plant breeder Carol Deppe has had them overwinter in the Pacific Northwest, and they can be planted as early as April or as late as July here and still mature a crop. Unlike peas and favas that don't like hot weather, and most dry beans that don't like cold, chickpeas seem happy no matter what. If you've only ever eaten store chickpeas, you'll be fascinated to experience homegrown ones — they are, in many ways, as big a revelation as homegrown tomatoes.

6. **Beets.** I know, I know, there's no vegetable anyone hates as much as the beet. Poor beets — they are so maligned. We should all be eating more beets — especially pregnant women, women in their childbearing years who may become pregnant, and those at risk of heart disease or stomach or colon cancer. Beets are rich in folate and good for you in a host of other ways. They store well, yield heavily, provide highly nutritious greens for salad and cooking and are the sweetest food in nature. If you hate beets, give them another try — consider roasting them with salt and pepper or steaming them and pureeing them with apples and ginger. Laurie Colwin used to swear her recipe for beets with angel hair pasta could turn anyone into a beet lover, while a recipe for beets with tahini has converted many of my friends. Really, try them again!

7. **Flax.** You can grow this one in your flower beds, mixed in with your marigolds. Flax is usually a glorious blue — the kind of blue all flower gardeners covet. But the real reason to grow it is the seeds. Flaxseed oils are almost half omega-3 fatty acids. A recent article claimed that we have no choice but to turn to GMO crops to provide essential omega-3s without stripping the ocean — ignoring the fact that we can and should be growing flax everywhere, and enjoying flaxseed in our baked goods and our meals. Flax is particularly valuable in northern intensive gardening, which tends to be low in fats. If you grow more than you need, flaxseed is also excellent chicken feed — my poultry adore it.

8. **Popcorn.** If I could grow only one kind of corn, it would be popcorn, which is particularly suited to home-scale gardening. There are many dwarf varieties, and many that yield well. And popcorn can be ground for flour (it is a bit of work, though, since it is very hard), or popped for food. My kids like popcorn as breakfast cereal, or, of course, as a snack. Popcorn yields quite well for me in raised beds, and is always a treat at my house. It has all the merits of a whole grain, but is "accessible" to people not accustomed to eating brown rice or whole wheat — a great way to transition to a whole-food diet.

9. **Kidney beans.** While kidneys have less protein than soybeans, they are very close to soy in total protein and yield more per acre. There are a number of pole-variety kidney beans that are suitable to "three sisters" polyculture as well, so you can grow the two together. If I could grow only one dry bean (I usually grow ten or more), it would probably be a kidney variety.

10. **Rhubarb.** Why rhubarb? Because once established, it will tolerate almost any growing condition, including part shade (most vegetables won't), wet soil and you jumping up and down on it to try to get it out. Rhubarb is tireless. It is also delicious, though it does require a fair bit of sweetener (stevia, apple juice or pureed cooked beets will do if you are avoiding sugar). We like it cooked to tart-sweet for a few minutes with just a little almond extract. But its great value is that it provides fresh, nutritious, "fruity" tasting food as early as April here, right when we are desperate for something, anything, but dandelions and lettuce, and goes on as late as July, happily producing spear after spear of calcium-rich, tasty food. I'm in the process of converting the north side of my house to a vast rhubarb plantation (OK, not that vast), because we can never get enough of it.

11. **Turnips.** Let's say you live in an apartment and want greens all winter but don't have even a south-facing windowsill available. What can you do? Well, you can buy a bag of turnips from your farmer's market. Eat some of them raw, enjoying the delicious sweet crispness of them. Shredded, they are a wonderful salad vegetable. Cook some, and mash them or roast them crisp. And take a few of the smaller turnips, put them in a pot with some dirt on it and stick them in a corner — east- or west-facing is best, but even north- will

work. And miraculously, using only their stored energy, the pots will go on producing delicious, nutritious turnip greens even in insufficient light. It is magic. If you do have a south-facing windowsill, save it for the herbs and put your potted turnips on the other sills.

12. **Maximillian sunflowers.** These are the perennials. They are ornamental, tall and stunning in the back of a border. They will tolerate any soil you can offer them, as long as they get full sun. They also produce oil seeds and edible roots, prevent erosion and can tolerate steep slopes, minimal water and complete and utter neglect. Don't forget to eat them!

13. **Hopi orange winter squash.** We all have our favorite winter squash, and perhaps you know one that I'll like even better. But this variety has the advantage of keeping up to eighteen months without softening, delicious flavor that improves in storage and high nutritional value. I have to put in a plug for banana squashes as well — they just produce a ton of food value to the space you allot them. Twenty-five-pound monsters are not unusual — and they store well and tolerate you hacking off chunks for a while without a noticeable decline in quality.

14. **Annual alfalfa.** Most alfalfa is grown for forage, and it has to be grown on comparatively good, limed soil. But alfalfa is good people food too, and even a garden bed's worth can be enormously valuable. First, of course, it is a nitrogen fixer. While you can grow perennial varieties, the annual fixes more available nitrogen, faster. It can be cut back several times as green manure during the course of a season, or you can harvest it for hay to feed your bunnies or chickens. Don't forget to dehydrate some for tea — alfalfa is a nutritional powerhouse. And if you permit it to go to seed, the seeds make delicious sprouts and last for years. I've found that the annual version will make seed at the end of the season for harvest.

15. **Potatoes.** A few years ago I did an experiment — I threw a bit of compost on top of a section of my gravel driveway (and by "a bit" I do mean a little bit — not a garden bed's worth but a light coating), added a sprinkling of bone meal, dropped some pieces of potatoes on the ground and covered them with mulch hay. Periodically I added a bit more and replaced the sign that said, "Please don't drive

on my potatoes," and in September, I harvested a reasonably good yield, given the conditions (about thirty pounds from a four-by-four-foot square). I did it just to confirm what people have always known — potatoes grow in places with rocky, poor soil (or no soil) that no other staple crop can handle. Don't get me wrong — potatoes will be happier in better conditions, but they can tolerate all sorts of bad situations and come back strong. And they respond better to hand cultivation than any other grain — until the 1960s, hand-grown, manured potatoes routinely outyielded green revolution varieties of grains grown with chemical fertilizers. If there's hope to feed the world, it probably lies in potatoes.

16. **Sumac.** No, not the poison stuff, but yes, I mean the weedy tree that grows along the roadsides here. That weedy tree, you may not realize, has many virtues. Besides its flaming fall color and value for wildlife habitat and food, sumac makes a lovely beverage. If you harvest the red fruits in July or August and soak them, you'll get a lemony-tasting beverage as high in vitamin C as lemon juice. Since sumac essentially grows virtually everywhere in the US that doesn't support lemons, this is enormously valuable. You can freeze or can sumac lemonade for seasoning and drinking all year round. Poison sumac has white or greenish-white berries, so it is easy to tell apart. Sumac's other value is as a restorative to damaged soil — densely planted sumac returns bare sand to fertility fairly quickly, as a University of Tennessee study shows.

17. **Parsnips.** If you don't live in the Northeast or do bio-intensive gardening, you probably don't eat parsnips. Me, I'm a New Englander, and the sweet, fragrant flavor of parsnips is a childhood joy. But even I hadn't ever had a real parsnip — one left in the garden after the ground freezes for its starches to convert to sugars. Parsnips are one of the most delicious things in nature, nutritionally dense and just about the only food you can harvest in upstate New York in February (though you do have to mulch them deeply if you don't want them frozen in the ground).

18. **Potato onions.** Onion seed doesn't last very long — and that's a worrisome thing. The truth is that if we can't get seed easily, and we can't grow out plants for seed easily because of some personal

or environmental crisis, we might find ourselves without onions, and what a tragedy that would be. Who can cook without onions? No, we need to have onions. Which is why the perennial potato onion, that simply stays in the ground and is pulled and replanted, is so enormously valuable. It tastes good too, and you can put them where you want, pull up what you need and ignore the rest. They'll give you scallions before you could get them any other way, and will provide a decent supply of small but storable and delicious onions.

19. **King Stropharia mushrooms** (aka winecaps). Mushrooms have complex nutritional values, and offer soil-improving benefits. The King Stropharia has the advantage of growing well in wood chip mulch in your garden, having few poisonous cognates (i.e., you are unlikely to kill yourself harvesting it), tasting great and being a natural nematodacidal. They give you something meaty and tasty from your garden and can actually improve total yields in a given space. If you fear fungi, this is an easy one to start with.

20. **Filberts/hazelnuts.** The best small-space nuts, these have an astounding range and the various varieties tolerate quite a number of soils. The nuts are delicious and fairly easy to grow, and the yields are generally high. In cold climates, oil-rich plants can be hard to come by — this is a useful exception Oh, and if you have chocolate, you can make that basic food staple, Nutella.

21. **Elderberries.** Got a wet spot? What doesn't care if it has wet feet, has incredible vitamin C value, delicious and nutritious flowers, makes a champagne-like wine and a red-like wine, grows like a weed, is ornamental and will feed the birds anything you don't want? Yup, the remarkable elder. What's not to love?

22. **Annual sunflowers.** Our local dairy farmers sometimes alternate cow corn with sunflowers as a winter feed. There is truly no more beautiful edible crop in the world than a field full of glowing sunflowers in late summer. They would be valuable enough if they didn't produce delicious food, high in vitamin E and a host of trace minerals, food for the birds and stalks that burn extremely well when dry and hot in your woodstove.

23. **Rice.** Rice feeds more people in the world than any other grain, and a surprising amount of it is grown in what we'd consider garden-sized

plots. While the far northernmost growers may struggle with this, rice is one of the few staple grains that is totally amenable to home-scale cultivation, and if you can grow rice, you might want to consider it. It is a nearly universal staple — studies have found that rice allergy essentially does not exist. While growing and harvesting it is some work (some cultures call it "the tyrant with a soul"), rice is worth the time and energy for many of us.

24. **Jerusalem artichokes** — I know, duh. Sweet and tasty, crisp and nutty, perennials that will take over your house if you let them — what's not to love? Those who worry that the bad guys are coming to take their food can plant these in their flower beds without fear that most people will recognize them as anything other than something pretty. When first harvested, the carbohydrates are in the form of inulin, so most diabetics can eat pretty freely of these.

25. **Kale/collards.** They don't mind heat — 100-degree days don't faze them once they are mature. They grow all summer, north or south. They don't mind cold — some strains will overwinter uncovered here in icy upstate NY, while almost all will overwinter covered. They are nutritionally dense and great cooked or raw in the baby stage. In the cold, their starches turn to sugar. Stir fry them with oyster sauce, steam them and toss them in vinaigrette, cook them with bacon dressing — it doesn't really matter, they are universally delicious.

Profile 4

Aaron and Jennifer Newton: Working it Through

By Aaron Newton

Facing up to the broad challenges of peak oil, climate change and financial disintegration is a daunting task but not nearly as daunting as trying to convince my wife we should maybe raise meat rabbits in our backyard. My name is Aaron, and several years ago this became my way of life; on the one hand trying to discern the situation facing my family at the beginning of the twenty-first century, and on the other trying to stay married.

I should start with some basics. My wife and I are in our mid-thirties. We have been married a little over ten years. We have two daughters, three and five, and we live in the Charlotte region of North Carolina. I should also be honest and establish the fact that most of the familial friction related to our response to the challenges mentioned above is rooted in my initial reaction. Peak oil and the realization that my future will be radically different than I had been led to believe freaked me out. And I shared my freak-out with my wife in less than comforting terms. I didn't actually immediately begin to stockpile cases of Spam and automatic weapons, but I might have mentioned zombies and I'm pretty sure I used the words "end of the world" at least once.

I also moved rather rapidly through the first three stages in the Kubler-Ross five stages of grief — denial, anger and bargaining — until I got to stage four: depression. Most unfortunately for my marriage, I decided to hang out here for quite a while. I experimented with some knee-jerk responses, including the bulk purchase of rechargeable batteries, the brewing of biodiesel (never mind that we didn't own a diesel vehicle) and front-yard sweet corn production. Worst of all I got caught up in the habit of self-medication, drinking alcohol not just socially but to dull the seemingly inescapable dread of impending doom.

All of this didn't exactly charm my wife, who later told me that it was my negative responses to these challenges that kept her from wanting to have anything to do with change. So she refused to better understand what we were facing, let alone help with making changes, and the rift between us grew.

I started blogging because my attempts to connect locally with others who shared my concerns proved ineffective. Writing did three things for me. It served as a release, a way for me to get concerns out of my head. It also helped me to connect with others, however far away, who shared my concerns and were searching for ways to respond. Lastly, writing helped me to move beyond depression and into acceptance, the final stage of grief over my lost life of over-abundance. It was in this mode of doing that my strategies for Adapting in Place began to take root, and my wife and I began to work together again to balance each other as we had done so well before.

Our two daughters were born during this time. I got more interested in the subject of agriculture and coauthored a book about it. I also lost my job. Up until that time I had been a land planner, working in part to try and develop more self-sufficient communities, a pattern the development community in my region was not ready to embrace. Then, in 2008, I lost my job along with a significant number of others in the development industry. Having helped write a book that called for a hundred million new farmers in America, I felt it only prudent to go out and become one of them. A program aimed at helping new farmers get established in my community had just begun, and I signed up and started farming full-time.

Ninety-five percent of our household income had come from my career up until my layoff, so my wife and I knew that now was the time to explore the idea of living differently more seriously. We started to juggle the finances and looked for ways to minimize expenses — reducing energy and resource use was no longer just about doing the right thing morally, it was also about keeping the bills low. We also started to juggle childcare, with neither of us working eight-to-five and neither of our kids in school. For almost two years I farmed mixed vegetables and took design jobs on the side. She developed a business teaching and coaching swimming and helped with a Community Supported Agriculture (CSA) program.

In 2010 my community took another step toward rebuilding our local food system, and county government hired me to coordinate that effort. I left the field somewhat reluctantly but with an eye on the financial stability of my family and took on the job of coordinating a food policy council and managing our community incubator farm. Again our lives shifted, together this time, such that I could earn more money and be better positioned to help our community address the issue of food in the post-carbon era.

Learning from the hardships of my layoff a few years earlier, we decided to stay diversified. I still grow some vegetables and raise laying hens and meat birds (chickens, ducks and turkeys) for sale in the local market. My wife has been able to develop her business further and make money in a few other creative ways. We have continued to invest time and money into making our lives more adaptive to the changing reality of life in a volatile time when the ease of cheap and easy energy and credit are falling away. I'll list here some of the changes we've made throughout that process that have been beneficial to us:

- Sealed and fully insulated our home
- Added an alternative heating system to our home
- Upgraded air-conditioning system
- Continued changes to our diet and sources of food
- Got rid of the television (which gave us back lots of time for making other changes)
- Invested money in tools, talents and other more resilient stores of wealth
- Localized our life to minimize car dependency
- Got comfortable on the bike (7K miles on my commuter since 2007)
- Installed smart meter and drove down electrical costs
- Got used to line-drying clothes (sounds simple but this was a compromise)
- Eliminated all debt except for our mortgage, and greatly reduced that
- Concentrated on making our home the focus of our time on Earth

This short list can't fully explain the extent of our changes and the ways in which my wife and I finally began to work together to Adapt in Place. It's a family effort now, with my five-year-old daughter recently reminding me that young new hens are still too little to fight off the aggressive older ones. Mostly what's changed is our mindset — my willingness to accept reality and respond to it rather than agonize and freak out; my wife's willingness to consider a different outcome in life and work toward a collaborative attempt at doing things differently.

My family fully expects the future to be full of truly unanticipated challenges, and we look forward to addressing them and helping others in our community to do the same.

Nine

All creatures great and small

I. Once you've got the chickens, you'll hardly notice the yaks

Talking about our farm projects, a reader, Claire, commenting at the other blog, observed that every animal we get seems to require another animal — that, for example, we use cats to control the mice, but if we aren't to be dependent on commercial pet foods, that means we need to raise a meat animal to feed them (hence, in our case, rabbits). To control a goat parasite that travels on snails, we got ducks, and so on. To Claire this seemed like a negative — one animal might lead to another, ad infinitum. In a small homestead or urban project, you do have to place limits upon that sort of thing.

I actually see this as both true and a positive thing — that is, I think it's a really useful illustration of why farms were once diversified, and why they probably need to be again. We could simply worm heavily. We could try draining the wetter parts of our pasture, or excluding all wildlife, or putting our goats in pens rather than on grass — these are other possible solutions to our problems. But they aren't the ones we want to use.

What animals live on a farm? Of course we can all close our eyes and make the list — and in the old kind of farm, many species lived there at once. This is in complete contrast to the modern farm, where farmers raise sheep, or cows, or whatever, but as an enormous preponderance of one animal. The classic small farm had sheep and cows, ducks and geese, cats and dogs. There are good reasons why our old vision of the farm has so many different kinds of livestock on it.

One is simply that diversification was better for the farm economy. Having different crops to take to market at different times of year spaced out the work, and the profit. Different animals and plants use different habitats and kinds of land. There are more complex reasons as well. Consider this — a pasture that will support one cow but not two cows will generally support one cow plus two to four sheep and their lambs. This is because the sheep will eat shorter grasses that the cows have already grazed, as well as some plants that are less palatable to cows. There are several advantages to this — the first, of course, is that you have lamb, wool, sheep's milk and sheep manure as well as milk, beef and manure from the cow. But your pastures are also grazed more fully and evenly, with fewer problems from unpalatable plants that would otherwise proliferate as the others were eaten down.

These analyses can get complex — the same pasture can probably also support an indeterminate number of geese, which will eat shorter grass still, or a few goats that will eat brushy weeds and clean out hedgerows. But do you want your hedgerows cleaned out? Do you have a market for geese? Might it be better to follow the sheep and cow on pasture with chickens that will eat pasture and insects and also help reduce worm pressure for the next cycle by eating worms and worm eggs? Or perhaps you want to use that ground for growing grain next spring, and should put pigs on it to till it up....

The low-energy farm often uses animals to do things that we now do with fossil fuels. Rather than kill the snails on my property with a chemical poison, I can use ducks. Besides not being toxic, I get to sell the ducks for meat afterwards. But they also require balance — too many ducks are not a good thing. I can't always do what I want. I might find that I need another animal to fill a particular ecological niche on my farm — say, guinea hens to reduce tick pressure on humans and dogs — even though I don't particularly want them, or even though guineas are less profitable than chickens.

My dog keeps down predators, but needs to be fed some animal proteins. Thus she and the goats are reciprocal — without Mac the

Livestock Guardian Dog, the goats would be prey to the coyotes that den across the road. On a traditional farm she'd be paid in a share of their milk — we do this, although she also gets some dog food. The cats keep our grain losses down — for them and the dogs we keep the rabbits, which make use of marginal weeds that otherwise would be pests to us.... The relationships are stronger when they are more complex and diverse, when there are more participants in each system.

Most of us grasp, of course, that monoculture is bad in general, but it is hard to viscerally grasp the consequences of reduced complexity, or of using one solution (fossil fuels and its outputs) to replace multiple resources. My own exploration of what our family needs for self-sufficiency plus income is a kind of reinventing of the wheel, and not coincidentally, it comes to look more and more familiar.

There's a price to be paid for all of this, as well as benefits — you can specialize, but only to an extent. You can pick and choose, but only to an extent. You will be more independent in many ways, but often not as profitable as a farm that chooses the highest-value crop and produces only that. There are costs in land use and resource use as well — the additional animals take space and time.

When we started out farming, we grew a huge garden and raised chickens. The chickens gave us eggs to put in the CSA baskets and for the challah we included in our baskets. They also gave us manure for our gardens. But we found that it was hard to get enough manure to support a garden big enough to run a twenty-person CSA — we were dependent on neighboring farms, which wasn't bad, but they didn't always have manure when we needed it. Or we were dependent on soil additives and fertilizers that we didn't make, and on the lawn mower to keep weeds from going to seed, since we didn't have enough stock to keep them down. Adding more animals made it better possible to grow the garden — but created new incentives to shape it in particular ways, so that we didn't trade one dependency (on soil amendments) for another (on the feed store). Diversity was better — but not just more diversity, the right combination.

It isn't just animals that work this way — plants do too. We know from research that in terms of output (as opposed to yield) diversified small farms produce more food, fiber and fertility per acre than monocrop farms. We know that polyculture is better for the soil, better for wildlife and soil life, better for people than monoculture. We know that different plants do well in different environments and that no fifty or ten thousand acres are precisely alike — trying to get the same amount of corn out of every single acre regardless of its conditions is not good for anyone.

This runs through pretty much every part of the diversified small farm (or garden or household), and it gets played out at the economic and social level — for example, running the diversified small farm with minimal fossil fuels takes people too. One way to do this, the traditional farm family way, was to have many children — but that's not all that was involved. Neighbors traditionally shared work during busy times, sharing tools, resources and time — effectively allowing a farm population of four or five to expand to fifteen or twenty when needed.

The farm economy was diversified as well — my family often stops at a historical re-enactment village that happens to be about halfway between our house and my extended family's. Once, while chatting with one of the gentlemen there, the village cooper, he observed that his shop would soon be closing, because he practiced cooperage only in the winter — spring through fall, he farmed. I was struck by this example of something that has always been true — only the most affluent farmers (or the ones in the best climates) actually farm all year-round; the supplemental income that is the norm for farmers now has been the norm for a very long time. Thus the cooper of 1830, my great-grandfather who farmed and taught school in Maine in the 1890s, and the guy who farms and drives trucks now are all part of a logical continuity — that there is time for paying work in the winter or the dry season, and that farm economies are stronger when they are diversified.

Does this mean that everyone who gets chickens is doomed to own a yak? No, of course not. But it does mean that once you open up a system to ecological management, the process of figuring out its proper mix of species isn't an easy one. Honestly, if I didn't want ducks and another dog, I'd find another way to do things. But the small farm of the past has lessons for creating a low-energy small farm of the future — there's a reason it has more species, not less.

We're still figuring out the right combination of creatures and practices for our farm — still debating whether we can make a living using our marginal wetlands as they are, what animals we should be eating down our pastures with and what will be needed as time goes on. But we're committed to this basic project, to the idea that it is possible to create an integrated, self-sustaining system where most of the interventions are productive rather than reductive — that rather than just poisoning the things we don't want, we can intervene in ways that create some kind of net improvement in our situation.

II. Against sentimentality — and for sentiment

It is pouring down rain — Tropical Storm Nicole is dumping five inches on us — and the dogs are barking out of control. I can't see a thing, but I suddenly realize what they must be barking at — I forgot to put Blackberry in the barn.

Blackberry, you see, is our pet rooster. He's so gentle that my children carry him around. Isaiah, who has a special rapport with animals, snuggles him under his arm. In the winter, the children tried to teach him to ski down the plow piles (note: chickens do not like to ski). In the summer, they come running when Blackberry roams into the road, which for some reason he does every day. The only way to keep him from his suicidal wanderings (besides the cars, he heads straight toward the coyote den) is to put him in the fenced side yard. Technically this is supposed to be a chicken-free zone, but Blackberry doesn't count. I try to pretend I don't notice when the kids feed him things from their plates — he's now learned to hang out under the picnic table.

Blackberry, who is the low rooster on the totem pole in our farm, doesn't really like to go into the barn at night until all the other birds are shut in. Normally one of us carries him in last thing. Apparently I forgot him — but the dogs didn't. They have him cornered under a downspout. They aren't trying to hurt him, just herd him out, but he's panicking a bit. I'm soaked by the time I gather him up, but he knows he's safe with a human's arms around him so he relaxes, wet feathers and all, as I carry him into the goat pen and drop him in a quiet corner. He'll nest under the hay manger for the night, next to one of the hens.

I have about fifty chickens, who provide eggs that we sell. It is getting toward winter, and I don't need as many as I have right now, so in a week or two I'll be doing a clear-out of odd roosters, older hens that don't lay well and a few ducks. My goal is to reduce the amount of chicken manure I'll have to deal with all winter long, and also to up the number of meals of coq au vin and chicken soup.

Blackberry is elderly, and there's a good chance he'll spend this winter the way he did part of last winter: persecuted by the other roosters and run down by the cold. I eventually moved him into a box in the wood-shed with a bantam hen for company. I don't really want a rooster in the woodshed for the winter, any more than I really wanted to go out in the pouring rain to gather up soggy poultry. But the chances of Blackberry going under the knife are nil. If the woodshed it must be, so it will be.

The real farmers who read this may well be rolling their eyes at me. This is proof I'm not a real farmer, right? After all, real farmers have to make their bottom line, they don't have room for all this messy senti-mentality about a pet rooster.

"No place for sentiment in farming." This was a sentence uttered by one of my dairy farmer neighbors. I'd stopped by to negotiate the price for some hay, and he was in the process of loading up three of his best — and, he admitted, favorite — cows to go to slaughter. They had escaped a fence and been loose for three days early that month and the mastitis they developed from not being milked had permanently damaged their teats. There was no place for them in the herd anymore. It was an eco-nomic tragedy for him, but he also spent some time telling me about the cows that he was losing — enough that you knew it was not just an economic crisis.

As he told me all this, I watched two horses stroll past in a pasture. I mentioned them and he rolled his eyes, noting that they had been his daughters' horses. I knew that his daughters had grown up and moved away many years earlier — before we moved to the neighborhood, and we've lived here a decade. I suggested that the horses must be getting on in years. "Yes, they are both near thirty ... but they were good horses and they've earned their retirement. Once in a while I put my granddaugh-ters on them and lead them around, y'know."

Sentiment officially has no place in agriculture, but I've met precious few smaller farmers who don't have a spot of it. Indeed, I've come to suspect that a sentimental attachment to things is in fact a requirement for good small-scale farming — and that equally, keeping sentiment in check is a requirement for the transition from "a few pet chickens" to "agriculture."

Keeping the sentiment in check is obvious — if your chickens are pets, it doesn't matter if they stop laying, you feed them and hope they start up again. If you make your living on your chickens, if they stop laying, your bottom line probably doesn't allow for extended periods feeding chickens that don't provide any return. The sensible thing is to eat them or sell them and get some chickens that will lay — going bankrupt and seeing the farm turned into developments isn't worth the trade-offs, no matter how much you care for any given chicken.

Less obvious, I think, is the value of sentiment — and by sentiment, I mean the logical emotions of love and attachment that emerge from knowing something well. Much of good agriculture is about paying attention — and attentiveness is easier when it is governed by feeling. Nor do I know any way to be attentive to living creatures, or a living ecology, without coming to love them. Feeling for the land, sense of place, attachment and love for one's animals — these are all necessities for close attention and the consequences of that attention.

Different people have different capacities for love, and different ways of expressing it — but we all have it, in our own ways. My ninety-plus-year-old neighbor, who farmed these hills all his life, is a man who doesn't express emotion much — but get him talking about the dogs he's owned over the years and you'll hear a genuine and profound passion. His pride and love, and sorrow over their loss, have not diminished, although many of those dogs have been buried for decades. Or consider the man we bought our senior buck, Frodo, from — David is a man in his sixties who used to run a goat farm with hundreds of goats, and he sold the majority of each year's animals. He's mellowed over the years, but as he told me of the death of Frodo's brother due to the mishandling of someone he had lent him to, there were tears in his eyes.

Here I would make a distinction between "sentiment," which is simply "emotion," and "sentimentality," which is cheap emotion, the substitution of a weak thing for something deeper. I don't think sentimentality has any place in agriculture — in fact, I don't think it has much place in life. Sentimentality prevents you from experiencing real sentiment.

Sentimentality in agriculture would be the refusal to put an animal that is suffering and has no future down, because you love it so much or don't feel you can kill something. Sentimentality in agriculture is the dairy-drinking vegetarian who expresses hostility to someone who dares to butcher a cute little calf — not realizing that that calf will grow up to be a large bull, that there is no retirement home for bulls, and that it is their milk habit that caused that calf to be born. These are sentimental emotions because they are cheap and weak — they don't require knowledge or love for specific animals, or a real understanding of the animals and their needs. Sentimentality is the meat-eater who doesn't want to know anything about the animals their meat came from, because it is just too hard to think about — and thus enables factory agriculture with all its horrors, because they don't want to know.

Consider, in contrast, the emotions of the farmer losing his cow. No, he can't afford to indulge his sentiment — thus he shakes his head and reminds himself and me that even though he feels terrible, there's nothing else he can do. He needs to do what keeps his (economically marginal anyway) farm going. He cannot, however, fail to feel for those animals — those animals who fed his family, whose calves he midwifed, who he cared for for so many years. There's nothing empty about this — the reminder that sentiment has no place in agriculture actually means the opposite, that emotion has a powerful place in agriculture. It is just that sometimes you have to do the rational, economically sensible thing, rather than the thing you want to do.

Sometimes, however, you don't have to do the rational thing. Sometimes you can allow love to take over. For the dairy farmer, it is those horses that remind him of his daughters' childhood on the farm. He can keep them in return for what they've given him — and for what all the other animals he couldn't keep gave him as well.

That same capacity to love is what makes him a good dairy farmer — and he is a good one. He's held on in a place where dairy farmers are wiped out every day, he's worked hard and harder even though neither of his daughters wants to come back and he doesn't know if the farm has a future. When other people retire, he still gets up to milk the cows, because he likes to milk cows and he loves the cows and the land and the way the land looks and feels. That's why he tends his land so well, not draining the marshy areas for extra hay pasture but keeping them intact. The same capacity for love and joy and memory and understanding that drive him to keep those horses also drive him to put the cows on the truck for slaughter — because he loves his farm more than any individual cow.

Most of my chickens don't have names — and that's intentional. My mother and stepmother have chickens, and they all have names. Their chickens are beloved pets, and there's nothing wrong with that. We love the pet chickens as well. But when we come home, most of the chickens are pretty much indistinguishable from one another. If one dies, we're sorry, but we don't mourn. We do honestly by them — they get good care, plenty of food, days in the sun roaming the property, all the scraps we can provide and more. I don't enjoy butchering chickens, but I don't feel I have done badly by them when after a summer in the sun or a few years of laying, we kill them as quickly and painlessly as possible, and eat them.

I realize this seems the height of callousness to some people — and I can understand that. I also recognize that there are other reasons than sentimentality that someone might find this evaluation of equity on both sides unsatisfying. I'm not claiming that everyone who disagrees with me is sentimental — nor am I claiming that there aren't other choices that could be honorably made. Maybe one's love for a place means recognizing that because you'll never be able to kill, you shouldn't have chickens. Or maybe one's deep sentiment means choosing differently. It is not my contention that mine is the only way — but I do want to draw a distinction I think is important, between honest disagreement and emotions that substitute for understanding.

And once in a while, a chicken like Blackberry stands out. We don't tolerate nasty roosters here — they become chicken soup on the theory that there are simply too many nice animals in the world for us to make space for the mean ones. Most of our roosters will tolerate us picking them up, and all are non-aggressive. Blackberry, however, is special. He is beloved. And the very fact that a rooster could be beloved, to me, seems a good sign — it means we are being attentive. We are watching closely enough to develop relationships. And we know our economic realities well enough to know that we cannot allow relationships to emerge in every case.

I want to stand up for sentiment in agriculture because I would argue that our industrial society discourages real sentiment, the emotion that emerges from knowing things, and exchanges it for sentimentality. This is an exchange that runs deeply to our detriment, in part because it enables us not to know things.

Sentimentality creates the factory farm — the sentimentality that says we are too weak to bear the pain of knowing animals and watching them die. This is what turns our food into Styrofoam packages and allows CAFO agriculture, where animals are carefully hidden from our view, the relationship of our purchases carefully concealed. Sentimentality allows us to care about the extinction of the preferred charismatic megafauna of our choice, ideally something with big eyes, but not see the connection between our purchases, our acts and the habitat destruction of the animals in question. Sentimentality enables us to care about the child Pakistani flood victim on nightly TV enough to send some money — but not enough to try and reduce the number of climate-related natural disasters by giving up some of our privileges. Sentimentality enables the patriotic fervor that allows us to not know how many Iraqi or Afghani civilians die in the interest of our national "greater goods." Sentimentality is the emotion that emerges from the condition of not knowing — and it is what you have left in a society that conceals real knowledge at every level. It too is both cause and effect — it permits great evil, and it facilitates lack of knowledge of the real.

Sentiment — love, anger, attachment, affection, real emotions — these derive from knowledge, and they can't be faked. And when you know things, the choices you make get more complex. The realities you live in get harder and grayer. Sometimes love means you have to kill something. Sometimes one love means that another loved thing get sacrificed. Sometimes you have to go against your feelings. But the only way that never happens is when you substitute sentimentality for real feeling.

We live in a world where sentimentality poses as real emotion, where we are often actively discouraged from understanding consequences, from developing real love for people and things, from paying attention. It is easy to miss the distinction between the two entirely — because we have blurred so many things together.

It would be easy to say that there's no connection between me carrying the rooster into the barn at night and the fact that my family tries to live on less each year, that there's no connection between my neighbor, trying to hold on to his dairy farm, and those horses. Neither is wholly consistent — and you could argue that I should subtract the feed I spend on Blackberry and the hay and oats he gives his horses. My energy bottom line would go down a tiny bit. His economic bottom line would be a little more stable.

That's just not the only way to look at it. The love that enables the farmer to give to those horses what he cannot give to the cows is something that needs a place to go. The love my children and my husband and I have for a rooster who gives back more than ordinary chickens is a way of expressing the love we have for our farm in general — fierce, protective, passionate. The whole thing is alive, and sometimes to keep it living we cannot do everything we'd like to. But we can express our love in selected places, keep an honest and just relationship with even the animals that don't get all our love, and pour into the land and its creatures the complex realities of our passion and sentiment.

III. Urban (and suburban) livestock

Despite the emergence of backyard chickens, I think most of us think of "livestock" as something that belongs on farms, that lives way out in the country. That's a comparatively recent point of view — both the US and Canada have long traditions of urban livestock raising. In fact, raising animals in cities and suburbs can help us make the best possible use of underutilized resources, including lawns, marginal weeds and food scraps. More of us need to bring small animals into our lives.

Meat, milk and eggs are problematic in our society because of ethical considerations — most of then are raised in factory-farm conditions, usually by feeding animals grain that could be used for human consumption. If we take as basic premises that we should and must eat less meat, eat only meat raised ethically and also, in order to feed a hungry world, raise our animal products with little or no grain suitable for human consumption, it becomes clear that pasture raising on marginal lands that are steep, erodible, rocky or wet in the countryside and raising meat, egg and dairy animals in cities on a small scale on food wastes are the two best options.

Many city dwellers grow gardens, and it would be wrong to under-
state their importance — they provide caloric and nutritional benefits,
allow people access to high-value, high-flavor foods they might not be
able to afford, and can provide some calorically dense vegetables and
even a few grains like sweet potatoes, potatoes, popcorn, etc. We know
that urban gardening can make an enormous difference in a city — for
example in Paris in the nineteenth century, 3,600 acres of garden plots
produced 100,000 tons of vegetables, more than the city itself could
consume. In 1944, US Victory gardens produced as much produce as
all the country's produce farms combined — half the nation's total. So
yes, as part of an urban aggregate, your five raised beds make a huge
difference.

But add livestock and the picture of urban food security gets much
richer. Those weeds growing in the vacant lots can be eaten by miniature
goats or rabbits — cut an armful as you walk by. Those gardens require
manures, and most urbanites lack a place for safe composting of human
waste, so rabbit and poultry manures are essential to sustainable gardening. Stop by your neighborhood coffee shop and pick up a big bucketful
of stale bread and salad leaves for the bunnies, or the leftovers from the
takeout Chinese place for the chickens (why Novella Carpenter and her
partner never actually made arrangements for places to save food for
them rather than dumpster diving was one thing I couldn't figure out).
And then turn that into nutritious people food, adding fat and dense
protein to your diet. In the process you can reduce your dependency on
feedlots, not just for yourself but also for your carnivorous pets.

Bees can sit on a balcony, rabbits on a back porch. Chickens are content in small backyards, and as Carpenter proves, you can even raise pigs
there, although she does get some complaints about the smell toward
the end (she notes that in 1943, London had 4,000 pig-raising clubs,
with 105,000 pigs kept within the city limits). Guinea pigs, quails and
pigeons and fish in tanks can also supplement the protein needs of urban
dwellers. Given the amount of imported dairy, I'd also suggest considering very small goats for milk and meat.

Cities will never be wholly sustainable by themselves — but neither will most rural areas, which will continue to rely on cities for the
manufacture of goods, from cloth to tools, and as import and transport

centers for items from around the world. We may relocalize, but it would be foolish to imagine that all trade and all cities will disappear. What cities must be, if they are to have a future, is as food self-sufficient as possible, part of a larger project of wide food access. We will find ways, over the long term, to transport dry goods like grains into many cities — that doesn't mean there won't be disruptions or, much more important, poverty, but there will be reciprocal relations between cities and the countryside. Vegetables and animal products are another thing altogether — they often require refrigeration, and without refrigerated trucking or train transport, those things are likely to become less available, or more expensive and more out of reach for many.

Moreover, we cannot permit food to be wasted on the present scale — that's why we need eggs, meat and milk that can be raised on food scraps in urban centers.

Our own livestock breeding projects focus on small-scale livestock for densely populated areas — small goats, angora and meat rabbits, chickens with good foraging ability, even small sheep. Not all of these will be suitable to the most densely populated areas, nor do I expect my farm to be definitive on the subject. But if you can take the girl out of the city, you can't take the city out of the girl — and that's a good thing. We need urban agriculture, and ties between city girls and country girls (and boys, of course) that help both places raise all the food they can, as ethically and wisely as they can.

IV. Fido and Fluffy and the meat conundrum

Most of us probably don't think much about what our dogs and cats eat — but that's a mistake. We know that meat production is responsible for nearly a third of all climate emissions, and that pets have a much bigger impact that we may have thought — for example, it would take one and a half New Zealands to produce all the meat US cats eat, according to at least one report.

There are compelling reasons to have domestic animals as pets. Many of us will have rodent problems over the years — and these are somewhat increased by the addition of food storage or a barn full of garden produce. Bred to kill rodents, cats and small dogs have an important role in many households — they are not a luxury item. Dogs also provide a measure of safety — they alert us to noises and work as guardians, shepherds, guide and assistive animals, etc. Moreover, for many people, animals provide unconditional love and physical contact — in a world where many of us simply don't get those things, pets are enormously valuable.

And yet, in a world that will struggle to feed the human population, where one billion people are hungry and that hunger is tied to rising prices for grain, it is sometimes tough to make a case for feeding animals better food than billions of people get. So what to do?

I am particularly happy to see this discussion beginning to open up because, in my research, I've come to believe that, in many ways, the pet food industry is the deciding factor that makes industrial meat production profitable. In the US, slaughterhouses reject one out of every seven cows in CAFO feedlots. These are animals that do not meet our rather minimal standards for slaughter, that are sufficiently diseased that the feedlot (which in many cases caused the cow's sickness) could not sell them.

Fully one-seventh of all cows are used to provide the protein in animal feeds, largely for cats and dogs. Cull chickens (i.e., ones that died horribly in confinement, often from disease) and pigs are used in the same way. If confinement operations could not get some of their money back from this extremely high percentage of lost animals, there are real questions about whether they would be profitable. Addressing the pet food question does more than simply reduce industrial meat production directly — it potentially calls the whole feedlot system into question.

Moreover, one of the feed ingredients in many industrially produced pet foods is euthanized cats and dogs — there's considerable evidence pet food manufacturers are willing to put just about anything into the animal food stream, including the corpses of our excess kittens and puppies. My concern about this (besides the fact that it isn't very aesthetically pleasing) is that we live in extremely close quarters with our cats and dogs, and every biologist I've ever mentioned this to observed that these are precisely the right conditions for inventing new and horrible diseases.

Now it would seem that choosing organic, grass-fed, free-range products to feed your animals is the best of all possible options. And this does somewhat reduce the impact of one's animals — most importantly, using entirely grass-fed meats reduces the pressure on the world's poor. Whenever possible, it is absolutely necessary that we not eat meat produced with grains — when we do, we place the rich (and their pets) in competition with the world's poor for food, and the rich and their pets always win.

That would mean buying beef, lamb or other ruminant-based food products whenever possible, ensuring that they are wholly grass-fed. This is not easy — finding all grass-fed commercial pet food is difficult and cost prohibitive. Organic itself is better than nothing — it reduces the emissions on the land in general by a small amount — but doesn't make a substantial reduction. Free-range chickens are still fed an enormous amount of grain for their body weight, so don't help nearly as much as you'd think.

So what is the answer? Well first of all, pets are a serious business. They should not be gotten trivially, should not be encouraged to reproduce (unless you are breeding working animals of some sort) by most people, and for those who are just sort of accustomed to having a cat or a dog, it might be worth asking, do you really want and need one?

If you do, you have a moral responsibility to reduce the impact of its food. And that means finding the most ethical and appropriate (to the animal and to your place) way of feeding your animal.

For the very poor, the elderly and the disabled, the only choice may be buying low-cost industrial pet foods — those folks derive more benefit from their animals than they do harm, and they get a pass. For the rest of us, just as we should do whatever it takes to avoid purchasing industrially produced meat, eggs and dairy, we should absolutely not buy those things for our pets.

Note that in the above, I said "purchase" and "buy" rather than "eat" or "feed." Because one option for feeding pets is to feed them at least in part on waste foods, particularly if you live in a densely populated area where large quantities of animal-suited scraps are available.

Here we get into the difference between dogs and cats. Cats are obligate carnivores — they have to eat meat. Dogs are not — they do need some animal foods, but they don't have to eat meat. Dogs are fairly omnivorous, and at least part of their diet can be made up of *healthy* food scraps from human beings. That means that if you have a bit of left-over stir-fry and brown rice, you can feed it to the dog and reduce their purchased food accordingly.

Restaurant scraps carefully culled can supplement your dog's diet too — think lean meats, green vegetables, small amounts of rice. You may be able to feed your animal high-quality pet foods by dumpster diving — split bags or damaged packing bags are generally thrown out. Obviously, you should do some research into diets and food safety for your animals first — but the reality is that all of us are facing a change in standard of care, and it is only fair that our animals absorb some of that, rather than the poorest human beings.

In some cases, it may be possible to get free offal — parts of animals that human beings do not consume and that are ordinarily discarded. Ideally, this will come from sustainably raised animals — and your local farmer probably does have enough chicken feet (don't feed them directly, make broth out of them) or lamb livers that she would sell at low cost to keep your dog and cat fed. Or you may be able to get some of this for free at your supermarket, in which case it won't be sustainable, but it also won't be supporting factory-farmed meats.

In the case of cats, you probably should not try and replace 100 percent of their diet with homemade, unless you are willing to do considerable research and purchase supplements. But dropping their dry or wet food consumption by half to two-thirds should be possible. In the case of dogs, it should be possible for their whole diets to be homemade.

Or you could raise other animals on scraps or wastes or grass. A large portion of the impact of our animals comes from methane, from ruminant livestock, badly handled manures and organic materials in landfills (all that kitty litter in plastic bags is a nightmare). You can reduce emissions at several levels if you raise small livestock for yourself and your animals on land that can't support vegetables, or by using waste land or scrap foods. Rabbits can be raised largely on grain scraps, grass and weeds, for example, and while rabbits do not have enough fat to feed other animals on their own, they can operate as the main meat source for both dogs and cats, with smaller amounts of supplements.

Raising rabbits, pigeons or other small livestock (or raising larger animals for human use sustainably and feeding pets the offal and scraps) can reduce the impact of a pet's diet in a whole host of ways — for example, by spreading out livestock production across many people rather than concentrating it, manures create a net benefit over time by enabling soils to hold carbon. Raising animals on scraps and marginal weeds means reducing the industrial agricultural land needed. And raising the animals that will feed your pets at home means that there are no transport emissions.

What, you don't want to raise butcher animals in order to feed Fluffy and Fido? Well, I think that's a useful measure of how much we do care about our pets — that is, if we only love them enough to open bags of convenience food for them but not enough to work at feeding them, well, that tells us something important right there. The truth is that keeping those you love — whether animal or human — fed isn't easy, and shouldn't be. We shouldn't be able to eat thoughtlessly, or feed creatures thoughtlessly. Whether you butcher your own or seek out better food, all of us need to be as involved with our pets' diets as we are with our own.

The truth is that our coming ecological crisis is not going to be good for the pets we say we love. There will be more diseases as the world gets warmer, and a lower quality of life for them, and more abandoned pets as we get poorer. There will be plenty of animal suffering to go with the human suffering in the storms and droughts, heat waves and floods. It is in everyone's interest, our pets included, to find ways of feeding and caring for them which dramatically minimize their impact. Our responsibility for them extends to their future as well.

Ten

Marriage and family

I. Seven ways to make your marriage sustainable

I GET EMAILS MORE OR LESS CONSTANTLY ON THIS SUBJECT: "I want to prepare for peak oil/live more sustainably/change, my life to deal with climate change and my spouse (and/or the rest of my family) doesn't want to, or doesn't think it is important enough."

This is something I've heard over and over — marriages struggling when partners have different ideas about what the right thing to do is. I've known several that have broken up over this issue, and a couple of others that are teetering on the brink. And besides the fact that divorce is always sad and traumatic, there are real and serious reasons that people are better off going into hard times with stable marriages and good support systems. Divorce impoverishes everyone, adds to stress levels, tends to reduce the quality of life for children and makes joint decision-making difficult. How, for example, will two intertwined but hostile divorced families decide whether a move to a cooler climate or a more walkable neighborhood is appropriate? Taking care of our primary relationships is really important.

On the other hand, I also understand the perspective of someone who feels frustrated and angry when they want to make changes they think are essential, but can't because of a spouse or partner. Eric and I have not always worked in perfect tandem, let us say. And yes, these critical daily life things really do matter — three hundred million Americans using all the water, coal-fired electricity and gasoline they want make a huge difference. So yes, it does matter how you do the laundry or what you buy. That doesn't, however, make change easy, or relieve the stress these issues place on marriages.

We will assume for the purposes of this discussion that the marriage is basically loving and healthy, and that if it isn't — if there are deep, insoluble problems, violence or other bad stuff — you'll either involve professionals or reconsider being married. We'll also assume (which I think should be obvious, but just in case it isn't) that when I say "marriage or family" I mean, "the person or people you love, care for, share stuff with and live your life with," regardless of gender, number or formal legal relationships.

I'm pretty lucky on the marriage front. My husband is a confirmed pessimist and deeply opposed to change of any kind, but he's also a professor of astrophysics who teaches things like planetary biology, environmental physics and geophysics. So when we met, Eric was already generally aware of peak oil and climate change, and concerned about them, although not enough to overcome his basic sense that change is bad.

Fortunately (or unfortunately), my husband married a perennial optimist who adores change, gets bored easily and believes in personal solutions. He has described being married to me as hanging on for dear life to a runaway freight train, and he regularly observes that if it were left up to him (we've been together fifteen years) he might be almost ready to pop the question by now.

Had I warned him when I was harassing him into getting married that a decade later he'd have four kids, a rotating cast of foster children, twenty-seven acres and a working farm, I'm pretty sure he'd have run screaming into the night. Right before my talk at the Community Solutions conference, while on the phone with my beloved, I told him I was praying for courage when I got up there, and Eric answered (with the exaggerated patience he uses when he thinks his wife is completely over the edge), "Honey, do you think you could pray for something you don't already have an excess of ... like common sense?" (This made me laugh so hard I couldn't talk for a while, which was helpful for me, and probably restful for him.)

All of which is just a way of saying that not only have I had the experience of disagreeing with my spouse about what should be done and when and how fast, but I also have some sympathy for him. The problems in marriages often come from both sides. I say this also as a person who has been divorced (brief, early marriage, still friends, but that doesn't mean it was easy) and who is the child of several generations of divorce. I have no illusions that dealing with this stuff is easy. Which leads me to axiom number one about the sustainable marriage:

Axiom #1: The problem might be you

Let's say you recently discovered peak oil, and you are aware that energy shortages are likely forthcoming. Or perhaps you are concerned about climate change and want to make radical emissions cuts. You want to preserve the future for yourself and hopefully your family, and it doesn't seem like you have a lot of time. Now your spouse of a decade has looked at a few of these things but hasn't done the dozens of hours researching you have, and after obsessively reading websites and trying to figure out what to do, you go to them and tell them, "OK, we have to get a farm. And ducks. And grow all of our own food. We have to get rid of your jeep right now and get a hybrid. And reinsulate the house, and start a community garden. The end of the world is coming. Stockpile food. Give up your hobbies. Stop going to movies. And I'm way, way, way too stressed to have sex." Now I hate to be the bearer of bad news, but this really does sound crazy.

Confronted with the realization that the world is changing and that they have to change too, a lot of people panic. It can be difficult for even the most loving spouse to absorb the new material, or deal with the fact that their darling has decided that they have to change their entire life and lifestyle *right now*. If there are kids, this can be even tougher, both because kids sometimes don't want their lives to be changed, and also because it can be very hard for parents to envision a future in which their children are deprived or in any way impoverished. While you may believe that the climate change/peak oil future means impoverishment anyway, and that it is better to prepare ahead, your spouse may just be hearing, "My husband doesn't want my kids to be normal/have as much as we had/be safe and secure."

The first and most important thing to recognize is that in any troubled marriage, some of the problem is almost certainly you. And since someone has to compromise, it might as well be you — at least half of the time, maybe even a little more. Remember, even if this stuff hits you like a ton of bricks, other people absorb things differently, and may need time. Back off a little. Let things go if you have to. Sometimes it isn't important to be right. You may be right, but the cost of being right may not be worth it.

So take a deep breath, go slow, and try again in a few days or weeks. See if the problem is your approach rather than your partner's intractability. I say this as someone who really likes to win arguments. It has taken me some time to recognize that it isn't always worth winning — and sometimes, winning is losing.

But let's say you have backed off, or that you approached the issue calmly to begin with. How do you get a reluctant spouse to consider changing? This leads me to axiom number two:

Axiom #2: The best techniques are the ones that already work

My husband is cheap. As a graduate student, in one of the most expensive housing markets in the country, he managed to accumulate savings of $18K over five years — never making more than that in a year, and paying nearly half his income in rent. Eric never met a dollar he didn't want to put away. And over the years, I've found one of the best techniques to get him to do things is with the enticement that it will save us money.

In other cases, you might connect with a spouse by emphasizing the excitement to be had, or the good physical exercise, the improved food, the weight loss, the shared time together, the more relaxed lifestyle, the family bonding, the spiritual benefits. Remember, your spouse isn't you — they aren't necessarily motivated by the things that motivate you. So even if you are driven by the desire to live ethically, remember that your spouse may be more inspired by the desire to live beautifully — and if you can phrase your argument for change in aesthetic terms, as a way of extracting greater quality from fewer resources, you might be more persuasive.

I'm not suggesting you manipulate your spouse, at least not sneakily (do any marriages exist without a sort of mild-mannered, friendly, self-conscious mutual manipulation?). But I have come to believe that carrots are usually better than sticks and honey better than vinegar, and if you've been paying attention to this person you love at all, you'll know what kind of honey to offer.

What if that doesn't work? Then comes axiom number three:

Axiom #3: Treat it as a hobby

If you want to make changes but simply can't get your spouse on board, you may have to accept that the onus for doing this stuff is on you. In that case, what you want is for your spouse to indulge you as much as possible. And for that, you need to present your new sustainability project as your wacko hobby.

The thing is, as long as you present this as a moral imperative, your spouse will keep arguing with you (or at least mine would), because if it's an imperative, there's no getting around it. But if you present your passion for off-grid living as your crazy obsession, your wife/husband can roll his/her eyes and tell his/her friends, "Yeah, some people's wives/husbands collect classic cars or re-enact the Civil war, travel around the country attending chili cook-offs or decorate their entire home in pig themes — my nutcase spouse believes that we're entering a period of energy depletion and rising global temperatures and wants to do the laundry with a hand washer and put solar panels on the roof. At least it is better than Lee's husband who insists on taking all their vacations to places where he can photograph radio towers. Sigh."

The beauty of this is that many people — most, even — have obsessions that cost their family money and time and about which their spouses roll their eyes and complain. But generally speaking, the eye rolling and complaining aren't too serious. This is what you want, if you can't get outright cooperation. That is, the goal is to have your spouse complain with a certain amount of amusement about the price they have to pay for loving you. What you do not want, under any circumstances, is for your spouse to feel that they truly do have to pay a high price for loving you.

It goes without saying, however, that you can only have one nutjob hobby at a time. So if you are going to be obsessed with preparing for environmental depletion, you have to give up your giant collection of salt and pepper shakers shaped like cartoon characters, your first edition buying habits or the three half-rebuilt boats on your front lawn. Sorry, but no spouse on Earth has to put up with more than one crazy hobby. Two is reasonable grounds for divorce.

Axiom #4: Give it time and get them involved with community

Give it time seems to me to be self-evident. Remember, the evidence that we were going to run out of cheap oil has been in front of all of our noses for decades — but a lot of us chose not to know. The evidence for climate change has been mounting for thirty years and more — but a lot of us chose not to know. And then, one day, it clicked. But it is important to remember that you, just like your partner, were in denial. And just because their denial hasn't collapsed yet doesn't make them bad, any more than you once were.

The thing is, the longer they live with you and the more they are confronted with evidence and reality, the better the situation is likely to become. I know several people whose spouses initially felt that they simply couldn't handle hearing all the bad news all the time, but who have gradually become more comfortable with it. Some people learn things slowly and gradually, and you need to give your partner time. This can be really hard when you feel like we may only have a short time of relative prosperity to prepare. But remember, you can begin preparing on your own, where you are, with what you have. You can start learning to dehydrate food, chop wood or grow a garden anywhere, even if just in a window box. You can buy less, do less, live more gently anywhere.

The other thing that works well, I think, is to involve your spouse in a community. Take them to a local environmental group, peak awareness group or conference. Let them make friends. It can be hard for people who have found community on the net to imagine how separate from this your spouse may feel without any such community. And some partners just aren't the net type — Eric isn't. He likes hands-on, direct contact with people. The first time my husband met another homesteader he was thrilled, because he finally knew, viscerally, that there were other people like us.

Sometimes all someone needs is a support network, or to see that they aren't the only weirdo around, or to add some people to their circle of friends who will validate what they do. Or perhaps they need to hear things from someone more authoritative than their spouse. I know this is hard for us to understand, but occasionally the fact that your spouse has seen you naked, scratching your ass, means that they might not be inclined to take every word that comes from your mouth as though it were conveyed from on high. It can be helpful for them to hear the same information from people who wear clothes and whose baby pictures they've never seen.

Axiom #5: Give credit where it's due

It is easy for the person interested in sustainability to say, "You don't care about the environment." And the other person ends up eternally cast as the bad guy, which no one likes. If you want your spouse to appreciate that you are trying to preserve a future for yourselves and your kids and future generations, you need to appreciate the things they do that are already environmentally sound and the places they are willing to make changes, but also *why* they are reluctant or concerned.

By this I mean that it is not only important to thank your spouse for doing things that matter to you, but also to understand that their motivations are as legitimate as yours are. For example, the spouse that doesn't want to see your children singled out and rejected because they can't go to McDonalds anymore, or who doesn't want to "look poor" and be pitied, has a legitimate concern, and deserves to be appreciated both for what they care about and what they do.

It is hard to make changes for your children, to live with less in a society that values more, to say to your friends "we're not going to do this thing we've always done." Your spouse is not bad because they are worrying about these things. The appropriate solution is to come up with ways around these problems or find communities that share your values. But this takes time, and it takes understanding. And when, despite their fears, a spouse does make an effort, they deserve to be loved and appreciated for it.

The hardest issues are the really fundamental ones, a lot of which are deeply tied up with peak oil and climate change. Things like, "What kind of home shall we live in?," "What shall I do to make a living and how much money should we have?," "What standard of living will we have?," "How often shall we visit our families?," "Should we have children?" or "How many children?" These are tough questions, and a couple that has been on the same page until now may find themselves unable to resolve them. Which leads me to the hardest axiom, number six:

Axiom #6: Sometimes it's better to lose the game and win the series

This is the only baseball metaphor I've ever used or am likely to use. It's awfully tough, and while I've got experience here, I really don't want to give it airplay. Suffice it to say that early on, my husband and I had a really, really bad time. And in the end, the thing that salvaged the relationship was that when we reached an impasse, I gave in, and did something I thought was not the right choice, simply because I loved him. I could have fought it as a scorched-earth battle, but I would have lost my not-yet-husband and, more importantly, it would have established a precedent that meant that next time, he would never have an incentive to give in. That's not why I did it — it wasn't a tit-for-tat thing — but ultimately, the marriage could only survive if both of us were sometimes willing to cede to the other for the other's benefit.

　Now all of this assumes that your marriage is worth the price, and if it is, I'd say that you should give in on at least half, and preferrably more than half, of the tough issues. That's not to say you should do things you think are morally wrong, but at the very least you should recognize that someone has to give way sometimes.

　Things get more complicated if there are children involved. What happens if you think that the choice, say, to stay on the Gulf of Mississippi might lead to your kids' deaths? Or if you feel it is absolutely wrong to bring a child into this world, and your spouse wants a baby? In those cases you are stuck between a rock and a hard place, and I can only hope that you and your spouse both love each other enough to find a compromise — maybe to move to higher ground in the region, or to adopt together. I don't pretend it is easy. But again, I think the best possible precedent you can set for one another is to have a long history of saying, "Ultimately, I care about you and your happiness enough to make some compromises."

Axiom #7: Make it fun

Extracting the most joy and quality of life from the fewest resources is really cool. Period. No debate. It is true that our culture hasn't much validated the optimization exercise view of life, but that's simply because growth capitalism requires the exact opposite — discontentment, and more of it. But the more you can make your spouse see how much pleasure there is in changing your life and living sustainably, the happier that life will be.

Keep in mind that there's really no reason to spend your spare time fixating on the darkest parts of all this, and the spouse who says they don't want to hear it all the time may just be protecting their own mental health. Instead of focusing on "The end of the world is coming, do this now," how about "Fresh salsa from the garden is so much better than this jarred stuff, and I've heard that bread made from wheat you grind yourself is much, much tastier." Or, "I miss the smell of line-dried sheets." Or "Wouldn't it be fun to walk together to the store and pull the kids in the wagon?"

My friend Robert Waldrop says he almost never talks about peak oil — he focuses on good food and good health, supporting local farmers and saving money. I think that's the right message for every spouse — tell them what is good about this and why they should be excited by it. Hook them into a community of people who are in the same place as they are. Let them roll their eyes, then watch their faces when they taste the bread and the fresh strawberry jam. Kiss them hard and share the taste. The rest will come with time in many cases, and if it doesn't, what you have may still be enough.

II. Some kind of help: Getting things done with kids who can't or won't help

When I speak of children who can't or won't help, I am referring to two groups. The first are babies and toddlers, who lack the capacity or temperament or understanding to be at all helpful. Babies obviously can't do much, and toddlers and most young preschoolers are so busy learning to be people that they cannot accomplish much else. Despite their significant differences, these groups often have a lot in common, and I'm going to treat them together.

The age at which children become generally helpful and both want to and can participate in your daily life varies a great deal — some especially calm and mature eighteen- or twenty-month-olds might actually fit the bill, although I have personally never raised such a child. In other cases, a child as old as three and a half might be unable to focus on helping much.

In developmentally typical children, it seems to me that the major transition occurs sometime between two and a half and three. At this point, though they may still slow you down because they want to help make the pancakes, hang the laundry or drive the car, children can at least participate in home and garden life, unlike younger children who, delightful and sweet as they are, mostly fall into the category of "hindrance" when you're trying to grow and preserve food, keep a home that will not be condemned or get much of anything else done.

The second category of children who can't or won't help are those with serious disabilities. Some of these children are those with neurological impairments that limit their common sense, impulse control, ability to understand danger or simply their interest in participation. Other such children are so severely physically or mentally disabled that their participation, while perfectly possible, requires an enormous amount of investment of time and energy by their parents or other caretakers. Helpfulness may come late, or in limited ways, or may never arrive.

I have had four biological sons and several baby and toddler foster children — my house usually has a cute little hindrance or two. And then there's Eli. My oldest son is autistic, and that means that his priorities and ours do not always match up, or even make sense to us. At least in our experience there's nothing tragic about having an autistic child — Eli is sweet-natured, with a merry sense of humor and a great deal of energy, but it is rather like going to the shelter to adopt a kitten and getting a puppy.

That is, Eli's worldview is different in fundamental ways from our own — thus he's not much interested in my attempts, say, to engage him with stacking wood; he'd rather whack the ice-covered branches that have fallen from the tree against the house. No persuasion of mine will convince him of the desirability of helping — he'll do it if I stand over him, but he simply cannot understand my own interest in this activity, and will abandon it the moment something else catches his interest.

It isn't that Eli is trying to be difficult — he genuinely doesn't yet grasp what is wanted or needed, or why we would care about these things. His world, his mind, are different, and it is hard for him to work through the distractions of autism to understand our perspective. He does, and we require him to do so, but there's only so much of that we can do in any given day, and have anyone have any fun.

I am not alone in struggling to get things accomplished with multiple cute hindrances around. And while I do take the time to include them, sometimes we just need to find a way to get things done around them. I'm excluding paid childcare as a choice here — I'm assuming that whoever is doing this is the parent or the paid childcare provider working out of their home. I figure "get a babysitter" is something you can figure out without me.

So here are a few suggestions I've come up with. Most of them probably involve a degree or two of bad parenting — but they get the jam made.

1. Let them make a giant mess

There's nothing that attracts a toddler — or for that matter, many older children — than water. Kids love to "help" with the dishes, but can't actually do them. So if I need to do a whole load of dishes, my favorite project is to put one of them in the tub with a dishpan of warm soapy water, some unbreakable dishes (enamelware cups are great) and let 'em go at it. They love it, and I might actually get a full load of dishes done.

I also feel strongly that sometimes it is worth letting the kids make a mess, if cleaning it up will not be too onerous, and it gets me a few minutes to work. So I am probably repulsively laissez-faire on this subject — recently three little boys were kept happily occupied slicing my husband's old exams into shapes (and then throwing the shreds up and yelling "Snow!"). I realize good mommies stop their children from doing this. But all I could think was, "Fine, I'll pick up the snow later, I get to make bread."

2. Don't look them in the eye

I have noticed that my children will be happily and productively self-entertaining while I am busy doing something else and nowhere in sight, but toddlers especially (and other kids too) think that if Mommy is in the line of sight, or, say, talking to him, this means "Mommy wants to pick me up." When you get those blessed moments of self-engagement

STAY OUT OF VIEW — if there are safety issues, that's one thing, but try and make sure there aren't, or recruit an older child and bribe them to come running if anything untoward happens.

This also applies to children with disabilities doing things for themselves. I find that much more help is needed if I'm available to do things for them. That's not to say we should allow children to struggle to the point of suffering to do something they are genuinely incapable of doing on their own, but I notice how creative they get when they think they are responsible.

3. Make use of big siblings — or even developmentally normal younger ones

I know this is a somewhat fraught issue. In some societies, siblings have enormous responsibility for one another, but we are less inclined that way. Still, I haven't noticed any negative effects — and have seen some positive ones, from giving Simon and Isaiah the responsibility, say, of helping a toddler up and down stairs, or keeping an eye on him in an enclosed space. Obviously, one has to be realistic about this — six-year-olds have limited powers of rationality. But I do think that the practice of being responsible for one another — mutually — is a good one in building family unity.

For children with physical disabilities, having a sibling be eyes or hands or feet can be empowering and positive for both of them, as long as it is done carefully. I have a friend whose ten-year-old with cerebral palsy cannot walk in the woods — so her brother brings the woods to her, each day returning with a collection of woodland artifacts: acorns and sticks, small tree seedlings, etc. They then make woodland fairy houses in the corner of their yard together, and wait for acorn seedlings to sprout.

4. Create enclosures

Particularly for toddlers and roaming older children, this is essential. We spent an awful lot of our inheritance from Eric's grandparents fencing a quarter acre of our front yard — and it may be the best money we have ever spent. Eli cannot be trusted not to roam, but he also is a pre-teen, with an appropriately low tolerance for his parents following him around all the time. This allows him some freedom — and I know that grants are available in some areas to low-income families seeking to keep disabled kids safe. I've heard of several people who fenced with such grants.

In the barn, we only have small livestock, so we don't worry too much about the kids, but a friend of mine who has draft horses and cows tells me that one of the best things she ever did was simply allot a spare horse stall to her kids. There are kid-sized barn tools, some toys and bales of hay to sit on, and a few old chairs and horse blankets to make tents with. That way, when she is working, her younger kids are out from underfoot. We don't have enough space in our barn for this, but if you do, it is a great idea. Even a small gated area can help, or a playpen.

Making points of access is also important for children — if you can, it is well worth spending money to bring the wheelchair into the barn, or move the chicken house to where your child can get to it themselves. She might not yet be able to go get eggs herself, and it may even be hard to imagine that she ever could, but making the coop accessible means the possibility is there, and many disabled children accomplish remarkable things.

5. Nurse toddlers as long as possible

I say this for two reasons. The first is that when they are in their "I am only sort of a person" stage, they have a lot of complicated feelings they cannot yet express. Often, the world just seems unbearable, and somehow nursing makes it less fraught. And it is amazing how much time you can save if you can short-circuit a tantrum by settling down together for some mutual comfort.

It also has a powerful tranquilizing effect on some kids — that is, you can get a kid to nap by nursing them even if they will no longer nap any other way. Since two of my kids gave up naps long before I felt they should, this was very important.

If you don't or can't nurse, create sleep routines and comfort routines. The idea here is to have short ways of sending various messages: "It's OK, the world is not falling apart just because you can't hold the credit card," or "Now it is time to go to sleep, even though it seems like it would be much more fun to throw the dog food." Think of it as keyboard shortcuts for your children.

6. Wear your baby or toddler

Not one of my four kids would ever tolerate a sling, backpack or other constraint after they could walk — not one. But I know many people all over the world do this. And it is good way of keeping your child about and contained. I laud those who can do it. Me, I never could pull it off.

7. Put them to bed early

We have a firm 8:00 pm bedtime at our house. They don't have to sleep, and they often don't, but barring an emergency, all children go upstairs and read or play quietly in their room — period, no discussion, no negotiation. Actually, there's no battle here — my kids look forward to bedtime, and their time together. We check in occasionally, they have water and plenty of books and toys, and often I find Simon reading aloud to the other three, or elaborate games being made up. But to bed they go — and Mommy and Daddy get to work on whatever project awaits us, until we collapse together. Alternately, if your kids are night owls, get up early and work before them.

On a related note, I'm a firm believer in tiring children out — all kids need plenty of physical exercise to get them ready to sleep, and I think kids who spend too much time indoors or being sedentary often have more behavioral issues. We find that lots of exercise is good for everyone — if everyone is too cranky, taking a long walk or a run around the local school track is good for Mommy, and for the boys. For children with physical disabilities, finding good exercise can be difficult — but it is important nonetheless. And it is good to find a fun form of exercise which will work for kids who do lots of physical therapy and are wary of such things. A friend of mine's wheelchair-bound son is very resistant to anything that smacks of "therapeutic" exercise, but will happily play catch from his chair.

8. Get a good dog or an alarm

For those children with escape urges, you need a way to protect them and still be able to look away now and then. Some kids really push those limits. There are both cheap and expensive options. One would be a well-trained dog taught to give the alarm if a child goes beyond a particular perimeter, and to go with the child. Not all dogs could meet this need, but many might.

Some children with disabilities might be eligible for an assistive dog — these are now available for a range of disabilities, not just blindness and deafness. I've even heard of miniature horses and monkeys being used in these capacities — obviously, this is a large decision and up to each family, but it is something to think about. Strong relationships with animals, and the experience of being in "charge" of something, are very important for kids.

Otherwise, you might consider either an alarm system in your house (if that's the issue) or an emergency alarm that attaches to the child and sounds when the child strays more than a short distance away.

It is also worth teaching your children "cue words" — many kids with disabilities have trouble with language but can learn a few key terms. By age two, all of my children knew that STOP meant stop NOW, without discussion. Any child capable of learning these things should have words or signs that indicate stop, stay and come. And if it's possible, mastering these should be a huge priority.

9. Integrate the child into the task at their level

We go berry picking, and Eli and the toddlers mostly eat. They are participating. We are happy they are there. They also occasionally contribute a squashed berry, and are lauded and praised extravagantly for this contribution (after which, the berry is discretely disposed of most of the time).

When we make a quilt, the little one can find the red cloth. When we fold laundry, Eli can bring me the towels. The trick is to find jobs sufficiently engaging to keep the child busy, while also not actually adding any time onto the project. This can be enormously difficult — but every investment of time and energy is an investment in future helpfulness. Your child may not be coordinated enough to pour the cat's water yet — but perhaps they can turn on the faucet while you hold the bowl.

10. Accomplishment is relative

The glorious thing about having a disabled child is that you learn to appreciate every step, however small. Toddlers do that too — one day they can't button a button, and the next day they can get it halfway in. One day they can't put on their underpants, the next day they can — and on their heads. The truth is, these are all steps forward.

If you are the parent or caregiver of a small (or large) beloved hindrance, remember that for you, too, the small accomplishments count. You, like them, do a little tiny bit more each day — some days. Some days it feels like you are taking a dozen steps back. But the truth is this — seven dishes done, up from six yesterday morning, is an improvement. Nine eggplants harvested before the tantrum is better than five last week. You, like them, are taking small steps. And just as the moment when the toddler who will never nap smiles and says, "I go sleep now, Daddy" or the child who cannot speak says "Mama" are moments of glory, joy and wonder, so too is the day when the jars of jam are on the shelf or the laundry waves in the breeze like a salute.

III. Helping kids Adapt in Place

I know all of us with kids or grandkids, nieces or nephews or just beloved child-friends are deeply worried about their future. We want to help them have a good one — and it is tough to realize that sometimes the best way to do this isn't always by insulating them from difficulty, but by helping them adapt to the world they'll be living in ahead of time.

I think a lot of people are saddened that they can't promise their children a perfect future or safety — because we've been in denial. That is, no parent has ever been able to truly promise those things to their children — but it can be hard to come to terms with parenting for a real future. The best thing we can do is offer our children a good and protected childhood that simultaneously prepares them for the future they will live in. That means we have to change how we parent.

1. BE THE GROWNUP

This sucks. I hate it a lot of the time. Every parent knows the feeling of wanting not to be the responsible one, not having to deal, not having to suck up their pain and frustration and fear — tough! This is the Mom and Dad (and Grandpa and Grandma) job — to bear the brunt of things, to do the hard stuff so the kids don't have to suffer, to not make your kids parent you or deal with your emotional inadequacies any more than strictly necessary. This doesn't mean you have to be perfect, noble or never feel anything or cry in front of them — it just means you don't indulge yourself at their expense. It just means that except when you just can't (and those moments can't be too often) hold it together, you can't ask your kids to take care of you — it isn't their job.

If you are scared, they are too. If you are sad, they are either sad or scared because you are sad. Your job is to face the future and come to terms with it so that they can too. That means being able to say, "I'm sad, and sometimes I cry, but now we're going to go forward." And act like you mean it.

This is a hot-button subject for me, because I honestly think a lot of our present problems can be summed up as, "No one was willing to be the grownup." No one was willing to have the buck stop with them, and to change their way of life — so now it gets harder. It is time for all of us grownups, whether we have kids or not, to act like we care about the future and be real adults. By this I mean not just when it is convenient but all the time. We will probably not enjoy it, but who cares? We have to live our lives asking, "Does this hurt the ability of future people to live and have a decent life?" And if the answer is yes, then no matter how many good excuses we have for doing what we're doing, things have to change.

I have no doubt that someday my kids will write an expose of "advice my Mom gave in her books and online and didn't always live up to." I suspect it will be a long and vibrant essay. I don't always find it easy to follow my advice either. But this is, I think, the first and most important job of preparing children for the future — giving them models of real adulthood. And the models they've got are us, so we've got to do better. I'm hoping my kids won't be able to say I screwed this one up too bad when the time comes — I'm trying.

2. Involve your kids in your adaptations in a kid-appropriate way

There is no need for children to know all the bad news, or your worst fears about the future. Sometimes you can tell all the truth to older teenagers, but I don't think younger kids need to be scared by things they can't fully understand. But the choice is not between "Do I wait until they are fifteen and spring peak oil and climate change on them then" or "Do I start them reading about doom at three?" There's a balance to be struck here.

Obviously you can bring them into the garden, bring them into the kitchen, give them chores to help you with your home economy, get them to help in your home business, teach them about ecology and environmental issues. I hope all of us are doing these things already, at age-appropriate levels. But there's more — one of the things we tend to assume in our society is that children should not work, and I think this is absolutely wrong. I believe children, like adults, need good work.

It goes without saying that young children should work appropriately and have lots of time for learning and play, but children not only can work, they should work. What they should not do is have to do the kind of meaningless work that drives adults to despair — that is, they need good work, and to understand why their work matters. They should feel proud that they can help their household, and know that their accomplishments matter, not in a fake self-esteem sense but in a serious way. To the extent they are able, children deserve to earn respect and serious attention for their work, and if they work with you, once they are old enough, they should have a say in how things are done, and a share in the rewards.

3. Respect what matters to them

I know it feels like you are trying to save the world, and they are worried about how crazy it looks that you are storing all this food or turning down the heat or doing some other weird thing. But that matters as much to them as your concerns matter to you. Try and be respectful. Sometimes the needs of kids simply have to be subsumed to family priorities, or their needs/wants aren't good for them. But sometimes they need to know that they count, and that you care about how they feel. So maybe it makes sense to do your shopping only at the store where your neighbor's son doesn't bag groceries, or to stockpile lip gloss and zit cream for the apocalypse. Just because you don't consider it essential doesn't mean they agree — and let's be honest, you have a few things in there that might not be totally essential, too.

4. Without taking everything away, make their new normal ahead of time

This is tough — on the one hand, we want our kids to be regular kids, we don't want our preoccupations to affect them, and since we know all this abundant cheap energy probably isn't forever, we may want to do a lot of special things now. That's not bad or unreasonable. But your kids will probably do best if they keep their lives about the same as the ones they lived before whatever happens occurs.

That means that most of the time, you should probably model the life you expect to live, plus a few things you want them to have that they won't have later. Too much of the latter and the new life will be a huge deprivation; too much of the former and the child will realizes their family is insane a bit too early — plus, you will lose things you don't have to lose yet.

Everyone's family is going to be different — but it helps if your routines and sense of what is normal are fairly adaptable. It's tough to replace "Christmas at Disneyland" with a lower-consumption equivalent — you just have to lose that one. But "We all stay up late and decorate the tree at midnight on Christmas Eve, and then open presents" can work whether you decorate with electric lights and tinsel or old wooden ornaments, and whether the presents are purchased or handmade. The more susceptible to adaptation, the better.

5. Kids need the people in their lives

I grew up in a family where my parents did a remarkable job of essentially creating joint custody long before it was widespread, but when it came to extended family, the issues adults had with other adults frequently intruded into the relationships kids had with those other adults. This is not something I approve of, except in the case of genuine danger to a child.

Kids who are related to people by biology or long connection have to keep up those connections. They have a relationship with grandparents and aunts and uncles that can and should be separate from the relationships the parents have with each other or with other adults in their lives. They shouldn't have to lose people because the grownups can't get along. This goes for divorce (and yes, I know some exes are assholes, and sometimes the courts choose badly and sometimes there is no good choice) as well as larger extended families. What your kids have going into this is their parents plus some other people who love them. Don't take those people away lightly.

I realize that sometimes this is unavoidable — parents have to move, people really can't find a good compromise. But in a lower-energy world, being far away from people you love is going to be a much bigger thing. Divorced parents choosing to live across the country from one another, or moving for that new job and uprooting the kids from Grandma and the cousins, will be depriving their kids of one of their primary sources of comfort, security, even long-term health and safety. Don't do it lightly. If you are divorced or divorcing, please try and stay near one another, and as difficult as it is, play nice. And if you can, get along with your relatives — because your annoying, intolerable father-in-law is also your son's beloved grandfather, and there are enough unavoidable losses coming — the kids don't need more.

6. Be prepared to educate your children

I was struck by Dmitry Orlov's observation, in his book *Reinventing Collapse,* about the way the people of Russia responded to the collapse of the Soviet Union. In a crisis, he says, education isn't less important but more. You may end up digging ditches, but if you also know poetry or music and have a head full of ideas, you can live in your mind while your body works. One of the most common misconceptions, I think, is that in the future we should only concentrate on professional, manual or technical education, and that every other kind of education is fundamentally useless.

This isn't true at all — certain kinds of technical degrees may still result in high-paying jobs when everyone else is poor, and people will need careers. But they will also need critical thinking skills, a connection to the world of, literature and music, ethical and moral principles, good reasoning skills, a deep knowledge of history, religious training if they want it and the ability to understand what the world looks like from other perspectives, to understand other languages and the cultures of the people who speak them.

Due to its high cost, college may be reserved for an increasingly small portion of the population, but you don't have to go to college to learn these things — there will be plenty of unemployed people who know about them, and books are cheap now, you can stock up.

Education as it is practiced in the US is very energy-intensive and centralized, and depends just like everything else on cheap fuel for buses, heat, a/c and driving commutes. It is likely to get less energy-intensive over time, often without warning. Many of our kids may need to be educated at home or in neighborhood cooperatives, and may have to find substitutes for college. And while it is important that they learn the manual and technical skills many of us lacked, they will also grow up gardening and cooking and fixing things — so their needs may be for art and astronomy, poetry and history and the life of the mind — skills they can practice while they weed and build and hammer.

7. Let kids be in charge sometimes

Turn some of the responsibility over to your kids — when they are young, they can help decide what non-essentials go in the emergency kits, or whether to make ketchup or salsa with the tomatoes. When they get older, give them more responsibility as they prove they can handle it. Let teenagers be in charge of the bulk order, or even the family food budget if they have the relevant abilities. And when you let them be in charge, let them be. Let them make mistakes, as long as these are not life-threatening. Treat them with respect, and when they make a mistake, let them fix it.

Also, if you want your children to stay on a piece of land or in a particular place near you, help them see a future there. They aren't going to want to live their lives as your assistant farmer or employee forever — make it clear that you will cede control. Help them start small businesses of their own, and grow them. Help them go forward, but also let them have their own territory, their own responsibilities, and let them do things in their own realm as they see fit. If they have dreams you think aren't feasible, well, help them get there anyway — but also insist that they have practical backup plans.

8. Enter the pass-down economy now

In most poor societies, children inherit what their family collectively owns, including all the improvements and investments their parents and previous generations have put into things. They can't afford to buy land or other major investments — what land they have access to comes from the stewardship of previous generations.

It is disheartening in some ways to realize that what may most define our children's future is what we can pass down to them — particularly when what we have is a bunch of debts and a lot of plastic. So it makes sense to shift into the pass-down economy sooner rather than later. That means buying things that are of good quality, trying to keep your life unencumbered and caring for what we do have of value, so it can serve future generations.

It also means our relationship to our children should be about passing on our values — not what we say we value, but what we really and honestly do care most about. And the way to do this is to live our lives according to what we believe.

9. Have fun with your kids

I'm not suggesting you should be their friend all the time — discipline is important, and being at the center of your parents' world is a little too scary for kids. But joy and fun and play are important for kids even more than grownups (and they are awfully important for grownups as well). So make sure you allow time for fun — if not the kind of fun you were accustomed to, the kind that doesn't cost money.

Moreover, **be fun** with your kids — don't let your fear or anxiety take away the pleasures of laughing with them, or dreaming about the future, or just being with them. It is reasonable to be worried — but not to let it overwhelm your life now, which isn't fair to your kids. Heck, it isn't fair to you, either.

Keep festivals and rituals in place, take time off even when times are hard, make jokes even when things don't seem funny, make time for play even when it seems like the work is endless — especially when it seems like the work is endless. Do it even when they think the rituals are stupid and your jokes suck.

10. Help them up when they fall down

Let them fall sometimes, either because they need to or because you can't stop them, but be there on the other end. Even in good times, they are going to fall. In hard times, they may fall harder and longer. There may not be as many safety nets. You can't protect them from everything, and sometimes you shouldn't. But with the exception of the occasional addict, what you should do is be there when they fall down, every time from those first steps to the first arrest (which ideally you'll get to skip entirely, or will be the kind of arrest you can be proud of).

Yes, it teaches them that you'll be there to save them. And for some small percentage of children, that's a bad message, one that says they don't have to be responsible. But for most kids, I think that helping them up, and maybe resisting the temptation to tell them what an ass they've been, lets the stupid thing be the lesson itself. All the lessons, all the judgments, don't have to come from you. At some point we can take our hands off and let them know that they have to do their own judging. That, I think, is that growing-up thing we're supposed to want them to do. And then maybe we'll have some more people being the grownups to work on the future with.

Profile 5

Lisa and Patti: Water in the rain barrel

By Lisa Coons

When I reflect on our family's ever-unfolding and broadening Adapting in Place process, I have to resist the urge to start listing. Our family of three is trying to look from all directions at our life system and the processes that sustain our lives (and others') and ask what we can do to use a fairer share of the world's resources. We know that adapting to a lower-energy future now is optimal, not only for us but for our child's future. This is an opportunity to rethink everything in our lives. We've undertaken many projects over the years, with a flurry of activities in the past two years that have added joy, simplicity and resilience to our family. Working adaptation and building resilience into our lives in a mindful way gives more meaning and purpose to some of our previous decisions, like saving energy by replacing windows and eating local food all year long (in chilly Minnesota). The challenge we set for ourselves years ago — to step out of consumer culture and stop buying anything new from stores — suddenly takes on greater meaning under the umbrella of adapting to a changing world.

This process has added new dimensions to our family life. We purposefully keep one set of feet in the formal economy and one set in the informal economy. This decision alone has allowed us to cut the use of many resources. We no longer need two vehicles or two professional wardrobes. Having one of us at home allows us to grow, prepare and eat food at home. We homeschool our daughter, saving the resources of packing a kid off to school each and every weekday. We spend more time together — gathering, chopping and stacking wood, gardening and canning, playing board games or sharing music instead of running to the mall for the next consumer fix. We are continually challenged

219

to change our ways of thinking, our ways of seeing and our ways of being on this planet. As a couple, we get to examine, question and rethink our ingrained American assumptions about family life, expectations and entitlement and just about everything else. We get to come together and ask, "What more can we do?" We have late-night strategizing sessions. We support each other in our new ways.

What's truly exciting is that working this process builds upon itself. It's a self-reinforcing system! When we power down, for instance, by turning our heat to 58 degrees, we stop investing so much of our finances in fossil fuel heat and we accomplish a few key things. We take resources away from an old system, invest in something different, and the money saved allows us to take our next steps. When we added redundancy to our home system by installing a wood-burning stove, we may not have saved money immediately but we gained other things such as the security of backup heat, another option for cooking and family togetherness as we all gather around the warmth of the hearth. When we installed three rain barrels to catch water off the house and garage, we saved money on the irrigation it takes to grow a large garden. The money saved allows us to invest in another rain barrel or some other adaptation tool.

We've done some good work and have plenty more to do. Having lived in our old folk Victorian house for nearly twenty years has meant many opportunities to make energy-efficient changes to our home. We've added insulation, installed new windows, reroofed with metal. We had a wood–burning stove installed to cut our use of and reliance on fossil fuels. Now after a storm, rather than see the "mess" of broken limbs, we scavenge downed limbs and trees from neighbors and friends to use as heating. We conserve resources, collect rainwater and save graywater for gardens.

Life-long learners already, the focus of our learning has changed to acquiring new skills and knowledge and reaching out to others who are interested in some of the same learning. While we have always gardened and canned, these activities have taken on greater importance in our lives. We doubled our garden size, then doubled it again the next year. Removing bushes and flowers, we've made more room for fruit and food. We eat from our pantry the food we preserve in the growing season. We teach others how to do this. Bartering labor, we acquire fruit from friends who have trees we don't have room for; my partner works on a CSA farm in exchange for our share. We've learned to dehydrate, pressure can and lacto-ferment and built a root cellar in the base-ment. We've learned about long-term food storage and worked that into our lives. We've even learned how to brew beer and make wine with an eye toward a future cottage industry.

We've done all these things but I think the most important "thing" we've done and continue to do is build community. We do not see our goals as com-plete self-reliance or anything close to it, as this is both impossible and, to us, undesirable. We believe that all of us will be more secure, resilient and adapt-able in community and in relationship as a community. We've gotten to know our neighbors and many in our neighborhood. We share food, lend tools and moral support. We bulk order supplies, food and grains for long-term storage and invite others to join in the ordering. We've broadened our circle by joining a faith community, finding spiritual connectedness an important part of "build-ing our reserves."

Using a fairer share of the world's resources has become one of our defin-ing family principles. Transitioning to a future with fewer available fossil fuels and more climate challenges involves a fair amount of courage to do the hard work — not the hard work of gardening or canning or making our house more energy-efficient but of looking critically at our lives as a whole and mindfully asking, "What can we do?" The answer, it turns out, is a lot!

Eleven

Father and Mother and Uncle John: tribalism and family

THIS MORNING, DURING SCHOOL TIME, Isaiah asked me just how many aunts and uncles he had, which led me to do some quick addition — and to a number that came out above seventy. Now Eric and I don't have that many siblings. In fact, I have two sisters, and Eric was an only child. Nor do our parents make up for it — each of them had one sibling. So how on earth do I get seventy aunts and uncles for my kids?

Well, we're a weird family — like a lot of families. Like many Gen-Xers, Eric's and my parents were divorced and remarried, so we have more than our share of inlaws and outlaws, and all of our family, because of this, are accustomed to making space for a lot of people. And one of the courtesies that accompanies this making space is the formal acknowledgement of relationship — when you can hurt someone with your title, welcome them in or cut them out by how you describe the relationship, you get careful about making space for people in both language and in person. Add to that our tendency to pick up chosen family, and, well, it makes for big (and fun) holiday dinners.

It also makes it a little confusing for kids. My sons have four Uncle Davids, two Aunt Rachels, three Uncle Jons, three Aunt Karens and two Aunt Sallys. Nor do titles tell you anything very clear about the relationship between my kids and the person in question. An aunt, in our family, could be a mother's sister or father's stepsister-in-law. She could be your great aunt, biologically or by marriage. She could also be a first or second cousin of your mother or father. She could be your mother's stepmother's cousin, or an old friend of either parent, or an old friend of Mom's parents, who *she* always called "Aunt."

In another sense, however, it tells you something very clear — this person is part of your tribe. In general, it marks a longstanding relationship, a formalized one. That is, most of the people who get the honorary title "aunt" or "uncle" get it by having that kind of near-family relationship before the children are born or when they are very young. There are occasional odd moments — I once introduced my "Aunt" Luana as "Aunt Luana" whereupon she, startled, observed "You know I'm not your aunt, right?" Well, yes, I do know that. I'm sure some languages have an official name for "my mother's lesbian partner's cousin who has functioned since you were a kid as approximately an aunt," but English is not among them.

Now in many cultures this wouldn't be strange — many cultures address nearly every adult in familial terms; "Tia" or "Grandfather" are honorifics applied to any older adult. In our own, however, where formal markers of relationships are often handed out more sparingly, I think it is a little odd. In our family, there's respect implied in these titles, but also an attempt to say, "You are part of us."

The boys and I talked a little about what all these people have in common. A relationship to my kids, of course — although a few have never met them, and some may never meet them. Some of them are very close indeed, and some very far away, both geographically and relationally. Sometimes it marks a distant biological or social tie that on some level may not matter much.

And yet, it does matter. I will never forget how nervous and uncertain I felt walking up to the houses of members of my husband's family, and how that changed when Eric's stepsister, who had only just met me, introduced me to her children as "Aunt Sharon," or when his grandparents asked me to call them "Grandma and Grandpa" and referred to me as their granddaughter. I grew up in a complicated family where relationships were never static — where family ties were made and remade, people married and divorced, you could suddenly acquire new siblings through marriage or foster parenthood, new relatives of all sorts, and it wasn't uncommon to meet a new aunt or uncle. And everyone was hesitant those first few forays into a relationship — but there's nothing like saying, "You are part of the family and here's your part," whether it is literally true or not.

Moreover, because my mother is gay, it was always possible to blight the relationship by failing to acknowledge it. It was always possible that someone could indicate in word or deed that we were not "really" connected, that some family did not count. To their enormous credit, most of my family tried incredibly hard not to do that.

I remember every snub, though, every time someone let it be known that my mother's lesbian partner's family wasn't like a "real" family, every time I self-consciously used a title that we weren't technically entitled to by force of law and custom, waiting to see if it would be questioned, or someone would disavow the relationship.

All of this hyper-awareness of who is in and who is out and how we place them gave me an appreciation for tribal ties — for the virtue of acknowledging, by title and action, "You are part of us." It also gave me a taste for big tents — for the inclusion of those who fit neatly in categories and those who don't. I would always rather welcome someone in than leave them sitting outside, with no spot at the table.

Our family has had a new opportunity to do so as we've become foster parents — children who have lived in our home might stay forever, or they might not. When they return to birthparents or to extended family, my children have to ask — are they still my brothers/sisters? We tell them that they are, that they will always be — that not all brothers and sisters live together, but you can always love each other as siblings do. We have been fortunate in that other families have welcomed the continued connection with us in some cases, so my children maintain relationships with their foster families, and our family becomes richer and more complex still.

I'm grateful that my children don't have to live through the pain of divorce, but I also appreciate the gifts of the fluctuating tribe, of the complicated family made by love, fosterage, marriage, adoption, trying again, everyone doing their best. Family is one of those things where everyone doesn't have to like each other or get along all that well, but where people try hard to make space for one another — the work of acknowledgment and space-making is just as important as love.

I think of this when I think about the adaptations that will be necessary in the coming decades — the tribe, I think, is due for a comeback. There's too much work for one person, or even a nuclear family. Sometimes the tribes will be biological in nature. Sometimes they will be mostly chosen. Most often, I think, they will be odd intersections of both, of ties that are formal and informal, broken and whole. Not everyone with a title will be connected — some ties will be lost in the mists of time and space. The big tribal tent is a place to start teaching my kids about how they are tied to other people — that a wide range of possible connections all matter. That you can be tied by love or liking, by biology or habit, by proximity or someone else falling in love. That you can tie and untie, but not necessarily undo relationships — that breakups and divorce, death and the failure of formal acknowledgment do not mean there is nothing there. I do know that when I counted for my sons all the names of the people who cared for them, the numbers rose higher than my littlest one can count.

I: Revisiting the brother-in-law on the couch

There are a few pieces of mine that have taken on a life of their own and been recirculated many times — one of them, reproduced in *Depletion and Abundance,* was an essay called "The Brother-In-Law on the Couch Version of the Apocalypse." I argued that the face of peak oil, climate change and the coming hard times for most of us may look less like our Mad Max fantasies and much more like our friends and family members losing their jobs and homes and coming to live with us. I joked that the reason moving in together got less discussion than ammo was that many of us are far more troubled by the idea of actually having to live with our relatives than we are with more extreme scenarios involving being gunned down for the world's last tube of toothpaste.

In the years since I wrote this essay, everything that's happened has just made it more clear that our future is communal — that we simply can't afford the 850 square feet of personal space we allot to the average American, or the ridiculous home and energy costs that went with this. We are already seeing this happen — the foreclosure crisis has already been bringing people together, whether they like it or not. The incredibly high joblessness rate among the very young means that moving back in with your parents is more common than ever.

This will only continue for many reasons — an aging population will need more help just as services are being slashed for them, leaving them little choice but to rely on family. More natural disasters will mean more refugees sharing housing.

We chose consciously to share housing with family — Eric's grandparents came to live with us on our farm, and stayed with us until their deaths. The space they lived in stayed empty for several years, and then we acquired a housemate to share resources with — Phil was a graduate student of Eric's and a friend of ours, and he lived with us for a while. We are currently seeking new housemates, as Phil moved in with his girlfriend.

These were planned consolidations. In the case of Eric's grandparents, we bought the house together with them for their future. We also very much wanted to do it — which doesn't mean it didn't come fraught with drama and emotion, both with other family members and those of us doing the living. Doing it on the fly out of necessity would have been ten times harder.

Which brings us to rule number one for making transitions easier — when possible, consolidate earlier rather than later. If you know it is coming, get the process underway. This won't work for everyone in every situation, but if you are facing hard times with your eighty-year-old mother living in another city a hundred and fifty miles from any of her kids, start talking with your siblings about getting her closer. No, she may not want to and you may not want to, and starting the conversation may be difficult. But with the exception of families that have abandoned all ties, dealing with this now is going to be a thousand times more pleasant than trying to get your mother into your home in the midst of an energy crisis and a blizzard.

If you know you are the one your feckless sister is going to rely on when she dumps her next boyfriend, start planning where she's going to sleep. If you know that elderly parents, disabled relatives or people with kids are likely to end up needing you, now is probably a good time to begin adapting your house, not just to living with your own personal needs in mind but to living with other people. Installing those shower bars, putting in an additional composting toilet in that extra closet, getting the kids used to the idea of sharing a room — these are things you can start now.

If it is you who will be moving, now is the time to think about how that might work — who will you share with? How would the logistics go forward? It can be quite hard to persuade people to adopt such arrangements before they need to — privacy is such a strong issue, and most of us see such arrangements as fundamentally defeatist. We mistakenly imagine that the ideal way of life should have us owning our own place, living autonomously as a nuclear family or an individual. This ideal should, however, come under serious scrutiny — most of human history was not spent this way. It is important to realize that this fragmentation of families and communities is enormously profitable to many of the people who have encouraged us to believe we should not want to share.

I write about this in more detail in *Depletion and Abundance*, but we should be somewhat suspicious of our sense that we need the huge spaces in most American houses for reasons of actual privacy — less than seventy-five years ago, the average American had sufficient privacy with about 250 square feet each; now the average is above 850. Is it really true that we have some biological need for that level of privacy? Or is it that just as we've been sold a whole lot of other things, we've been sold this idea that we can't live in close quarters and should regard doing so as a move of last resort? Not that the "room of one's own" doesn't have merits — but Virginia Woolf was not talking about a 1000-square-foot great room of our own, but a tiny garret.

Figuring out how such family members can be integrated into your lives — or you into theirs — is another thing you can do now. What role are they going to have in your household? How are all of you (and those providing the home are not off the hook on this) going to compromise to keep everyone happy and working together? Being the homeowner gives you some privileges, such as establishing basic home and safety rules, but tyranny is neither nice nor a good idea, unless you want to live in constant conflict.

It is also worth remembering that, in many cases, the arrival of family may not be an imposition on you, but your salvation — more and more of us are already struggling to pay the mortgage and keep up with the other bills. The only way we may be able to heat homes and keep payments up is by bringing in others to contribute. We may only be able to get a home by buying out a share from a family member in the future. Even if you don't need them financially, there's going to be a lot more work to do in the lower-energy future — the things we used to use energy for will now be done by people. The nuclear family or single life are not especially optimal for this scenario, so you should probably leave the "this is my house and you'll do as I say" thinking at the door. If you are moving in with others and they don't grasp this, try and address it head on from early days.

It isn't always clear that the person with the best "homestead" skills will necessarily be the most useful person — what if they can't get along with others, are so caught up in other issues that they can't utilize their skills, or even if what is most needed is not another person who knows how to can food but someone who can hold down enough of a job to keep the mortgage payments coming? It isn't always clear how things will work in hard times — keeping one's options open for the people who matter to you is always helpful. Don't prejudge others.

It probably goes without saying that all of us would prefer useful, helpful, kind people we get along with — those mythical cousins who are professional gardeners and cabinetmakers, and their grown son who can lift a refrigerator straight over his head and never complains about anything. Instead you will probably be getting the real cousins — a computer programmer who doesn't like to go outside because of all the bugs, his testy wife who spends two hours a day doing her hair, their surly teenager who wants nothing to do with any of you and an elderly, snappish and incontinent dachshund. I'd throw you a pity party but I've got relatives of my own.

The challenge here is to find the good and useful skill set and the fine traits underlying the obnoxious ones. Sometimes this is simply not possible, but you'd be surprised how often it is. The computer programmer may not be great at outdoor work, but may be tireless at tending and teaching the young kids in the family. His wife may not shine in the mornings during hair time, but is a hard worker and great at organizing a new business. The teenager may not want much to do with you, but set to finding ways to save money on food, he may come up with a plan that keeps everyone eating. And perhaps the dog will heroically scare off a burglar someday. A certain optimism and good humor is necessary in these relationships.

Some of this is, of course, less likely than others. Some people are just twits. But that's another argument for taking in the less twittish parts of your family early on — so you can say to your sister in Peoria, "Sorry, I've got Mom and Uncle Tito and cousin Maria. That means you get Kim and the three little devils … er … darlings."

It will help, in all of this, if you can find ways to structure your house that give everyone some space and privacy — although not necessarily as much as they were used to. That might mean knocking down a wall to make dormitory-style accommodations for four girl cousins, or at least hanging curtains so that families can have a little privacy. If you can divide family space by floor, or by using separate entrances, it may make the transition to closer quarters easier.

A large part of the practicalities are personal for the people involved — you cannot necessarily predict their reactions. What is important is that people be respectful, that they work on making roles and accommodations for one another, and that they do their best to let go of past assumptions. Honestly, many of us spent some of the happiest times of our lives living closely with others — in service, at college and after becoming independent. Simply determining that such relationships could be positive, the symbol not of a loss but the reclamation of something, might help ease the pressure and anxiety we feel about them. At least until the incontinent dachshund arrives.

II. A pallet on the floor: preparing for refugees

> Well, I was broke and so dissatisfied
> Yeah, I was broke and so dissatisfied
> I was broke and dissatisfied
> I damned nearly died
> And then you made me a pallet on the floor
> Yes, you made me a pallet on the floor
> Yes, you made me a pallet on the floor.
> When I had no place to go
> You opened up your door
> And you made me a pallet on the floor.
>
> — *"Made Me A Pallet on the Floor,"*
> traditional folk song covered by the likes of Doc Watson

After the last few years, does anyone really need convincing that they may someday have to be prepared for friends, family or strangers they want to help to arrive at their doorstep in need? All over America, people were fleeing — floodwaters in the Midwest, wildfires in California, hurricanes in Texas, New Orleans, New York and Vermont, ice storms and extended power outages in the Northeast, blizzards in the mid-Atlantic. The pace of "natural" disasters is rising rapidly and that means more evacuations, more people in crisis. And in a crisis you go to those you know will care for you — or if you have no one, you are cast forth on the kindness of strangers.

What can those who are prepared to stay in place do for those who can't? I'm going to explore the practicalities of dealing with people who arrive, often on short notice, sometimes after experiencing great trauma or physical harm, and who first and foremost need, as the song goes, "a pallet on the floor." There are issues to dealing with long-term refugees as well, but this gets you started with those in real crisis.

Only you can know how many people are likely to see you as a potential refuge, and how many you are prepared to accept — my own feeling is that, in a short-term crisis, many of us can make do with fairly tight conditions for some time. Moreover, while some people tend to take a hard line and say, "You didn't listen when I told you to prepare, so I'm not going to help you," this is a tough stance to maintain when you have to shut the door on an injured family member who approaches you for help. I suspect most of us, whatever internal resentments we may have, will sigh and open up. Me, I've never even pretended I would take a hard line. We never know when it will be us who needs to evacuate or move rapidly, so compassion is a wise approach.

Now is the time to do some counting. And when you count, remember that your family (as always, I mean both biological and chosen "family" — the people who count in your life and count on you) has family too — that is, you sister's partner may not be able to evacuate without bringing her elderly mother along, and your brother-in-law may show up on your couch with his brother-in-law, his sister and their two kids. Yes, it may seem strange to count that way, but if the situation is dire enough, if all the motels are full, if they've been through hell — what are they going to do? Abandon those who matter most to them? In one sense, it may seem like this simplifies the idea of "extended family" — in other ways it may complicate it.

Most short-term crises that require mass evacuation are regional — but it isn't inconceivable that larger-scale crises could occur. And if your family and friends are comparatively concentrated, you may have large numbers expecting to rely on you, especially if they know that you are the "prepared one." It is also worth remembering that such arrivals don't necessarily require a natural disaster — in some families, someone's sense of shame might mean that you didn't learn about a foreclosure, divorce, abusive marriage or eviction until they need a place to stay *right now*.

OK, first of all, how can we prepare in advance for the population of our homes to double, triple or quadruple? Some of us can't, much. Either we are operating so close to the bone that we don't have any reserves for this hypothetical or we have so little space we can't prepare much. But since the average American has more than 850 square feet per person, there probably is room for many of us to make preparations for such a contingency.

In order of priority, I'd say the preparations should go like this:

1. Food

Having more food in storage is a good idea for many of us anyway, and it is important to remember that in a crisis, you may be better off than others, but not able to engage in normal activity — the stores may be closed at your place too, the power may be out, or you simply may not be able to afford to buy food for seventeen, while your visitors may have left without cash.

Having some simple-to-heat-up foods is a good idea for evacuation bags, but may also be wise for those first hours when refugees are arriving and simply need to be fed. Remember, if a crisis is widespread enough, or the evacuation notice short enough, you may be close to the disaster yourself and without power or other resources.

Besides some quickly prepared food, it is good to add to your general stocks as well. Basic staple foods mean that you can feed twice as many people fairly easily — more rice in the soup, another box of pasta. These things can mean everyone eats. I go into much more detail on this subject in *Independence Days: A Guide to Sustainable Food Storage and Preservation* than I can here.

2. Beds

How many people can you sleep now, if you tighten and consolidate sleeping arrangements? It should go without saying that children can be moved out of their beds to sleeping bags on the floor, the parents' bed or consolidated into sleeping together to allow older adults more comfortable arrangements. If you have the space, replacing couches with sleeper couches or futons, adding these to extra rooms and acquiring extra mattresses that can be stored, trundle style, under beds can be a good prep — and useful for weekend parties or other fun causes as well. All this gear is often inexpensive or free (people give away futons, mattresses and old sleeper couches all the time on my local Craigslist and Freecycle) for the hauling and can make your experience a lot more pleasant and comfortable for everyone.

Once you are maxed out on beds, the next step might be the proverbial pallet on the floor — a tatami mat, carpet remnant or camping pad with a sleeping bag or set of blankets on top. Air mattresses are OK, as long as you have the tools and time to fill them manually, since power may be out. Futons can be double layered in many cases — making the bed more comfy while they aren't needed, with the extra pulled out and moved to the living room when called upon.

Extra blankets, sheets, towels and other bedding are often cheaply available at garage sales and thrift shops — and, thanks to an AIP student's tip, one good way to store them if you are tight for space is between the mattress and box spring of your bed, laid flat.

3. Medical supplies

We'll talk a bit more about medical issues in the next chapter, but at a minimum refugees are likely to be exhausted, stressed out and suffering from wicked headaches. In the worst case, they may have been burned, have walked for miles, have serious injuries, be starving or dehydrated or suffering from hypothermia, heat stroke or the lack of a needed medication. And again, it is worth remembering that your place may not be free of consequences either — just because you are *safer* doesn't mean the power is on and the hospital isn't packed, on skeleton staff and miles away by foot. While you can't meet every need, you will be useful if you can evaluate the situation and, if it's not too urgent, provide basic solutions — painkillers, a splint for a sprained ankle, warmth, rehydration, bandages.

4. Clothing, baby stuff, toys and other optional extras

This is one of those things that can usually be finessed, so I put it on with the recognition that most people may not need to worry about it much. If she has to, your mother, who is five feet tall and weighs ninety-three pounds, will wear your five-sizes-too-big clothes, as will your eleven-year-old nephew. If worst comes to worst, your six-foot-three, three-hundred-pound cousin may not fit into your five-foot-nine, hundred-and-forty-five-pound husband's clothes, but there's probably some big guy in your neighborhood who can spare a sweatshirt and pants.

But if you have the space and energy to deal with it, it isn't a bad idea to do a quick evaluation of who might end up your way, and pick up flexibly sized (i.e., stretch waists, cotton T-shirts, sweatshirts and sweat pants, cardigan sweaters) clothes that might meet their basic needs of those most likely to come your way — or if they are friendly to the idea, invite people to leave an outfit or two at your place. Everyone will be happier if they are warm and wearing clothes that neither expose intimate bits nor leave them freezing or frying, and the clothes they traveled in may be unusable. My suggestion for this would be bag sales, often held on the last day of large rummage and garage sales — people want to get rid of stuff, so around me they offer "fill a bag for X tiny sum" (often 50 cents or a dollar), and the bag is often a garbage bag! (This is also a good place to get interesting fabrics for patchwork quilting, old sweaters for unraveling to knit with, and felted sweaters that can be cut up to make felt mittens — oh, and clothes for you and your family.) I'm not sure I'd devote a lot of energy to this — but it isn't hard to get sizes for people you love (mention birthdays), and if you keep a list and run into cheap clothing in quantity, having an outfit or two (shoes included, if possible) for any likely refugees will make things go smoother.

The same is true of baby things, a few toys and any special needs items for medically fragile or disabled family members. No, we can't plan for everything, but if there are a lot of pregnant women and young kids in your family, bag sales that offer cloth diapers and small clothes, some toys to distract the kids (these are also useful when they come to visit) and a few children's books can go a long way to making things nicer. But if you don't have the space or the time, this is the time to call upon the neighbors. A few decks of cards or board games might be smart as a way of organizing and distracting a large crowd that is also listening in terror to bad news or watching their beloved home be washed away on TV.

OK, let's say, prepared or not, your family is here, now. What do you do?

1. Triage their situation

What do they need right now? Medical care? Food? A place to rest? While some evacuees may arrive in a good situation and mood, most are likely to be extremely traumatized, and as mentioned above, some may be injured, in shock or otherwise in serious trouble. We will assume that you already know minimal first aid, and how to evaluate someone's conditions. If not, please learn — and check the reference section in the back of this book. If the hospitals are operational and can be reached, and aren't a greater risk than staying home, someone should be deputized to take the injured for treatment. If not, get out that collection of medical books, make people comfortable and do what you can for them. Learn to recognize the signs of shock. Warm the cold and cool the hot gently. Rehydrate them. Pay particular attention to children and anyone unable to articulate their situation.

If someone is in a serious medical condition but cannot get to the hospital, do what you can to stabilize them and begin working with your community to arrange transport as soon as possible. Know which of your neighbors are doctors, nurses, EMTs or other practitioners and call on them if needed.

If someone arrives ill with some obviously contagious (and serious) illness, you will need to make arrangements to isolate them immediately, and assign someone to care for the sick person, who will also remain in isolation from the rest of the household. You will need, at a minimum, a room, and ideally a bathroom (although a bucket toilet and plenty of water will do), as well as lots of bedding, gloves and masks if you have them, bleach to disinfect and a place for the caregiver to sleep. If there are a few of them and the illness is highly contagious, you may need to quarantine a whole group — so think about how to allocate space (people who are not sick but have been exposed should be kept separate from those who are actively ill, to reduce the dangers).

2. Start out by being a refuge, a place to recover

The first hours or even day is no time to begin laying down anything more than the minimal necessary rules — provide as much quiet as you can, food, a chance to talk about the experience or the option not to, as comfortable an environment as possible, support and kindness. Feed everyone something comforting if possible — soup or something else familiar and not too difficult to digest. If possible, you might give up your room, at least for the first twenty-four hours, to allow exhausted adults a chance to sleep. Continue to keep an eye on children, who may express their feelings about the experience in unexpected ways. This period may need to last longer for the seriously injured or those who are quite elderly, medically fragile or disabled.

3. If the situation goes on for more than a day or two, you are going to have to begin the work of actually living together

Especially if there are a lot of people in close proximity, this is likely to be annoying at times — everyone will need time and space when they are not around each other. Visitors may seem ungrateful or demanding, while you may be impatient and frustrated with the disruption. The first and perhaps most important thing you can do is to take some deep breaths and recognize that for now, you are stuck with each other, and that fighting and expressing every feeling you have will not help you. Courtesy is paramount here, and in most families, a polite measure of shutting up.

There are some extended families that can lovingly and respectfully discuss their disagreements even at the worst of times, when everyone is under enormous psychological stress — they do not constitute anything even remotely like a statistical majority, however. I'm going to suggest that in the very short term the appropriate way of handling most of our emotions is "suck it up" — I realize that this flies in the face of the conventional psychological wisdom that self-expression is good for you, but in this case, we are attempting to achieve the greatest possible good for the maximum number of people.

This is also NOT the time to discuss or try to resolve old problems. Table them for now and, to the extent it is possible, decline to revisit them even with determined family members. Any discussion that begins "You always ..." is probably a bad one to have now.

So how do you live together in the long term? What if this all goes on for a while? This is obviously a longer subject than can be covered fully in one chapter, but here are some strategies.

1. Post the rules you really care about — write 'em out, post them publicly, and enforce them equitably

Yes, I know you understand that your kids are acting out because they are under stress, while your SIL's kid is a little monster all the time. Tough patooties — everyone has the same rules, barring inability to understand or inability to physically obey them. But resist the urge to be a complete control freak, or to make sure that your life runs exactly the way it always has. If this is something you suffer from as a matter of personality, do your best to suspend it. Yes, it is appropriate to make rules about lengths of showers and washing out your breakfast dishes. No, your house isn't going to be as tidy, your kids aren't going to be as well behaved and things aren't going to be normal for a while — too many restrictions lead to mutiny and failures and more crisis.

2. Give everyone as much space and privacy as humanly possible

Everyone is likely to be feeling cramped and sick of one another — so try and give them a break. Someone has to go grocery shopping? Be gracious — take your kids and theirs and leave the other couple alone for a short while. Plan on being outside as much as humanly possible, given risks and climate. Remember, your spouse or kids or housemate may be having a lot of trouble too — give them some space as well. Send the kids off to a playdate, let the boyfriend run the errands alone.

3. Bring in more people — really

You and your family in a tiny lifeboat alone may be awfully tough — so invite the neighbors over. Yes, they take up space too, but they'll talk to your mom for a while so you can do the dishes, and maybe they have a suggestion for a local apartment or a senior center event that people might want to attend. Giving your family other people than you to talk to is good.

This goes doubly and triply for children. If you aren't used to kids, you may think that the idea of inviting three neighbor siblings over to play with the three kids invading your house already sounds like hell on earth. But six kids can be easier than three bored kids who want you to entertain them and have nothing to do but express their trauma with their parents and relatives. Bring over the neighbor kids and they may suddenly disappear out into the yard or the basement to entertain themselves and give you some much-needed breathing space.

4. Let people know what you like about this, and them

There may not be much, but there are good things about an extended in-house camping trip with your family. They are likely to be feeling vulnerable, like they are a burden. They may be tiptoeing around you, afraid that you'll throw them out and leave them with nowhere to go. Letting people know that even though this is annoying, you love them and appreciate that they do the dishes and keep the kids quiet in the morning so that you can sleep in, that you like having them around and wish the visit could be under better circumstances, is good — especially (but not exclusively) if it is true.

In many families, giving people useful work and a way to contribute will go a long way to relieving the sense of burden. Let them make dinner or help you fix the roof, if they can. Part of generosity is not making people feel overly beholden — do what you can to allow people to feel part of your family and routine, as if they were participants.

5. Expect trauma and fear to manifest themselves

People who have lost their homes or don't know whether they have one, people who are missing family members or who have been through hell and back, are messed up. You would be too. They are likely to be angry sometimes, weepy, afraid, oversensitive. They may do stupid things. The kids may seem badly behaved, act like much younger children, be hostile or fearful.

As much as you can, chalk up the difficulties to this, even if you have your doubts. Give them the benefit of the doubt you'd want in the same situations. Make clear that some responses are utterly unacceptable — there will be no violence, no drug or alcohol abuse. For those who seem to be moving into pathological responses to trauma, get them help as fast as you can.

OK, how do you bring this situation to a logical conclusion, assuming you don't want to make it permanent?

If the problem disappears on its own — the rain comes and reduces the wildfire risk, the floodwaters recede and the house is still OK, the disaster was largely averted — it may be as simple as helping them pack, giving hugs goodbye and waving as they drive back to their normal lives. But what if it isn't like that? What if the house was burned, the area is contaminated and uninhabitable in the long term or your family members refuse to ever go back, for fear that it might happen again?

Then you need to help them get established somewhere else, or begin to really live together. Some people may be able to take the initiative on this themselves, or the living conditions may be all the incentive they need, but the elderly, the very traumatized and people who simply aren't go-getters may need help settling in. You might need to devote some time and energy to helping them find an apartment, apply for needed services, look for a job. If yours is the only car, phone and computer, you may need to share more than you'd like. Remember, it is for a good cause.

If this is a crisis that is symptomatic of our larger one, now is probably a good time to encourage your family members to think about that for the long term — to suggest that instead of rebuilding somewhere wildfire prone, they consider a safer area, or to suggest that if the relationship is good, maybe they stay near you (or if it is bad, that they relocate to some distant city with opportunities; now is a good time to think about how to avoid this happening again).

You may, at some point, have to be blunt. After a reasonable grace period it is appropriate to tell people, "Look, we need to get you settled in a place and the kids enrolled in school, so I expect you to start looking for next month, if that's possible, and I'll expect you to take that part-time job you were offered while the kids are in school, and start paying rent." In a few cases, you may need eventually to evict people who have moved from "refugee" to "freeloader." If so, all adult permanent residents should agree and send a consistent message: "We were glad to have you while we could, but we simply can't anymore." Do try not to punish children for the sins of their parents, however.

Will all this advice make the sudden descent of ten of your closest friends and relatives seem like unmitigated bliss? Probably not. But it may make the thought manageable, and might help you shift from thinking about how overwhelming it could be to how grateful you are that you can help, that your loved ones are safe, and that they probably will be leaving soon.

Giving care

For someone in her thirties, I have a fairly large experience of being someone's caregiver. In high school, I began working in a nearby nursing home. I can't remember quite what drove me to seek that work out — it was not the kind of work that most teenagers I knew did. I think what intrigued me about it was its importance — as a teenager seeking meaning, caring for people at the end of their lives seemed urgent.

It was only later that I came to realize that taking care of the elderly and disabled was, in our society, viewed as not only not urgent, but not integral or important, either. Even as a teenager, I couldn't understand why it was treated as unskilled labor, when it seemed to require such a complex measure of compassion, kindness, physical strength and humor. Why weren't my fellow caregivers, most of whom were supporting families, better paid? I never did come to fully understand it, in all the years I spent working in nursing homes and hospices.

Later, as an adult, my husband and I chose to care for his grandparents in their last years. This was by no means easy, and devoured a large portion of our existence at a time when we also had very small children and infants. It was exhausting, stressful and sometimes very sad. It was also wonderful in many ways — a gift to my children to know their great-grandparents intimately, a gift to us to know them so well, a gift to us to understand that what we were doing is part of a cycle that they had done for their parents. Acknowledging that something is a gift does not mean it is always easy or pleasant or joyous, but I have no regrets and would do the same again in a heartbeat, because it needed to be done.

Parenting is not caregiving — one gives care to one's children, but within expected parameters as they grow and increase in strength and ability. My oldest son's increases do not work the way most children's do, and one of the measures of his development is how we gently approach the day in which I will shift from the ordinary work of parenting to the less typical (but still very common) work of caregiving to my adult child, who will probably never live fully independently.

This comes with some sorrows and ambivalences, of course — and with the recognition that, someday, this responsibility will have to pass to someone else, when Eric and I can no longer care for Eli. This is a scary thing. But on the whole, caring for Eli is also a gift and a delight — even when it is messy, tiring and stressful. I know it will be my work for the whole of my life in one way or another, and that does not frighten or horrify me — although it occasionally seems exhausting, since my son is rather like a two-year-old, but with the physical abilities of a very large twelve-year-old, and will only get bigger. Still, the rewards and return of loving Eli are enough, and we try to frame our future as the project of making a life that includes our child and meets our needs as well. It is an art project, this life we make.

There may be more caregiving roles in our future. My husband is an only child — and it is he who will face the responsibility of any care his parents need (G-d willing little and long from now). Eric and I have agreed to act as guardians for a child in our extended family, a little girl with serious disabilities, like Eli, and a mother who is a full generation older than we are. Again, someday, hopefully long from now, we will be responsible for her care and helping her navigate her life. We are also foster parents who hope to adopt — and foster children have higher rates of disability and mental illness than the average, so caregiving may be part of as-yet unanticipated relationships as well.

I cannot say we look at each of these future obligations with delight, but we wish to live in the kind of family, the kind of world, where families make a place for people who are not able-bodied or fully able to reciprocate, and in order to live in that world someday when I need care, I must begin to make it with my own hands.

One of the questions that comes up more than any other in our Adapting in Place class is what to do about aging and retirement, how to avoid being a burden on another person, particularly if they cannot count on their retirement savings cushioning their experience. I don't have a good answer, but the ones I can come up with are these. First, it is not necessarily inherently burdensome to need help — that is merely a responsibility, and if they can be lived and handled gracefully, responsibilities are not crushing.

Moreover, in the course of our lives, every one of us will be dependent upon someone else — perhaps for only a few moments, perhaps for many years. Many of us will be disabled, elderly, ill, fragile, injured. It is an illusion to think that by saving money and hiring people, we can avoid "being a burden" — instead, what we can do is shift our dependencies onto professionals. If those professionals are fairly paid and enjoy their work, they may not find you to be a burden. I can say from experience, however, that sometimes they do. Money doesn't make you less burdensome, it merely makes people less free to tell you that they find you burdensome.

I point this out because I think we misframe the relationship when we speak of this as a choice between "money to pay for assistance, no money to pay for assistance and thus a burden." Instead, I think it is important to remember that dependencies are mutual — and that the relationships that are burdensome are not based on reciprocities and acknowledgments. That is, it was not a burden to care for Eric's grandparents because even though I had not been raised and cared for by them, my husband had that experience, and I had the experience of being welcomed, included and loved by them. It was also less of a weight because I knew they understood what the experience was like — they had done the same for Inge's parents and could see it from my perspective. And in talking and listening to them, I could see a small view of my future, and how I would want to be treated and cared for myself. Doing this for them was a way of doing it for myself, in anticipation.

For a whole host of reasons — demographic, economic, energy-linked and environmental — giving care is going to be a more important job in the future. More of us will have to care for one another, where institutions could once do so. More of us will have to rely on people we know rather than our savings. More of us face the terrible fragility of those questions — who will care for me, how will I manage to care for them?

And for all that I do not find my own work as a caregiver to be unpleasant, I know that it can be hard. I've been fortunate — we were able to integrate Eric's grandparents into our lives, and our son, as autistic children go, is easy. I tell everyone that Eric and I won the lottery. I know people who deal with complex medical situations, with recalcitrant and angry Alzheimer's patients, with mental illnesses that simply are unmanageable. I wish I had a good and magic answer for how we're going to do this. I don't. All I can say is that many more of us will be struggling with this project, trying to do the very best we can. More of us will have to begin earlier — having conversations and speaking to one another and, more importantly, creating the kind of deep relationships of biology or choice that make it possible to take without reciprocating based on a long and deep history of generosity, a well of shared experience and love that makes it possible to draw deep when there's nothing left.

Ultimately, I think giving care is part of what makes us human, of what makes us moral. I hope that institutional responses to our coming collective crisis will be sufficient to help those who need it the most, although I am not wholly optimistic. But for those looking down the reality that all of us age, suffer illness and face times of needing care, the only real answer I can give — and it is no solution, just a part of the answer — is that we must begin to conceive the act of giving care correctly, as part of our lives, begin to speak of it and make space for it, and most of all, find our way to navigate this essential and yet not fully visible path in our lives.

None of us, if we think of it, want to live in the kind of world where there is no place for those who cannot participate fully. And that means that each of us has an obligation to do the work of making this harsher, warmer, poorer world still a place with space for those who are old, who are weak, who are ill, who are disabled. We need to make sure that they are fully integrated into our lives, because they deserve it, because we know that someday we will be them too, and our only hope is living in a world that gives care.

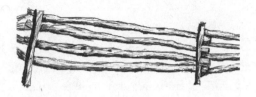

Twelve

Is your love enough?

Everybody wants to live the life of kings and queens
But nobody wants to stay and plow the fields
Everybody wants to tell their neighbors how to live
But nobody wants to listen to how they feel
And it goes on and on and on and on and on
For a thousand years, a thousand years I say
And it goes on and on and on and on and on
What language are your tears?
But what I got to say right now
Is love enough yeah, love enough?
Or can you love some more?

> — Michael Franti & Spearhead,
> "Is Love Enough?"

I. Towards an economy of love

VARIATIONS ON THE OBLIGATION TO LOVE ONE'S NEIGHBOR show up across both the religious and secular spectrum. They tend to provoke a range of responses — from those who attempt to sort out what loving people who are not part of your immediate tribe would mean to those who reject the necessity outright. This is not an easy idea, and even if you can sort out what it means to love people you may not know well, or like much, or even trust, or know how to get to knowing, liking and trusting — it is a damned hard thing to put into practice. I will also talk about practical strategies for loving one's neighbor, but here I want to say a bit more about why we even use the word love and why we might want do the hard work of finding a way to love others.

Because rather than talking about "working" with your neighbors or "getting along" I want to talk about the problem of actually loving them, despite the difficulties that the word love raises. It is the right word — it is no accident that we speak of moral obligation in these terms. In this case, I would suggest that we all think about "love," not as a particular feeling you have to evoke but as a larger structure for our relationships, a way of organizing our world.

The danger, of course, of speaking about love is that it evokes a range of things — religious beliefs, romantic and familial feelings, and occasionally a certain dippy, intellectually vacant lack of specificity, the idea that our relationships will all be productive if we do group hugs and sing in a circle regularly.

However, I'd make the case for a language and world of love that is as rigorous as any mathematics, as formally structured as any economy. That is, it is not loving people to express things lovingly all the time. It is not loving one another simply to articulate your common ground, or to allow everyone to "express" their differences, or to be universally supportive, or to fall backward off a chair. Love is needing each other — not in easy or cheap ways, but really, truly needing one another. It does not require that you share beliefs, or even like each other — all of us can call examples from our biological families that support this fact.

In this, love is not a feeling or a particular social practice. It is the replacement, at least when possible, of a world that thinks in terms of maximization of personal profit and extraction with one that maximizes interdependence and the well-being of the group, not just the individual. And it requires that we risk depending on one another — that we give up owning every single item we might ever need personally and trust that our neighbors will share with us and we with them. That we trust that our children will care for us when we grow old, and they trust that we will help them as they get started. It requires, that is, that we extend our need outside of our most intimate world — and allow others to fulfill it, knowing that things may never come up truly even.

The most frightening thing about the loss of our fossil energies may be that we will again be thrown back upon our own resources — and if we think of our personal lives as having to replace each and every watt and gallon, we know we can never make it happen. So "our own" has to expand into a larger community. We have to be able to risk that to survive. And that risk is ugly and frightening if we think that all it is is a risk — but it changes when we begin to think about that vulnerability as both creating the conditions to be loved and creating and increasing the capacity to love, too.

I think a lot of people find the notion of being dependent upon others frightening, and not without reason. Other people are sometimes less reliable and more complicated than lawn mowers, dishwashers and private cars. And when, as often happens, the balance of what they do for me shifts and I've done less and they've done more, we're grateful, but uncomfortable with the necessity of gratitude at times.

Risking owing someone more than you can pay is frightening. Indebtedness to real people rather than abstract companies is difficult. No one wants to be the one who owes more, and most of us are on some level afraid of being taken advantage of as well. More than being owed, I think we're afraid of owing. We have this notion that all debts must be paid, when in fact, the only way all debts can be paid is if you live wholly and purely in a money economy — it can never happen in the economy of love. We probably cannot love one another if we are too afraid to share. And we cannot go forward by replacing a full set of low-energy, private infrastructure in each private home. As Auden put it, the stakes are simply these — we must love one another or die.

The economy of human love is what we're moving toward as we give up our electric tools and our reliance on the grocery stores and replace them with reliance on our neighbors, our families and our communities. That is the basic nature of community or family — an unbalanced, imperfect, inadequate set of exchanges. Barter and sharing and community are, as people often point out, far less efficient than money. And that lack of efficiency is entirely the point.

Money allows you to figure out what things are "worth" — with barter or simple sharing, there are things that can never be quite worked out. Is that firewood equivalent to twenty dozen eggs and a bushel of plums? Was it really enough for me to babysit in exchange for the help getting the gutters cleaned out? Should I make some cookies too? What is the correct repayment to someone for loving your child, or helping care for your elderly parents, or chasing the local pest dog across an icy field to rescue your chicken, other than someday doing it for them, or for someone else in need?

Things never come out evenly. You always have to be grateful, and thus, dependent. If we give up all the things that have stood as barriers between ourselves and the people we need, that have enabled us never to be dependent, we're never again going to be square. The only hope is that the person you are working with or bartering with or sharing with is secretly afraid that she/he hasn't done his fair share either.

But then again, that's what love is, isn't it? I've never met anyone who loved someone or was truly loved by someone else who didn't secretly think that their spouse (or parents or child or friend) was crazy to love them, that if they could really see all the way through to their depths, they'd realize how inequitable things are, and how little they deserve that love. So you end up just being grateful, feeling damned lucky that this time, you got more than you ever deserved. A gift appeared to you, and someone loves you — how miraculous is that?

Now we may never feel love for the guy down the street who leaves his motor running all morning in the same way we love our partners or children or parents. But we can have with him and with most people (not all, but most) those same moments of feeling we haven't done enough to deserve the help we get, the trust we can have in him when he drops off the kids at school or helps you fix the roof. You don't have to even like him to feel that moment of certainty — that you have gotten better and more than you truly deserve. Then you find a way to return that feeling, to make him say, "Well, they are weird and they dress funny, but we're lucky to have them."

That is the love economy — the sense that you can never quite be even, that you never get only what you deserve or what you earned. It is hard to articulate what it is that you do get — that along with the eggs or the hands or the shoulder to cry on, came something that most of us know now only through lovers, children, parents, G-d, if that's your sort of thing. I think the easiest, although religiously laden word for it is "Grace."

I am not claiming that the money economy is going away, or that we will all have the energy to live entirely in the world of love every moment, or that loving our neighbors as ourselves will be easy, or that every exercise in dependency and community will be a success. What I am claiming is this — that we will learn to love each other, or we will face a much harder and darker world. And our success in that world will almost certainly depend on the space we can find for an economy of love in the economy of money, and a culture of love in the culture of distance.

Sometimes all you and your neighbors will have is, "I've got honey, will you give me carrots?" And sometimes all neighbors are people you can ask to help pound the fence pole in. And sometimes all friends are the people you sit down at the table and laugh with. But the day you start to trust that your neighbor will remember that you need some carrots, and the day that your neighbors step away from their own work, no matter how urgent, because keeping you secure and your sheep in is more important than their work, and the day that the friend sits at your table and shares the fruits of her garden and you the fruits of yours, and you eat and you eat and you eat and you are full together of what you share, you have achieved not just community, but grace, and an economy of love.

II. Love, schmove

Above I waxed philosophical on what it might mean to love your neighbors, and how we might build a love economy in our communities. This is important, but now let's get down to brass tacks. How do you deal with the neighbors who you not only do not love yet, but can barely tolerate — and who haven't expressed any particular desire to love you, unless you count letting their dog poop in your yard? How about the ones you already can't stand — or who can't stand you?

This is one of those things I feel proud of our family's ability to do — build community, not just with those carefully selected for like-mindedness but with real neighbors. I have a good relationship with my neighbors — we've shared a lot of things over the years, including childcare, a car, our washing machines, stress, gossip, meals and time. I trust that I could get their help in a crisis — and I hope they trust that they would have mine — in part because we have helped each other through various things.

Does this paradise of neighborliness exist in a place where everyone shares our values and opinions? Not hardly. We cover the range of political opinions from far left to far right to "don't give a damn." We cover a reasonable religious range — protestants of several stripes, from AME to Lutheran to evangelical, to Catholics, pagans, atheists and us, the neighborhood Jews. As for visions of the future — well, at least one neighbor reads my blog, but most of them either don't know what peak oil or climate change is, or politely think I'm a loon. We disagree strongly on everything from what should be taught in the public schools to what constitutes a good diet to whether Syracuse making the finals is a cause for celebration.

What we do have is a good deal of common ground on other issues. It is just a matter of finding it — and generally speaking, we find it at fairly basic levels. We all eat, and higher food prices are pinching everyone's purse. Those of us who have kids or grandkids or children in our lives all care about those kids' future. We all want to keep safe, and ensure a decent future for ourselves. We all like being happy, and all of us want a good life.

Now it is absolutely true that some people will have differences about how to get at these things. But it is also true that usually, with most people, you can find some common ground, if you dig around. Yes, they may be mostly concerned with the rising price of sugar cereals and you with your morning bowl of quinoa porridge. But now you have a talking point — your shared concern about food prices. And maybe, just maybe, you have the beginnings of something else — the chance to say, "I'll pick up your sugar-frosted Loopies if they are below X price at my supermarket — will you check the quinoa bin to see if it costs less than this?" And there probably is something you both eat. Or maybe you worry a little bit about gas, and you could share a ride in to the supermarket.

I've only very rarely met someone with whom I could find no common ground at all — and I'm not perfect or unusually good at getting along with others. But there's always something you can share — always.

What about the awful people with whom you are already at war? Sometimes these things can be fixed — sometimes you can learn, if not to get along, to tolerate each other, and work together when absolutely necessary. Saying "I'm sorry" even when it was their fault, or even when you are still mad, can be a starting point. On the other hand, sometimes it isn't going to work. If too many bridges have been burned, the next step is simply to work on your community with someone else — move on to the next house on the road. Nothing I say about community will ever mean that everyone is always working shoulder to shoulder — you can build community, but some people will want nothing to do with it, or only on their own terms. Sometimes there will be factions, or anger, or feuds. The best strategy is to let it go and move on — concentrate on the people who are willing to put differences aside, or those who don't require so much effort. We've all got to decide how to use our energies — chasing the person who hates you may not be the best choice.

I am going to say something that may be a little controversial. Back when I was dating, I met some guys who would tell me about their romantic history, and it turns out that all their ex-girlfriends were either crazy or evil in some way and every relationship had ended badly. And I developed a rule that I pretty much think applies to community building as well — everyone is entitled to one or two or maybe even three (depending on the length of the history) experiences with wackos and bad people. It happens to the best of us. If all their ex-girlfriends are psychos, if not one person they ever dated was someone they could like enough afterward to have a civil relationship, much less a friendship, with, the general rule of thumb was that it wasn't just the other people — it was them.

I realize many people may not like to hear this, but I find this rule useful when people tell me about how they hate all their neighbors, they can't get along with anyone, everyone always betrays them or is trying to hurt them. That stuff happens. It is real. There are bad people out there, as well as fools and creeps, etc. If, however, it happens all the time, either the problem is partly in your ability to have relationships or your inability to prevent being a victim, and you need to do some work on that end as well. That may mean learning to let things go and believing that other people aren't trying to be unkind or hurtful but are simply doing their best. It may mean learning to stand up for yourself and not be a victim. It may mean learning to get along better with people — to not say what you think or demand to do things your way all the time. Sometimes community building is about fixing yourself. I know it sometimes has been for me.

How do you get started, if you don't know your neighbors? Well, one way is to enter into existing community structures. Your community has them — churches, synagogues, mosques, the PTA, the library board, the garden club, the local political parties, action groups for various issues, etc.

I think there's a tendency to underestimate existing community structures, to decide, "Oh, those couldn't possibly be made to serve our goals." But that is what happened, for example, during World War II — existing neighborhood associations, church groups and other community structures were brought together to work on the war effort and help people adjust to big changes like rationing. Often there's more interest than most of us would expect — for example, for years, I mostly kept my work and my synagogue life separate, because I wasn't sure how well they would overlap and I didn't want to seem too pushy. Finally I pushed a little harder to get some green stuff going, and what I've found is that there's more enthusiasm than I had ever expected, and I'm the one telling people to slow down. The moral of the story is that sometimes it is easier than you think to harness the power of extant institutions.

Or perhaps you do need to start something. How do you get your neighbors together? Well, how about some food? Some music? Beer? Nothing builds community like inviting the neighbors over for a meal. Start talking — and listening — to what people are thinking about.

Once you know what they care about, you've got the key to finding a big tent way to start working together — instead of bulk purchasing quinoa, you need to think about finding something everyone uses, or someone else who eats sugar-frosted Loopies to share a bulk order with. What about a clothing swap? A neighborhood-wide yard sale? A babysitting co-op?

Remember, you don't have to tell everyone everything to work together. You can bring up peak oil and climate change, and when the neighbors say, "Well, Newt Gingrich says we have all the oil we'd ever want and that we're approaching an ice age" — let it slide. It doesn't really matter whether your neighbor is buying in bulk to save the planet or to save up for their Disney vacation — you are working together. The idea that people who disagree with you are bad is probably the single most destructive cultural problem in America — don't buy into it.

Sharing stuff is new to a lot of people — and new things are hard. So make sure you keep trying. It might take five times to get an elderly neighbor to agree to let you pick up a carton of milk for her on your way home — the first few times, she might think it was polite to say no, or that you were judging her, or assuming something about her. It might take five times — or even ten — before she realizes you are serious.

Make it fun. If you can get your neighbors to sit down and talk about preparing, or getting ready, make cookies or bring beer. If you are going to share a bulk order, make the night you sort it all out into a party. If you want to start getting together to get work done in your neighborhood, make a big meal and provide games for the kids. Give people the benefit of community right away — don't make them wait for it.

Keep pushing the envelope, even if it is hard. First you borrow a cup of sugar, then you lend one. Next time, when your neighbor mentions her vacuum died, you can say, "Why don't you share mine — I only use it on Tuesdays."

Expect rejection — and don't take it personally. You might have to try a dozen times to come up with something that meets their needs, or they might not care as much as you do about another thing. This is disappointing — but it doesn't mean that they are bad people or they don't like you just because sometimes you have to work to find the right buy-in. Try not to be too judgmental — the guy who mows his lawn in a Speedo probably thinks he's improving the neighborhood aesthetics, or maybe he's just hot. Consider it part of your vibrant local culture.

Most of all, keep at it. Eventually, you won't have to do so much work — community takes on a life of its own.

III. Changing the rules

Over the last fifty years, food and zoning laws have worked to minimize sustainable subsistence activities in populated areas. Not only have we lost the culture of doing for ourselves, but we've instituted legal requirements that make it almost impossible for many people to engage in simple subsistence activities that cut their energy use, reduce their ecological impact and improve their food security and their communities. In some cases, these laws were instituted for fairly good reasons, but in many cases they happened for bad reasons that associate such activities with poverty.

In fact, scratch most of the reasons for these things and you'll find class issues just under the surface, in the name of "property values."

There are ostensible reasons for these laws, but generally speaking, they derive from old senses of what constituted wealth — and what constituted wealth was essentially having things that don't do anything of economic value, but show that you can afford them anyway. It is important to remember that many things we think are ugly because of their class associations are not inherently ugly — a lush garden is not inherently more ugly than a lawn (quite the contrary), for instance, nor are colorful clothes hanging out on a line inherently unattractive. We wear the same clothes on our backs for admiration in public — why is seeing them damp on a blowing line bad? What we find beautiful has to do with our culture and our training in large part.

Among the basic subsistence activities commonly legislated against by towns, cities and housing developments are:

1. Clotheslines instead of dryers. Reason: Looks poor. Might suggest you can't afford a dryer. Plus, you might see underwear that isn't your own. This is a major cause of sin.
2. No livestock. Huge pets are acceptable. Reason: Ostensible reasons are health-based, but one has to suspect that the real reason is that pets, which have no purpose other than companionship and cost money, are a sign of affluence, while livestock are a sign of poverty because they provide economic benefits. No livestock is as dangerous to human health as dogs, which are generally permitted.
3. No front yard gardens. Reason: The lawn is a sign of affluence — you have money, leisure and water enough to have a chunk of land, however tiny, that doesn't produce anything of value. In many neighborhoods it creates, as author Michael Pollan has observed, a seemingly contiguous but basically sterile and safe-seeming "public" green space that is actually privatized and not very green in the ecological sense. Gardens, on the other hand, have dirty wildlife and bugs in them, and might grow food, which is bad because it implies you can't afford to buy food — even if you can't.
4. No rainwater collection. Reason: This is mostly in dry places in the Southwest, for fear that the tiny amount of available rainwater that might be shifted into barrels might not reach people who hold arcane water rights in perpetuity. A few other municipalities do it

for fear of West Nile virus because they seem never to have heard of screens or mosquito dunks. Oh, and barrels look like you can't afford to water your lawn with sprinklers, even when it is raining. In fact, most dry-area cities have trouble with storm overflow water being lost, and rain barrel collection would improve the situation.

5. No small home businesses, cottage industries or home commerce of any kind. Reason: This often does not include white-collar telecommuters who can make money out of their homes all they want, or upscale white-collar professionals with home offices. Instead it means people who want to sell food, do hair, fix things from their home or put up a discreet sign. This is deemed ugly and bad, as it's a visible reminder that some people may not be able to keep warm by burning their money and might actually need to earn some.

Now I realize I'm being a little unkind. People have real aesthetic concerns — but a law that outlaws even tasteful gardens or small signs that say "eggs" on them, or a town that tries to keep its "traditional," "colonial" or "small-town" feel without actually allowing any of the characteristics of traditional, colonial or small-town life is creating a sterile Disneyland as well as destroying long-term environmental, economic and food security.

The reality is that clothes on the line aren't empirically ugly. Neighborhood cats carry more diseases than backyard poultry. If you can put a political sign on your lawn, you should be able to put a sign that says "fresh baked goods" on it — food security is political!

That means that these laws can't be allowed to stand, and neither can homeowners association agreements that undermine our right to live sustainably in our communities. One of the first things you or your community, your transition group or your neighbors can do is to push to change your zoning laws or your neighborhood covenants.

That means you need to get involved. Go to the town meetings. Get to know your zoning board. Talk to your neighbors. Strategize — can you find some people who want chickens to get together with? Find out what the objections are and address them — if people are afraid of bird flu, remind them that bird flu is largely a problem of industrial production. If people think that lawns are beautiful and food gardens are ugly, show them otherwise. Show them that other towns are doing it.

If the law won't help you, consider whether you are willing to consider civil disobedience. Unjust laws need to be overturned — and you don't have to go to jail to be Thoreau, sometimes you just need to plant some kale. But before you do that, do know the price you may have to pay and make sure you are willing to pay it. Someone with courage who is willing to pay a price may have to go first — and if you are willing to be the one to fight that battle, well, all honor to you.

The reality is that some of the zoning restrictions and covenants will fade as times get tougher, but we really can't afford to wait for things to be really bad to get our chickens — because it will likely be harder to come by diverse stock then. We can't wait to grow food until we're already hungry. We can't wait to collect water until our well is dry. It is worth fighting these battles right now — particularly since many of them truly are rooted in ugly prejudice against the poor, and separation from our agrarian past.

Most Americans couldn't get much more separate from our agrarian roots, so that's sort of silly. Bit by bit, people are bringing clotheslines and front yard gardens back, and making them cool again. But we can't wait for that to happen — because the reality is that many of us will be poor and will need the utility of these activities to soften our poverty.

We can't wait until everyone sees a garden full of food as beautiful and lush. Instead, we've got to make sure that even those who still think it looks old-fashioned and dirty don't get to control something so basic as our future anymore. We're going to need to address zoning questions early in the process of adaptation, but the question is how — right now those battles are being fought in cities and suburbs all over the country, piecemeal, one by one.

There is potentially a better way. An increasing number of rural areas have "right-to-farm" laws that protect farmers who are engaged in the normal practice of agriculture when suburbanization or urbanization enters the picture. The assumption is that if it is part of the normal practice of agriculture, the neighbors can't complain or file nuisance lawsuits.

Right-to-farm laws came about in response to increasing development of rural areas. As more and more suburbanites moved out to the country and came in contact with the realities of farm life — manure and roosters, hay wagons and cows — they complained. Farmers rightly argued that they needed protection. The rule became "sniff before you move" — that is, if you are going to move into a house next to an existing dairy farm, you should make sure you want to live there.

Now obviously, in city centers, standard right-to-farm laws can't be applied wholesale. First of all, most of the farms are long gone — that is, we're not talking about protecting existing farmers but enabling new ones, so the "sniff before you move" test can't be applied here. Second, we can all reasonably agree that some kinds of agricultural and livestock production are probably not appropriate in urban environments, and that living in cities requires a high degree of accommodation of others.

That said, five of the six largest US cities permit chickens in backyards. Many have minimal or no restrictions on urban livestock — there are goats in LA and pigs in Brooklyn and chickens nearly everywhere, and people manage to get along quite well. A friend of mine has five acres in an affluent suburb of Boston (it wasn't affluent when she bought them); she has horses, goats, a pig, chickens, turkeys and geese, and you'd never know they were there. I know another person with three cows inside the city limits of Evanston, Illinois, a suburb of Chicago.

There are also cities that permit no livestock, not even poultry — as Gene Logsdon has put it, "You can have a barking, crapping dog the size of a pony, but not three quiet hens." Other cities may have elaborate and excessive laws that benefit neither residents nor the city that has to enforce them — for example, in a small city near Boston where my mother and stepmother keep four hens, they were required to get permission from every single one of their abutters, have their property inspected and get a yearly inspection by the town vet. Any increase in flock size requires more queries, more permissions, more visits. Meanwhile, the next town over has a "six chickens per household" flat policy — no inspections. Given the cost in time and effort to her city, as well as the barrier having to approach your neighbors offers, this process really ought to be streamlined.

The same goes for gardening — some cities and suburbs restrict front yard food gardening, or don't allow sidewalk marginal strips, to which ornamental gardeners have full access, to be planted with food plants. The reality is that growing food is at least as beautiful as flowers, and we need to change those laws.

We also need to clarify regulations about water use and capture that make home-scale agriculture possible in the dryer parts of the US — rain barrels should be permitted in every state and city. In many cases, the driest parts of the country are subject to heavy rains, and when these come, much of the water is lost in flooding on asphalt and overflowing storm sewers. Allowing homeowners to capture this rainwater is an essential part of creating sustainable cities.

Moreover, some cities make no distinction between lawn watering and food garden watering. In *Coming Home to Eat*, his book about living the 250-mile diet in one of the driest areas of the country, Gary Nabhan cites research that confirms that sustainable home food production uses less regional water than trucked-in produce — the high water cost of most electrical generation means that growing in your backyard will use less water overall than buying produce that was shipped and held under refrigeration.

Small-scale home businesses that are quiet and don't alter the landscape — the right to sell your bread or your eggs from your home — should be protected. So should the right to hang your laundry. What is needed, then, is a set of consistent legal parameters that can be applied in cities and suburbs throughout the country — that can be pointed to as a reasonable norm, that protect the neighbors of city dwellers within reason, but that also balance that protection with the right to practice subsistence activities and the recognition that urban dwellers already accept nuisances of all sorts as part of having neighbors.

That barking dog next door, the cats that pee on the back fence, the rumble of trucks delivering to the grocery store, the traffic pollution are all accepted parts of city life. If we're going to complain about the smell of a neighbor's rabbits, it would have to be an abnormally strong smell — not the earthy smell of reasonably kept rabbit cages, which is less strong than the smell of diesel exhaust to which most urban dwellers are accustomed.

In our increasingly poorer world, it cannot be left to an accident of geography — where our jobs or our family are — to decide whether we are to have enough good and safe food to eat. Just as farmers affirm their right to farm, so urban dwellers should have the right to meet their basic needs.

Thirteen

Skills, work and money

I. Competence

> A human being should be able to change a diaper, plan
> an invasion, butcher a hog, conn a ship, design a build-
> ing, write a sonnet, balance accounts, build a wall, set
> a bone, comfort the dying, take orders, give orders,
> cooperate, act alone, solve equations, analyze a new
> problem, pitch manure, program a computer, cook a
> tasty meal, fight efficiently, die gallantly. Specialization
> is for insects.
>
> — Robert A. Heinlein, *Time Enough For Love*

I HAVE AN EMBARRASSING CONFESSION TO MAKE — I'm not handy at
all, and I have absolutely no excuse for it. You see, unlike my husband, who grew up in an apartment where a super handled any fixing,
I grew up with two parents who were both extremely handy. There was
my dad, who smelted his own bullets in our furnace, fixed things and
taught me to handle a knife, an axe and screwdriver early on. Just in case
I should try and get away with whining that I didn't learn because I was
a girl (total nonsense, my dad would have had no truck with that), my
stepmother is an extremely talented woodworker who I got to watch
renovate our home more or less by herself through my whole adoles-
cence. Sue is incredibly talented — I have beautiful bookcases, my sons

have beautiful wooden toys and a gorgeous toy box, and whenever she comes to our house, she runs about fixing everything that Eric and I are ignoring.

Both my parents tried hard to pass on their skills — and it didn't take. As a teenager, I was busy getting ready to live the life of the mind — the fact that even minds get broken toilets and funky wiring didn't really register until after I left home.

Basically, the reason I'm not handy is that I've never bothered to really get the skill set in any coherent way — somehow when I was younger I wasn't paying enough attention and didn't realize what I was missing out on, and then I was busy getting other skill sets into order, busy learning gardening and farming, food preservation and mending.

Eric has the same lacks, with better excuse, although it is more embarrassing for him, since he's a guy and thus "supposed to" know how to build stuff and fix things — particularly out in these parts where most of my neighbors pretty much could build their own houses from scratch with a MacGyver-like collection of odds and ends. We, on the other hand, could probably make a plastic model of a house out of my son's Lego — but I wouldn't bet on it not falling over.

We joke that there are two kinds of people in the world — the ones who have a window that won't open and immediately rush over to fix it, because it shouldn't be that way, and those who say, "OK, I'll just open the other window." We're both the second kind, and there's a price to that kind of laziness.

Now we've both been forced to learn some basics — we've gotten fairly good at small engine repair maintaining the ragtag vehicles we've had over the years, and we can build simple, box-shaped things, though these tend to look a little funny. For a while I avoided most woodworking because I was pretty constantly pregnant or nursing and didn't want the chemical exposure, but that's not been a good excuse for a while now.

And one of my New Year's resolutions is to fix this gap. I keep putting it off, though, because I really hate feeling incompetent. I remember when I was first learning to knit — I knew that eventually it would become as natural as breathing, but boy did I hate every single second of the period before it did. It was so frustrating, so maddening. I don't like to be bad at things — and of course, you need a period of being bad at things in order to get good. It is easier not to try, to complain I can't do it.

This was banged home to me when Isaiah, who was then five and in kindergarten, echoed my own internal whining. You see, Isaiah was learning to read — and it isn't his favorite thing. He's a natural at math and science, but unlike his big brother Simon, who picked up reading at three and never looked back, this language stuff was work for Isaiah. Now don't get me wrong — we were in no hurry, and we weren't pushing him hard — we believe it is perfectly normal for a five-year-old not to read yet. But we did make him practice his letters and pre-reading activities, and do a little bit of practice sounding things out — maybe ten minutes a day in total.

Then Isaiah told me, "I'll do my reading work tomorrow. Or the next day. I'm not very good at it." I told him that I thought he was doing just fine, actually — that he was doing very well for his age. And he told me that he liked math better, because it was easy, and he liked being good at things, so he didn't want to learn to read if it meant not being good. Out of the mouths of babes, as they say.

And I heard myself telling Isaiah that while it was OK that he didn't read yet, reading was one of those things that everyone needs to learn. Barring some very serious disabilities, we pretty much accept that everyone is supposed to learn to read. I heard myself saying gently that there are certain things everyone needs to know, and reading is one of them.

And, of course, fixing things and being able to adapt your basic environment is too. I don't want my kids picking up the notion that learning how to do that isn't just as important as learning how to read. I want them to be as competent as they can be with language and with hand tools.

I was struck by my own cowardice — like Isaiah, I don't want to be bad at it, so it is easier not to do it. But the difference is that Isaiah was only five, and he didn't really have to read just yet. We could let the whole thing go for a year or more, and be none the worse for it. On the other hand, we might not have the money to pay people to fix our stuff soon — and I'm well past the age that I should be doing the work.

Periodically I hear others (and I do this myself) say, "I'm not good at X." For X you can insert just about anything — growing food, sewing, cooking, repairing things. Now sometimes this goes to a real physical disability that has to be overcome — or can't be. There are things those of us with physical or intellectual limitations may never be able to do — just like there are people who will never master their times tables or learn to read. Barring such disabilities, there are some things in life that the general consensus requires us to have a minimal skill set in. For example, children may come to reading or arithmetic with great difficulty or great ease, but the assumption is that they need to learn to read and do their times tables. They may never find math easy or loveable, but they have to be able to do math up to a certain point — talent may shape their future, but they don't get off the hook for lack of it.

There are many basic subsistence skills that we really need to put in the same basic categories as reading and math — things that every adult person should have a certain level of minimal competence in, barring a true physical or mental barrier to them. I'm not sure I'd use Robert A. Heinlein's list quoted above, but you can come up with a decent one that isn't too far off and that prepares us for this new world where we can't buy our way out of so many problems. All of us need to know how to cook a decent meal, handle basic medical concerns, tend a sick kid, fix a broken step, darn a sock, dehydrate a tomato, tell a story, grow a potato, build a sun oven, bake a loaf of bread, put up a fence, season cast iron, mend a rip, care for a dying person, sing a baby to sleep, clean a toilet, knit or cro- chet a sock, fix a roof, use a weapon, plant a tree, immobilize a limb, make someone understand a counter-intuitive idea, save seed, sharpen a knife, chop garlic, have courage, fix a bicycle tire, make soup, give a pep talk....

The truth is that for most people with most things (and again, I know there are exceptions), "I'm not good at it" is a cop-out. The real- ity is that most of us aren't going to be very good at everything — some things will always be struggle, and as long as we've got the time and money and energy to find alternative ways of dealing with them, it is perfectly fine to say that I want to reserve my struggling for things I care more about. What's not OK is telling our kids or ourselves the lie that it is OK to use our fear of failure or our hatred of being bad at things as an excuse for not picking up skills.

The other excuse that isn't OK is division of labor, particularly by gender or class. That's not to say that there aren't jobs it won't make sense to contract out to a partner or someone who needs the money — there's nothing wrong with saying, "I have more money than time right now, I'm going to get someone to build in those pantry shelves." Nor is it bad to acknowledge that your six-foot-three, two-hundred-pound husband is probably better at hauling hay bales than his five-foot-one, ninety-pound spouse.

But the reality is that spouses sometimes go away, and things happen when they aren't around — and occasionally, they die or marriages break up. Sometimes spouses are away just as the cattle need feeding, and the money dries up even though you really need those shelves. The wrong attitude here is, "My wife does the cooking, so I don't have to" or "I'm very important and I make lots of money, so I don't have to know how to fix my bike." Instead, the idea is that all of us be able to handle the basics — we can hire our friend who is a talented seamstress if there's cash, but if rips need mending and there's no money, we need to be able to make our clothes wearable. All the men and boys need to know how to do "women's work" at least to a competent minimum, and vice versa. Everyone gets up on the roof, at least enough to be able to know how to keep the rain off — and then, if you are fortunate enough to have someone else in your life willing to go up in the rain and fix it, well, you can be grateful, but not dependent.

I'm going to bet that every one of us has a little guilty spot right now, a thing they know they should learn, a skill they've been avoiding picking up, something that they've already tried and put down in frustration because they sucked at it. So I'm about to give you folks a bit of a challenge — I invite you to take a look at the holes in your own competence, pick one that needs filling, and get to work filling it. Trust me, I'm right there with you.

I. Everything you need to know, in order

Never let it be said I'm not ambitious.

A student in my class asked me for a list of skills we need to get ready for peak oil, prioritized. I admit, it took me about a day after she asked to stop thinking, "Holy crap, how do I figure that all out!" But it is an interesting question and I thought I'd take a shot at it — and the larger question of whether it is possible to make a useful list of this sort of thing.

Now I'm not going to get everything, but it did occur to me that we could break it down a bit, and then subcategorize. So what the heck, here goes. In order of priority — the main categories are numbered, and the skills in each category are lettered. Here's the beginnings of my list.

1. How not to panic

This is probably the most important skill set — when stuff gets hard, you need to focus and do what needs doing. In order to do this, you need:

a. To feel like you are able to handle things, because you have mental contingency plans and you have built trust in your own competence. The best way to get this skill is to plan, to talk and think out scenarios so you know what you would do, and to practice doing stuff until you are reasonably confident that not only can you do familiar things, but you can also learn new ones as you go.

   Think about how fire safety training works for kids in school — first you learn that fire can be dangerous. Then you learn "Stop. Drop. Roll." Then you practice fire drills and finding the exits, testing doors to see if they are hot and getting low. That is, you identify a scenario in which you might need this information, break down the skills you need and practice.

b. To have the skills to control your own reactions — these may be strong. You need to be able to put your anger, grief or fear to the side long enough to make everyone safe and to meet immediate needs. Meditation, biofeedback or simple compartmentalizing may help with this. It is also extremely useful to develop the ability to accept that sometimes you will make mistakes and fail at things.

   My oldest son is severely autistic. At twelve, he's tall and able to climb our eight-foot fence or open doors. This is scary as heck because Eli wanders — he's gone and sat in other people's cars, walked down the road and headed to the creek when it was at flood level. All those things have happened despite the fact that we have locks on every door, pay attention and constantly ask, "Does someone have an eye on Eli?" We do everything we possibly can to keep him safe — and we also have to acknowledge that someday, we may fail to do so, because you cannot watch someone every single second for their entire lives. Coming to terms with that is very, very hard, and I'm still not done with it — but I do have to recognize that sometimes we may fail, despite our profoundest caring and best efforts, and accept that, even as I redouble my efforts not to.

c. To help other people remain calm, respond appropriately, and find a role for themselves. Some kind of leadership training, community response training or just practice organizing people will help here. Some folks are not good at this — if you can't be a leader, that's OK, maybe your job is to find someone who is totally losing it and help them stabilize. But you certainly need to know how to help your immediate family and neighbors, so you think about how they may respond and how to help them. For children, it might be helpful to give them some training, or plan out specific jobs for them to do to help them feel powerful and useful.

2. How to learn things — and how to teach them

You are never going to learn every useful skill. It won't happen. It will be very helpful, though, if you figure out how you and members of your family learn, and think about how you might make it easy for you all to learn more things as you need to. If you are a book person, get books. If you need diagrams, get diagrams. If you learn best from people, find out who knows what in your area. But the basic skills of learning things are all pretty much the same — most of us can learn to do almost anything. So learning how to learn — how to research an issue, how to pick up a physical skill, how to help another person do that, how to analyze a problem and find a solution, how to avoid major errors of logic, what the necessary basic tools are — will really help you expand your skill set.

3. How to get along with everyone else

I sometimes get emails from people telling me that everyone around them is an asshole, and that they can't possibly get along with their neighbors. I've already discussed my rule of thumb developed while I was dating — when I see a pattern like this, I think the person talking isn't very good at getting along with others. Now I don't mean that people who are content without a large community are necessarily bad at this — some people are just introverts. And some people who are bad at getting along in the course of things either can do better in a crisis, can find one role they can fit into, or can be protected by their families, who they can get along with.

But if you aren't great at getting along, learning to be tolerant, learning to listen, learning to like other people even when they seem weird and, perhaps most importantly, learning to judge them gently (and I am not always the natural master of any of these skills either) is really, really important. Do it now. This is especially important if you have trouble getting along with your relatives, and might end up sharing housing with them.

4. How to deal with an immediate medical crisis

a. Basic hygiene, safety, self-care and nutrition. How to make a balanced meal, and to provide a balanced diet, how to make an oral rehydration syrup, how to wash hands, how to sterilize things, how to cook safely, how to keep water from being contaminated, how to deal with contaminated water, how nutritional needs vary by age, sex and medical condition. How to care for teeth, skin, etc., without commercial preparations. How to prevent pregnancy and disease. How to use tools safely and keep children and others safe in their presence. Sounds obvious, will kill people if you don't know it.

b. Basic first aid and triage of a situation — everyone needs to know these things, period, no discussion. Maybe you'll never use it, but you should be able to stop bleeding, do CPR, help a choking victim, evaluate whether someone can be moved, help clear an airway, and decide whether medical treatment is necessary. This comes up all the time regardless of whether there's a crisis on.

c. More advanced medical care, when to use it, and when not to. This is particularly likely to come up in a localized disaster, an epidemic or a transport crisis. If you can't get someone to the hospital, if the emergency rooms are overflowing with people, if the hospitals are closed or evacuated or if there's no way to get someone somewhere because

of a gas shortage, snowstorm, ice storm, hurricane, earthquake ...
you need to be able to meet emergency medical needs — to observe
a concussion victim, make a temporary splint for a broken bone,
birth a baby, ease the pain of a dying person, etc. At least one person
in every household, and preferably everyone old enough, should get
some or all of these skills. At the very least, know who in your immediate area already has them so you can call upon them.

5. How to feed yourself

a. How to cook simple foods, and make them tasty and appetizing.
   How to adapt your cooking to changing availability of ingredients.
   How to deal with special diets that you are likely to encounter.
b. How to grow and forage simple, easily accessible foods. These vary a
   lot by climate and culture, but the indigenous foods of your region
   will give you a good idea of what grows well. Includes how to save
   seeds of these plants, what kind of soil conditions they need, the
   basics of soil science and how to harvest and preserve the plants, as
   well as how to recognize safe wild foods and how to use them. I will
   discuss foraging and gardening later in the book, but even if you
   imagine you won't have to garden or have very little land, learn these
   basic skills.
c. How to store your food so you will lose as little as possible to predators, mold, bacteria, theft, etc. Includes security, hygiene, good
   storage practices, rotating, maintaining, checking, managing stores.
d. How to secure your food from predators, and if you are interested,
   how to be a predator — how to hunt, trap, fish and butcher wild
   and tame livestock. Even vegetarians may want this skill set to feed
   their pets, if the cost of food or its availability becomes prohibitive.
   Includes understanding the rules of hunting as well as gun, bow, dog
   and trap safety. Also must include humane practices, when not to
   take animals and the best strategies for predator removal.

6. How to have a sense of humor about stuff, and how to shake off your distress and go on

How to be kind when you are pissed off and grumpy, but it isn't anyone's fault.

7. How to wring the most out of everything

Extreme thrift.

a. How to minimize waste and minimize expenditures — reducing need, using care and good management skills.
b. How to take care of your stuff so it won't break, and how to repair and patch it if it does.
c. Repurposing of now useless things, making do, creatively compensating for things you lack.

II. What are you going to be when you grow up?

OK, everyone who thinks that your job will still be there in five years raise your hands. For those of you with your hands up, how sure are you? How secure are you in a deep, systemic crisis? Seventy percent of the economy survives on consumer spending — what happens if 50 percent or 80 percent of that dries up — if really all we're buying is food and oil, and not that much of either?

The truth is that the one thing that all of us should be planning for is a job loss — and by this I don't mean a short-term job change, but a job loss in a deep Depression with extended, widespread unemployment — where there is no unemployment insurance anymore and most of your neighbors can't get work either. Is this inevitable? No, merely probable, I think. But probable enough that we should be prepared for it to happen.

Now I realize this scares the hell out of most of us — and not much less me than you. My family buys groceries too. But that's what happened in the Great Depression, where more than a few people think we're headed. We can all be happy if we don't go there, but we should be ready for the formal economy to stop feeding and housing us.

So the question becomes — what are you going to do to keep body and soul together? What are you going to be when you grow up — how are you going to feed yourself and keep a roof over your head? As the formal economy begins to tank, we have to look to the informal economy — that is, the economy made up of subsistence work, criminal acts, barter, under-the-table work, domestic economics and self-employment in cottage industry. That doesn't mean none of us will work in the formal sector, but all of us need to be able to shift as much as we can to the informal economy — to save our precious cash for the house payment and thus provide food and heat by barter or subsistence work.

If we do have formal sector work, it may be in businesses we set up for ourselves, as more and more employers begin making layoffs. In many cases, even though it is a pain in the ass when you are doing too many other things too, we may want to start the businesses now — begin doing a bit of extra work on the side in your potential cottage area so that you'll have a customer base and experience when the time comes.

How do you decide what to do? Well, it is possible you already have an obvious and marketable skill — either you could do the work you do now for yourself or you have a useful skill set you aren't using. Maybe you used to buck trees and can set up a firewood business quickly, or your current skills as a nurse could be applied to a community clinic you set up. In these cases, the solution may be obvious.

In other cases, it may seem hard to figure out — what will the job market for marketing professionals look like? What will construction workers do in a housing bust? Now might be the time to reorient yourself, gently or broadly. Instead of building new houses, get in on some retrofits and start learning home reinsulation; instead of corporate marketing, consider setting up a business providing something useful — bulk food, water filters, fishing worms and equipment, warm clothes, farm-direct products — or perhaps local marketing help for those products, to your community.

The one thing I warn against is allowing your enthusiasm for some project to warp your perspective about its future. I've met a number of people who blithely expect to make money marketing high-value organic produce or their exquisite hand-knit objects or somesuch. And while there certainly will be markets for some knitted goods and food in the future, the truth is that what we are seeing is rapid economic deflation — money is disappearing. That means people aren't buying stuff — and those who have, up to now, been paying extra for quality may not have the spare cash to do so. So while it might make sense early on to rely on high-value, high-effort products, the idea that enough people will be going out to expensive restaurants to allow them to pay $25 a pound for your basil or $40 to give you a fair living wage for knitted socks is unlikely. The same is true if you do crafty cute stuff with no real use —

funky beer mugs and wall hangings are lovely, but they are salable in an affluent society, not a poor one.

Nor should you be duplicating immediately things we have a lot of — in many cases, people will not be buying adult clothing, for example, because they have enough in their closets for a lifetime. Eventually making clothes may well be an important project again, but short term and long term may well be different, and we all need to be flexible. Think *practical* and be adaptable — be able to produce not just a high-value product but an immediately useful one that people might need.

What might people need in the short term? Food. Warm blankets. Firewood for heating. Insulation. Childcare when both partners are working multiple jobs. Elder care. Medicine. Distractions — theater, gambling, alcohol, sex, dance, drugs, music, things to make them laugh, newspapers or the electronic equivalent, cartoons (and yes, even struggling people will find some money for these things). Shelter. Shoe repair. Security help. Toiletries — obvious ones like soap and toothpaste, and things to make them feel attractive — even under the Taliban, women used perfume. Education — people will still want better for their kids, and training to get new jobs, but it may not be the same model of education we use in a cheap-energy society. Tools. Anything that breaks and wears out easily. Handymen, plumbers, midwives, doctors, nurses, ministers of every faith, anyone who can fix, mend and repair. Livestock handlers and dog trainers. Gardeners and people who can teach us how to adapt to low-energy life.

You may need to do more than one of these things — in the short term, the money may be in helping those who can afford it retrofit their homes, for example, while in the long term it might be in growing food. Or you may find yourself doing several seasonal things — cutting firewood, growing plant starts, building furniture or sewing in the winter, milking spring to fall. The informal economy is going to require multiple skill sets rather than the single job we've been used to — and our ability to get out of the mindset that says "I have this one job, and that is the only thing I can or should do" may be the thing that defines best how well we do in the difficult times ahead.

It is worth thinking about what you will do in this new economy — maybe only watch and thank G-d you got to keep your job. But just in case, it is worth making plans, and perhaps putting a foot into the informal economy, testing its waters and building the beginnings of a new personal economy along with the old.

III. Money

OK, time to talk finances. I have to say, just as security isn't my favorite topic, neither is "what you should do with your 401(k)" — because while I'm a generalist, rather than a specialist, I feel that I'm especially general on this subject, because the exact parameters of the future are pretty hard to parse. I don't want to be responsible for someone liquidating their retirement funds and cursing my name later, so please take what I say with several large grains of salt.

At the moment we are experiencing steady price increases for things we need, like food and energy, but also some signs of deflation — that is, the overall money supply is contracting rapidly, as is the availability of credit both at the personal and corporate level. That means, from the looks of things, that we are headed into a Depression rather than a period of, say, hyperinflation. A lot of folks see a recovery right around the corner, but that's far from certain. That doesn't mean it isn't technically possible that things could shift, but the present trends suggest that our real incomes and access to money are shrinking, while our basic costs are going up.

Because of this, we seem to be headed into a period where money is hard to come by. That means that debt is potentially a much bigger deal than it is in a period where credit is easy to come by and you can always borrow off your Mastercard to pay your student loans, or refinance your home, or even just get another job. Not enough jobs, pay cuts, no credit — these mean tough, tough times for the indebted, and of course, their number is rising rapidly. Most Americans can't live within their salaries — and since their inflation-adjusted income is shrinking, that makes sense.

So the first advice is "get out of debt." But that's one of those "duh" things — yes, you know this. And presumably you would if you could — or you've been playing the odds that one more month on the credit card bill won't really hurt — or you don't have much choice but to use the card to cover that broken arm and buy groceries. But if you can, get out of debt.

What if you can't before the axe falls? Well, next you have to decide whether to negotiate directly with those you are indebted to, declare bankruptcy or walk away from your debt. Those are pretty much the choices.

If you have one major debt you can't handle — say, medical bills — the best bet is probably negotiating repayment if there's any chance of it, because this option won't hurt your credit or your ability to get jobs that depend on good credit (lots of employers, especially federal and state ones, check your credit history, and academic jobs may depend on the ability to get an official transcript, which is tough [but not totally impossible in some cases] to do if you are in default on student loans). It will also save you wage garnishment and loss of your economic stimulus package.

You can declare bankruptcy, but this will not get you cleared out quickly — student loans and child support are almost never included, and you will certainly have to repay some of your debts under new bankruptcy laws. It costs money and it leaves your credit trashed. The good thing is that in five to seven years, you should have credit again (assuming there is any).

The third choice is to dump your debt. This means that anything you may have that you default on will be repo'd — but that may not matter much if you'd lose it anyway during a bankruptcy. This actually might be a better option for people wanting to keep their home — if you can keep up your mortgage payments and live with the fact that it will be a long time, if ever, before you can get another one, you can probably give back the car and any other big-ticket payment options, turn off the phone to avoid the credit card people, accept that you'll never get that federal job (they can't repo your education) and just live with it. This is not an easy option, but I suspect it will be the dominant model in the future. Someone is going to get screwed because of the mass extension of credit, and it would be a nice change if it was the credit companies, not the average person.

OK, what if you have money, not debts? This is good, no?

Well, yes. But what should you do with it? How to preserve your retirement funds? How to preserve your kids' college savings?

Honestly, I think the most certain bet would be to stop looking at your money as the only means to a particular end, and concentrate on the end itself — that is, if you are saving money so you are not hungry, cold and lonely in your old age, perhaps you might put some of that money into a house for your kids who can't afford one right now — perhaps one very near you. Perhaps you should think about helping them develop an economically resilient local business. Or maybe pay off your house, invite good friends without a house to live in it and trade them help as you need it. These are risky choices, of course, but so is leaving your money in your 401(k).

If you want an educated child, perhaps the best option would be to add to her college fund a budget for lots of books, and a chance to build relationships with local college professors or knowledgeable people she might apprentice to. That way, she gets an education even if she can't go to college. Unless you have the money to spend without loans, I'm not honestly sure that I recommend college right now for most kids — the choice to go and come out encumbered with tens of thousands in debt is simply too dangerous. Education can be had a lot of ways.

I think that gold and silver are probably overvalued right now, and will come down, so I don't know that I think people should buy them. I do think that investments in oil wildcatting, alcohol, prescription sedatives, pornography and escapist videos probably will do well in the coming years, if the stock market is your sort of thing.

Otherwise, I think that putting money in things that are likely to cost more later, or have value (not necessarily the same value) in the long term, is probably wise. For example, I think that food-producing land will continue to have value (not necessarily the same as now) if you can buy it outright. So will investments in local businesses, food and local energy production. And now is the time to buy or barter for the goods or equipment you will need for your future business.

Will state sources of income keep being there? I wouldn't be certain of that — one hopes that disability checks, pensions and social security will keep coming, but we all know how tremendously fragile our economy is. This creates a powerful burden on each of us to support local safety nets for those who cannot secure their own future — each of us needs to ask what we are doing to help care for those who may fall through the cracks.

Fourteen

Security matters

WHEN I TEACH ADAPTING IN PLACE CLASSES, I find that the sub-ject most of my students worry about most is personal safety and home security — they know that economic and political unrest can make the world a dangerous place, and it seems so hard to know how to respond. To a person, they are afraid of a world that is less safe than the one they live in now — and yet such things are part of poverty and conflict. The question of how to preserve a decent quality of life in a difficult world is one of the hardest parts of adaptation.

I'm writing this from America, which means I know that for most of my readers, there is an expectation that this chapter is going to talk about guns. Unfortunately, we live in a culture where "security" often translates as " everyone get a bunch of guns." Especially in the US there's an immediate leap to "guns = security." Now in saying that, let's be clear — I'm not anti-gun. Guns are tools on a working farm, and in many cases, I think they are a component of personal and community security. But only one component. Before we start to talk about weapons, and the loaded (so to speak) discussion that leads to, let's remember that the gun comes into the security discussion quite late — if you are pulling a weapon, you are already well past many things you could have done to keep yourself safe. Not getting to the weapons stage should be the focus of everyone's relationship to their own security.

The truth is that while my pulling a weapon on a person might be useful in some situations (when I am being treated aggressively by one or two people, and all other better responses have failed me), and assuming I am resolute enough and quick enough not to have it taken away from me and used upon me (and this happens), doing so also escalates a situation in a dramatic way. There are plenty of scenarios one can imagine in which my not seeming to be a threat could be just as valuable as my ability to appear like one.

I know at least one woman who had a gun in her glove compartment when a man got into her car and threatened her. There was a decent chance she might have gotten the gun quickly and turned on him — but she might also have failed, and her reading of the situation was that she was better off emphasizing that she was a mother, that her children would be alone and vulnerable. She did so, and the man let her out of the car. In another case, with another person, she might have been wiser to go for the gun. In all scenarios, however, she would have been wiser if she'd kept her car locked and not pulled up to search through her purse in an unlighted area without any protection. As in almost all cases, reducing risk would have helped the most.

I'm also going to mention that this is one of many issues in which there is no one-size-fits-all answer. A lot of it depends on who you are — your personality, level of physical ability, psychology, age, gender and time of life, as well as your neighborhood and other factors: who the person or persons or animals threatening you are, their motives are the situation.

One of the things that shocked me when I became a mother is how fearful I became for myself — I'd never worried much about dangerous things, or feared death much in any conscious way, and now I realized I was terrified that something would happen to me or my husband. I was puzzled by this, though I have found that now my last baby is turning into a big kid, my fear has eased off again. And now I see it for what it was — a perfectly reasonable recognition that as a pregnant or breast-feeding mother, I depended on my husband's survival in many ways (because it wouldn't have been easy for me to take up the economic responsibility) and my child depended physically on my survival for his. Now that my babies are not babies anymore, I find that while I certainly don't like the idea of my death, or my spouse's, I can breathe a bit when I have to contemplate them.

That's simply because my children are no longer physically dependent, and I'm no longer in such a vulnerable stage of life. I mention this because I think that a pregnant woman, for example, has a different set of vulnerabilities and potential responses (and remember, the person most likely to be assaulting a pregnant woman is not some random criminal but her husband, boyfriend or lover) than, say, her husband, or an unencumbered male. That is, what we can do and what we need to do vary quite a lot.

The truth is that how you deal with security issues depends a lot on where in life you are — a mother with several young children has different choices to make than someone with older or adult children. And those choices aren't certain — a woman in her fifties whose children are grown might be able to commit to organized non-violence even at the expense of her own life, while a woman in her thirties with three small kids might feel she had no choice but to defend them. On the other hand, a woman with small children might feel that escalating the violence could endanger them, while a woman with no kids might not feel that same fear pulling her gun. All situations vary a lot and it is impossible to talk here about every imaginable scenario.

It is also true that most of us are going to make our choices on the fly, in response to stimuli and without fully understanding what we are doing. That is, most of us aren't going to have time to make considered choices, to do the right thing every time, and mostly, we aren't going to know what is right for sure. I often talk about the choice my husband's great-grandmother made for her daughter — they lived in Nazi Germany and Jews were being rounded up to the ghetto, but as yet, there were no major death camps and the violence against Jews seemed mostly non-fatal. At the same time, the Germans were bombing Britain heavily and were close to conquering the country. Jewish parents had the choice of sending their children on the kindertransport, a train traveling through France to England — that is, putting your children, now comparatively protected in Germany and under the protection of their own parents, on a train that would travel through a war zone, to a country being heavily bombed, to be cared for by people who did not know or love them, in a place that, odds are, was likely to be conquered shortly anyway by the same Germans. Or they could keep their children by their side and hope that German anti-Semitism didn't escalate into widespread mass murder. Of course, it had before, but there were also plenty of examples where, well, it hadn't.

I remind people of this because it seems so obvious now — Eric's great-grandmother put her daughter on the kindertransport and sent her off to England, along with one cousin. A third cousin elected to stay behind. And of course, that third cousin died in the concentration camps. In the same sense, the Warsaw Ghetto survivors make it seem so obvious that Jews should have taken up arms early on in the Nazi conflict against the Germans.

But if there is any truth about history, it is this — no one knows how it will work out when events are happening. Security is something that each of us is going to navigate from a different perspective, and from a different place. And at some point most of us may have the horrible thought — damn, I could have done that better if only.... The truth is that most often we are going to decide what to do at climactic moments with not enough information, just our guts and what we do know — and sometimes, we're going to be wrong, or make mistakes.

The best thing most of us can do is reduce our level of risk — lower the number of those moments as best we can by planning. The second best thing we can do is to prepare for such moments — make sure we won't be overcome by panic and have the tools (whether they be a barking dog, a neighbor on speed dial or a gun) to deal with them, and to know what our choices are. We must remember that we need to not only protect ourselves from those who might do us harm, but also protect our loved ones from access to dangerous things and others who might become accidental victims in the heat of the moment from injury.

I want to remind people that all of this — all of the process of adaptation, of which security issues are a part — is about skewing the odds in your favor. It is not about eliminating all risk. It is not about ensuring that no one will ever die, or make a mistake, or have something horrible befall them.

And perhaps the beginning point of talking and thinking about security is talking about something none of us really like — death. Our own deaths, the deaths of people we love and rely on. These are not fun things, but they are important. American culture sells us the idea that we can all be magically insulated from death — we can sue if by some chance someone dies from something, because, after all, we can achieve immortality through the medical system; these are things we are told in a thousand ways.

But the odds are good that in a lower-energy world, one that is poorer and harder and probably has more violence in thus-far protected areas, some of us are going to die sooner than we'd like. The odds are that most of those deaths will not be from marauding hordes but from diseases we can't afford to treat, but some of them probably will be from violence. And having some sense of how we face this reality, scary as it is, is probably the first tool we need. There are things we can't protect ourselves against, and some things we could protect ourselves against in the hypothetical, but that will run up against our real imperfections. And people die anyway, even while we're told no one should. All of us need to hold in our heads the truth that death is a reality for all of us, and sometimes sooner than we would like.

I once was a noble idealist, and could think of things that (in the hypothetical, since it was never asked of me) were worth dying for, and that I hoped I'd have the courage to die for. Then I had children, and for a while, courage meant staying alive at any price, to ensure their survival. Today I can just barely begin to see around to the day when I might think that there are principles that would be worth dying for again. Now don't get me wrong, I very much prefer to live for my principles. Both of those perceptions are real and rational responses, one to a youth with that glorious sense of immortality, the other to that sudden recognition you have flesh in the game. Both are reasonable. And neither perception allows for the fact that one is just as likely to die ignobly, and that those who need to be immortal never are.

When we talk about security, even before we begin minimizing our risks and talking about our options, we have to recognize that there is no perfect solution — you can reduce various risks but never be perfectly safe. All the scenario planning in the world, all the thinking and choosing we do, will get us only so far, and will probably never get any of us back to the level of security that most affluent Americans experienced quite recently. That doesn't mean we're all doomed, or that the zombies are coming anytime soon. What it does mean is that we will never be secure enough. We can use some or all of the tools in our hands, we can plan and think and prepare and train ourselves not to panic and how to respond, but we will never be wholly safe, never know what the perfect choice is, except in hindsight. All of us will die, some of us sooner than we'd like — and that has to be part of our planning as well. I don't like it and I'm sure you don't either. But security only goes so far — we can plan and hope, but sometimes things go wrong, and we do the victims and the dead a great disservice if we imagine that death can always be prevented, mistakes can always be avoided and failure is something for other people.

It is almost always cheaper, easier and more efficient to devote most of your resources to personal and community PREVENTATIVE measures than to devote them to responsive ones. That's not to say you shouldn't have a way to respond to violence or threat — no preventative works all the time. But if you have limited resources, preventative measures are usually the easiest way to start, and the most effective overall.

Most threats are based on a fairly rational risk assessment by the person posing the threat — they think they'll be better off stealing from you or hurting you than not. Now some criminals are morons and can't tell what their risks are, and some people are sociopaths or motivated by compulsions beyond rational control — but the odds are good that the person looking to steal from you or attack you and take your money is looking to do it with minimal risk to themselves and good odds of success. If they do this as a regular hobby or a living, they are probably pretty experienced at it. If they don't do it very often, odds are they are quite nervous about being caught. So anything that slows them down (and thus increases their chance of being caught), makes you and your family appear to be a less attractive victim, or raises their risk of being caught or hurt, reduces your risk of being a victim.

I'm talking mostly about criminal assault here. And I think the odds are that increasing poverty will increase the crime rate, although differently in various areas. It is worth remembering, however, that while individual or small band criminal assault is a fairly common scenario, it is not the only possible one. I would remind all of us again that domestic violence is far more common than external violence. In a lower-energy world, most of our problems will probably come from people we know or who live nearby rather than the bands of roaming marauders some people worry about. This is particularly important when we talk about guns.

One of the reasons I don't recommend guns to every household is that for people who are victims of domestic violence by husbands, lovers or boyfriends (or, less frequently, girlfriends or wives), having a gun is probably more dangerous than not having one. Someone in an abusive partnership has already failed to use the most potent weapon they have — getting out of the relationship (this does not necessarily apply to those who have left abusive situations and have to fear a partner coming after them). If you can't leave an abusive partner, odds are you won't shoot them either. On the other hand, abusive partners often kill the people they abuse, sometimes with their own guns. All people need to think about not just "the stranger trying to jack my car" but other, more intimate realities.

Another real and serious question is the issue of suicide. This is a particularly big issue for men — the disruption of male economic roles tends to cause depression, anxiety and stress-related illness and a lot of suicide, especially by middle-aged and older men. Teenagers are also vulnerable. Having the gun available in the house means that you don't need a sustained desire for suicide — a brief period of despair will do. For those with a history of depression or concerns, the benefits of guns may well be outweighed by the dangers of having them. I do not recommend guns in the house of anyone who has ever had any kind of serious bout of depression or mental illness.

Finally, there's the issue of children. If you have young children, it is wise to keep guns and ammo locked up — there are rural families who live in ways that don't allow this, and police and military parents who need to use other strategies, but most parents will be safer if there is no possible way for young children or children with disabilities that limit their ability to understand the consequence of guns to get ahold of them.

The other scenario worth talking about is state-supported violence. If you are black in the US, you are already probably pretty clear on this one, at least at one scale. A lot of us tend to leap immediately to the idea of "camps" or something as the logical face of state-authorized or -created violence, but simply the idea that you have to be as or more afraid of the police than criminals is one form of state violence. This can occur at any level — town, state, federal. There are people for whom and places where police will never be your allies. The US military, the police and the state can be used against you, and have been. The last charge of the US Cavalry, for example, occurred not against a foreign enemy but during the Great Depression, when impoverished veterans of World War I marched peacefully upon Washington and set up shanty-towns demanding that they be paid a promised subsidy. The fear of the state is perfectly reasonable. This does not mean that agents of the state are bad — or that they can't also be a really good thing. It merely means that even the best and most humane agent of the state always risks being misused by an immoral government.

That said, what you should do about the fear of the state is a tough question. Personal solutions will probably only work in very rural areas where the state has few representatives, and while an armed populace represents something of a deterrent, it honestly isn't clear to me how much. In the case of widespread federally supported state violence (and I should note by this I mean "more than now" and not to imply it doesn't exist now), probably the best solution is a revolution, preferably a non-violent one. But this involves a level of community organization I'm not quite prepared to cover in this book.

Personal preventative measures

1. Self-confidence, or at least the appearance thereof

It isn't true that all victims look like victims, but it is the case that if someone is calculating whether to attack or steal or do something illegal, they are probably calculating their risk too. The stronger and harder to intimidate you appear, the less likely you will be to look like an easy target. For some people this is easy — for example, I'm six feet tall and not thin. I'm a big woman and I walk and act like I take up space, and this is to my advantage. But I've known very small and very elderly women who also have this quality. It may not truly be the case that all bullies are cowards, but some are, and you can put off some assaults with a cer-tain measure of self-confidence and by not responding fearfully. It isn't magic, and it has to be carefully balanced with the instinct for self-preservation, but it can help.

For women facing domestic violence, I realize this is much easier said than done, but part of this has to include the ability to say that it is never permissible for anyone to touch you violently, even if they love you, and that you will leave immediately, not the second or third time it happens, but the first time.

2. Common sense

Don't make yourself unnecessarily vulnerable. Walk with another person when possible. Stay close to other people if you are out alone. Don't flash cash where no one else has it. Don't punch your ATM card in clear view of everyone. Don't leave your bags unattended. Don't start bar fights you can't finish. Don't let your kids roam around alone if there are lots of human or animal predators around. Be aware of your surroundings, pay attention to other people, avoid people looking for fights or trouble. Use your brain — that's what it's for.

3. The ability to shift the ground and understand the person you are dealing with

This may be about slowing things down, increasing the perception of risk by the criminal, making you seem a poor choice of victim. Or it may be about making them fear being hurt (use this carefully). If the threat to your security is a person, sometimes you can change the threat by talking to them or dealing with them. I've already mentioned the woman I know who got out of a carjacking by talking about her kids and their need for her. But I've also met a woman who got out of being raped by claiming she had her period, and Derrick Jensen talks about his sister getting out of it by saying she had VD. That doesn't mean things like this always work, but they are tools you have.

I've also met an elderly nun who rather famously disarmed multiple soldiers on several separate occasions. She lived in a nunnery near Sarajevo, and soldiers would come to the nunnery to steal, intimidate or, at least one time, bent on rape, and she would talk to them, joke with them sometimes, guilt trip them others, remind them of their own mothers, and every single time it ended up with the soldiers leaving, and a couple of times she was holding their guns by then. This is a gift, obviously, that not all of us have, and that some people are not susceptible to. But some are, and language, persuasion, emotional manipulation, identification, even humor — these are tools people can use and should view as such.

4. Basic home security measures that slow someone down and make it more likely they will be caught

Good locks. Actually lock them if things get risky (I live in an area where locks are not presently used much). Stout doors. Bars for the doors. Heavy metal screens or window bars for particularly dangerous areas. Fences to keep things out of sight. Padlocks on sheds. Locks on your gas caps. A safe place to move animals to.

5. A dog, geese or guinea hens

These raise the risk of a criminal being caught and hurt. I don't suggest that most people get trained attack dogs, but some kind of animal deterrent that can alert you to unusual situations is a good idea. A dog is the most common choice, but geese have some real advantages — they are also excellent watchdogs, and in some ways, your average criminal may be more afraid of an aggressive gander than a dog, simply because it is more unfamiliar (and they eat grass, which is cheaper than dog food). Basically, you want something that hears and smells better than you do, and will give you some warning time, while also discouraging the large number of people who want an easy target.

I don't recommend this one if you don't like animals, can't take care of them or don't have a plan for supplying them with food in the longer term. The world does not need more abandoned or euthanized animals. If you have kids, the dog must be gentle and good with them, ideally raised from a puppy, and you must not leave young children alone with dogs ever. But if you are prepared to do this wisely and carefully, watch animals can reduce your risk and provide you with some warning of trouble.

6. Electronic security systems

These depend on electricity, money, monitors, police infrastructure and cars that can get to your place quickly — they are an option while things are good, but I wouldn't bet on them unless you are quite wealthy and you and your neighborhood can afford to maintain the infrastructure behind them. Even then, the "gated community" model doesn't particularly take my interest, so I'm going to skip over it.

Community preventative

1. A community

This is one of those "duh" things, but it is useful to have those relationships built before you need them — that way if things change quickly, you've got this in place. And honestly, a non-car community — a place where people walk and bike and talk to each other and sit on porches or interact regularly at meals and occasions, i.e., where there are people around and connected to each other — is itself a deterrent. That is, a neighborhood with people isn't as easy pickings to a burglar as a place without them.

2. Neighborhood watch

This is related to the above. Getting together, keeping an eye on things, having people out in the streets, showing presence — these things help make you look less vulnerable. Obvious neighborhood unity is protective against state violence as well, because if the police have to deal with a large community en masse they will be less powerful than if they can deal with isolated citizens. A neighborhood watch that looks within may also prevent domestic abuse, discretely enabling victims to get away or making it clear to perpetrators that they pay a public price as well.

3. Bells, code words and other alert methods

Jews in urban New York City use a Yiddish codeword. Carnival operators yell "Hey Rube!" In some places, "Help" or "Socorro!" or some other equivalent gets the response. Other places may use whistles or loud bells. The idea is that when the alarm is sounded, everyone drops what they are doing and comes running, ideally armed with whatever is at hand — a stick, a rock, a loud voice. This works on any kind of violence or criminal activity (and is especially effective if neighbors can bring themselves to do it in the case of domestic violence, which relies heavily on the tacit silence of neighbors and their fear of intervention).

Numbers have power! Two criminals with knives are scary if they are facing a few people — against thirty or so angry neighbors, they aren't quite as scary.

4. Public and private security, and a good relationship with them

There are places where police have little relationship to the people they serve and protect — and many times this can be remedied. Getting to know the police and having them build a relationship with your neighborhood or community group can be really helpful. Their presence can provide a deterrent, slow crime down and increase the chance of a criminal paying a price. In some post-collapse situations, societies rely on private security — you may have no choice but to do so, as in some places the choice is "hire" protection or need protection from those you might otherwise have hired. Having people whose job it is to see to security is a good thing, assuming they are good people with the (whole) public interest in mind.

5. Walls, gates, lights, speed bumps, etc. — barriers to entry

While I'm not much interested in the wealthy gated community, in some neighborhoods reducing car or pedestrian access to certain areas, providing motion-sensor lighting, etc., make a lot of sense. Do an evaluation of your area and its needs.

6. Organized nonviolence

This can be an extension of much of the above, but also can include passive resistance strategies and a host of other things. I strongly recommend Mark Kurlansky's excellent *Nonviolence: The History of a Dangerous Idea.* This is potentially the most effective strategy ever against state violence, and can be used quite effectively. It does require, however, that you have a strongly organized and consistent community that pretty much agrees to this policy — it can't work without strong community ties.

Personal responses

Everything in this category is totally pointless if you don't know what you are doing with it. Seriously, if you can't take the time and energy to deal with learning how to use this properly, when to use it, when not to use it and a host of other things, don't bother — concentrate on the above. Because having a weapon that can be taken from you and used on you is a bad idea.

It is just as important to know when *NOT* to use these weapons as when to use them. For example, self-defense trainers teach people not to hang onto their purses during most purse snatchings — you have to learn how to let your purse go. The reason is that most purses don't have anything worth risking your life for. If you respond to a low-level threat with a strong response, maybe you'll end the situation — but if it goes wrong, or you make a mistake (and mistakes happen, no matter what), you may find yourself facing a much greater threat. One of the classic peak oil worries is the question of the marauding band. My feeling is that if there's someone after my food, and I have young children, it doesn't matter if my band is bigger and meaner than the food hunting band — the minute the shooting starts, I risk the loss of someone to crossfire, which kills as many people as intended violence when bullets are flying. There are situations where each of these tools can be useful — but plenty of situations where they are not, and telling one from the other is a bigger problem than I can handle here. So if you are going to pick up one of these methods, think hard about when you might want to use it and when not.

All of these options act as deterrents as well as actual responses. But the problem is that if you aren't prepared to use them, they can be easily used against you. It is never a bad idea to gently let people know that you are familiar with self-defense methods (the only exception to this is that in some kinds of crowds, I'm told that certain martial arts create a guy kind of "I have to try and take him" crap, so keep that in mind), or perhaps to not make your nonviolent proclivities the subject of public discussion. If you are resolutely nonviolent, you might consider an unloaded shotgun which can still be 'pumped' — because the sound is such a visceral and powerful one.

1. Self-defense or martial arts training

This ranges hugely, from purely defensive techniques to aggressive ones, from basic police-sponsored self-defense training to serious martial arts.

Almost anything you will get is better than nothing, assuming it comes with a competent trainer who can help you evaluate your situation. In the broadest possible terms, even very basic self-defense training will help you make yourself a lot harder to hurt or attack. It won't fix everything, but again, assuming that people who want to hurt you in part rely on the fact that you will be frightened, panicky and not know how to hurt them, this helps a lot. It is also a huge confidence booster — I was friends with a woman who used to teach self-defense to elderly women who lived in urban areas, a terribly vulnerable population, many quite frail and disabled, and she said their tracking showed that assaults halved, mostly not because the women could do terribly much harm, but because they acted like they could and made it difficult for their attackers.

2. Blunt objects

I really like these. A good, heavy, blunt object has a lot of uses in icky times. Baseball bats, Maglite flashlights, axe or hatchet handles, even good canes for them that use them. Now knowing some commonsense use is really helpful — it is easy for a strong attacker with a long reach to take this away and use it on you (this is true to varying degrees of all weapons). Still, if you can figure out how to use them productively, they are cheap, widely available and useful at close range. You can get training in the use of the blunt objects traditionally used in stick fighting of various sorts, and this is not a bad idea. But often in a non-weaponed conflict, simply the sight of a stick or other weapon makes you look like a bad target.

3. Pepper spray

I've heard very mixed things about this stuff, and must admit to no personal experience with it. It has the advantage of being usually (but not always) non-lethal, painful as hell to the attacker and cheap and widely available. I've known several people, however, who didn't realize just how close together you have to be to use it successfully. Two of those people used it so far away that it wasn't very effective, and one of the attackers was REALLY pissed off. So like everything, KNOW HOW TO USE IT. It is also worth noting that pepper spray can cause death by asthma and is incredibly painful — so you might not want to use it in uncertain situations.

4. Tasers

These cannot be classified as a non-lethal, as they do cause death some-times. They are legal, including for concealed carry in many states, and they do work rather well — but shouldn't be used casually. They do tend to end a confrontation quite rapidly, but they depend on fairly close proximity and decent aim. They are not legal in my state for civilian use. It would be wise to treat a Taser as less likely to kill than a gun, but as potentially as dangerous.

5. SCA weapons

I'm unfairly putting bows of all sorts, swords, fighting knives and a host of other weapons in this category. I am not doing so because I dismiss them, but because they are not things to fuck with unless you know what you are doing, and generally speaking, the Society for Creative Anachronism (SCA) isn't a bad place to master them. The problem with the SCA as I see it is that there are a certain number of gamer geeks who think that once a week waving a sword about makes them quite some-thing, and who are totally wrong. That is not universal, but I think it would be easy, with the wrong people, to get the sense that your weap-onry is more useful than it is, or that you are more skillful than you are. If you are going to rely on SCA weapons, train extensively with multiple people and know their limitations and abilities.

6. Knives

An emergency backup — if you are using your knife in a conflict, you are already pretty screwed. Knives, like everything else, can be taken away from you, and most people know this. If you are already in close quarters, getting out a knife and using it will be awkward, but if you can do it, might be as effective as all hell. But stabbing someone is not phys-ically easy (bodies do not penetrate as easily as on TV). Not the worst reserve item ever, but not easy to use.

7. Guns

Who shouldn't have a gun? Kids who still think they are immortal and those with mental or psychological disabilities, anyone likely to seriously consider suicide, anyone who hates and fears guns, anyone who doesn't think they'd use a gun, morons who think guns make them invincible (although those last people probably already have them) and anyone who is vulnerable to violence from someone they love. Who might want to consider them? Anyone with animal predators around (and packs of feral dogs are a likely consequence of a poorer society), hunters, women, especially single women, and older women and couples. Anyone who is good with guns and will take the time to use them carefully. Anyone who needs a long-range weapon and who can effectively use a gun, never pointing it unless they are prepared to use it. Anyone who can disconnect themselves from TV and the popular culture relationship to guns and treat them as tools of limited usefulness.

I don't buy the idea that isolated armed homesteaders will be secure in the future, but that doesn't mean that I don't have guns or am a pacifist — I'm not. Among other things, I live in an area populated by bears (of course, the official maps say not, but the bears say otherwise), at least one large cat (we didn't see it, but from the sound of its movements and its noises, not to mention the fact that it scared the poop out of my very intrepid dog, we most likely have a bobcat — which also aren't supposed to live here) and assorted mid-sized predators.

We also have poultry, small goats and sheep to protect — so weapons are just tools of our trade, along with shovels. We don't hunt, but I'm not opposed to it. I'm not working on that skill set simply because my eyesight is so appalling that I think the odds of my hitting a food animal are pretty small. But I can hit a target pretty well at the distances needed for humans and animals, and I'm reasonably confident that I'd do so. I learned to shoot when I was a child, taught by my father for self-defense, and I remember well helping him make bullets in the furnace of our house. So no, I'm not opposed to the careful and wise use of guns.

I don't honestly buy the bullshit that is passed around about the evils of guns. I certainly believe it is quite possible for guns to be used stupidly, and I have no problem with the regulation of certain kinds of weaponry and gun ownership generally. I think different countries can and should have different approaches — but in the US, we have a heavily armed populace and guns are part of our reality. They have their uses.

Statistics show quite clearly that women, particularly women living alone, may be safer in the US if they carry a weapon and know how to defend themselves. The best discussion of this issue I've seen is by Joe Bageant, in his great book *Deer Hunting With Jesus,* where he debunks most of the standard, urban, liberal perceptions about guns. That doesn't mean that it isn't possible to kill your own kids with a stupidly managed gun, or that guns are the answer to everything, or that everyone should own one — quite the contrary.

Community responses

1. Organized collective non-violence with media attention

I mentioned this above, but I think it works both actively and passively. It is worth noting that nonviolence is not the same as "non-resistance" — it does not mean accepting outcomes, but thwarting violence before it happens.

The reason I mention "media attention" is that perhaps the most important things nonviolent resisters can do in a violent situation is draw attention to the realities, make people see what they do not see. One of the points of Mark Kurlansky's book is it is very easy to say, "Oh, nonviolence wouldn't have saved the Jews under the Nazis" — and that is almost certainly true. On the other hand, nonviolent forms of resistance did save the Danish Jews, who virtually all survived. There is no question that if the Allies had opened their borders to the Jews early on, most of the loss of life would have been prevented. That is, violence became inevitable once we closed down every other choice — and that may well happen to many of us. But that doesn't mean that nonviolence is pointless or has no role in the lives of people who are not pacifists — sometimes, often, especially when states are involved, it is extremely effective and powerful. It is not, as some argue (including Kurlansky, and I think he's wrong), the only tool — but it is a tool and an important one. It is most effective when used early in a crisis, not after violence has already erupted, and on state-sponsored or institutionalized violence.

2. Militias/community self-policing

This works best if you are trained by someone who actually knows what they are doing — I don't recommend it otherwise. Getting a bunch of people together to practice using weapons is kind of pointless, if no one has ever thought critically about strategy, or when not to use weapons or fight. Half of such work is knowing how to disperse a crowd, distract a drunk and send him home, or recognize trouble waiting to happen and intervene. If the police are unavailable, corrupt or absent and private security untrustworthy or too expensive, get someone with serious training to teach you. While the mainstream media often overstates the risks of guns, I think the risks of weekend warriors waving weapons around without a lot of training couldn't possibly be overstated.

OK, now that we've talked about money, death and violence, on to sex and taxes, right?

Fifteen

Putting it together

TEN YEARS AGO TODAY WE MOVED TO OUR FARM. We brought with us some boxes of stuff, some furniture, four cats, our then fifteen-month-old son (Eli, now twelve and five-foot-seven tall), Simon (packed conveniently in my pregnant belly) and my mom (who went home after a day or two of helping us with the little guy). I was twenty-nine, Eric was just about to turn thirty-one, and we were about as unprepared for life on a farm as any two (or three) people could be.

Eric had grown a garden once or twice as a kid with his mom in various apartment buildings. I'd had balcony gardens all through college and grad school, and once a year my family had made strawberry jam. Neither of us had ever milked a goat. I'd held chickens back when I was ten. We had been living in various apartments, and our entire tool collection consisted of a hammer, three screwdrivers and a measuring tape that Eli liked to play with. Not one minute of our combined almost-forty years of education had covered soil science, botany or agriculture. I was pretty sure I knew what a stamen and pistil were, and Eric once had heard a lecture about the development of the moldboard plow in a history of technology class. He wouldn't have actually recognized a moldboard plow if one had come and bit him on the ass, though, and neither would I.

What brought us there was a combination of factors. The first was Eric's grandparents. Shortly after Eric asked me to marry him, he told me that he expected to care for his grandparents when they needed it. The rest of the family was far away or unable to do so in other ways. He had long expected it to become his job, and he wanted to make sure that I understood that. I did, and I was willing. That previous fall Eric's grandfather, ninety-one, vital, energetic and funny, had suffered a series of microstrokes. Eric's grandmother was frantic trying to care for him, and when she recounted trying to carry him to the car when he became ill, it was a wake-up call for both of us. Something had to change — and our plans had to include them, and a place where they could live in their home until they died. We wanted that for them desperately.

The second factor was my desires — we were living in an apartment in an old nineteenth-century mill building in Lowell, MA. It was a great small city; diverse, funky, beautiful buildings; great culture, a strong Southeast Asian immigrant community, everything we wanted. Except, of course, that we had no dirt. None. Not even a window box. Shortly after we moved in, I realized it was making me crazy — my original plan had been to eventually get some land. Now I felt like I was being smothered. I wanted a garden so badly, some animals, a farm. There was a three-year waiting list for a community garden. Had I known then what I know now about urban agriculture, I'd have found some. But then I just wanted some dirt — preferably lots and lots and lots of it. Even though I intellectually knew that an acre was a lot, I wanted as many of them as I could get to compensate for the fact that I had none.

The third factor was Eric's desires. After finishing his PhD in astrophysics the year before, Eric had taken a convenient job in the same building. Over the years he'd spent doing his thesis, he had realized he didn't want to do bench science but wanted to teach instead. Science education was what excited his imagination. So when the job designing museum exhibits and educational materials opened up at the Center for Astrophysics, Eric was excited. But he found sitting in an office down the hall from where he'd been a graduate student depressing, and hated being in front of a computer all the time. Our new baby didn't add to his dedication to a job he loathed. Screw it, we thought, he needed a classroom, and we'd be growing all our own food, so who cared about the 70-percent pay cut?

Finally there was the fact that both of us believed that our rather conventional way of life had to change. We both had done the math on resource use, climate change and energy — we knew that it wasn't possible for billions of people to live like Americans — and yet, billions of people wanted to. Somebody, we reasoned (OK, I reasoned; Eric rolled his eyes but admitted I was right), had to come up with an alternative life model, and some Americans had to try and live on a fair share. Why not us? How hard could it be?

Eric's grandparents agreed to look for a house together. Eric gave notice. I began dreaming of dirt and buying books about farms. There were some caveats — Eric's grandparents had a European sense of geography (they were post-war immigrants) and knew in their hearts that Massachusetts and the rest of the New England states were cold and far away (they'd lived in the New York/New Jersey metro area for more than fifty years), so they flatly refused to look in Massachusetts. New York or New Jersey were the only choices, once we narrowed things down. It had to be a place with a job for Eric, and a place we could afford. This did not leave many options.

We settled on the Schoharie Valley in New York and its surrounding areas. We made three trips before the final move — one to scout locations, one to see twelve houses in three days and one, with Eric's grandparents, to see the house. And now we were moving in. Completely unprepared, still achingly sleep-deprived from Eli's early colicky months, with dreams of cows and chickens, huge gardens and wool to spin and a baby coming, plus an addition to build for the grandparents. For assets we had a teaching job in the State University of New York system for Eric, the last semester of my tiny graduate stipend (and my dissertation that never would get finished) and a complete lack of comprehension about what we'd gotten ourselves into. That last was the most useful thing we had.

And, as William Goldman put it in *The Princess Bride*, from one thing and another, ten years passed. Maybe you've read a bit about one thing and another here — there was a CSA and some books, some poultry and goats and a couple more babies and a bunch of foster children and a lot of screw-ups — the kind of things that constitute a life, I guess.

Two days ago, there were five families at my farm, and I was showing them what we've done over those ten years. Some of it wasn't that impressive — I showed them where we screwed up designing the garden beds and where we are now finally fixing the screw-up we lived with for five years, and explaining what the root cellar would look like if it wasn't May. Some of it is kind of interesting — we showed them the cookstove and how we've gotten off heating oil, and the ways we are using willow and other tree crops to feed our livestock. I talked about how we've come to produce all our milk and eggs, almost all our own meat and a majority of our produce and staple starches (i.e., potatoes, mostly). We have no debt but our mortgage, and not much of that. We get more independent of the feed store every year. Our use of fossil energies has fallen every year, and we're now approaching our dream — using one tenth as much as the average American household. It isn't perfect. It isn't everything. But I still think someone has to find some kind of good life with a lot less.

It isn't the idealized, sustainable life I dreamed of — we use about one tenth the average American's gas, but we still own a car. We heat with wood cut sustainably and locally, and use comparatively little, but it still makes emissions. We eat local and sustainably, know every chicken our family consumes, but we let the kids make s'mores too, and I'm pretty sure Hershey's and Stay Pufts aren't local. Periodically someone points out that it isn't really as sustainable as it looks — and they're right. It is a hybrid, a mix of what life is like now and what life can be, with emphasis on making sure that when (I don't say if here) major changes come, we can be as comfortable as possible, go on as best we can. But I cherish no illusions of a life without vast trouble. The question is just how much insulation we can give ourselves and our children, how much help we can give to our neighbors and our friends, and ultimately, how many other people we can help do the same for themselves, their children, friends and neighbors and loved ones. It isn't perfect at all — it is just a tiny start of something deeply flawed, and as much as we have managed.

In a decade this has become home. Shortly after our move, the rabbi of a synagogue we were considering attending gave me the email of a woman about my age, with two children just a little older than mine. We started corresponding by email, and now my children and hers are playing together, and we are talking about her eldest's bar mitzvah — and shortly to follow my own first son's event — with the ease of old friends who know the insides and outsides of each other's lives. When

Eric and I occasionally talk about the pull of eastern Massachusetts, where most of my family is (now that Eric's grandparents are gone), we talk about how hard it would be to leave our close friends here, our good neighbors, our synagogue, and so far the anchor here has been stronger than the pull from there.

Of the children, only Eli has ever lived in another place, and he doesn't remember it. Both Eric and I, the children of divorce and mobile childhoods, have now lived on this piece of land longer than we have ever lived in any single place. Sometimes children come in and out of our lives through the foster system — we are still hoping for children who will stay forever, but the anchor of this place still has power to heal and stabilize, even if they don't stay.

Every year we know it better. Every year we restore it a little more. We count more bird species, more wetland creatures every year. The families that came to see what we have done sat outside with us, and we saw a pair of tree swallows, the first time that they have resided here. Yesterday I found their nest, which makes ten different species of birds raising babies on our land, from the yellow warblers in the lilac bush and the barn swallows in the barn to the cedar waxwings in the spruces and the phoebes on the front porch.

When we came here, we did not know what we were getting, what we were choosing. We had no knowledge or skill or concrete training, only improbable, ridiculous dreams, energy and enthusiasm and passion. The people we dreamed it with are gone, but they live on in our memories, and new people have come into our lives. I am not sure how well we have accomplished all the things we intended, and no idea what the future holds, for good or ill.

But through a combination of good fortune, the kindness of strangers who became friends, good luck, energy, hope, optimism, too many books, barter, trust, too many mistakes, sweat, stubbornness, curiosity, joy, anger, ambition, fear and delight, we have made it into something. It may not be for me to say what. I still shake in my boots every time I invite strangers to our place, tremble for fear that we will look too small, too disappointing, that our insufficiencies will overflow what we have accomplished. But I keep doing it because whatever else it is, it is real, it is what we have done.

It changes every year — I showed people where the cistern will go, and the hoophouse and more tree crops. I talked about the sheep that we hope will come soon, along with the ones we have shared for years, about how important sharing has been and hopefully will continue to be. I showed them where I hope the new dreams will grow — the bedroom waiting for a sibling group that needs a home. My children have grown enough to have their own dreams and goals here too. This one thing I know — ten years is just a beginning, and the new projects, the changes, the adaptations are just starting. And most of all, from it wells up a stream of new stories that I tell here, and a stream of new friendships that flow out from it. And that alone would be enough.

It is a rainy day on June 1. Last year there was frost on the same day. Two years before that it was blazingly hot. We need the rain, and the boys are in the house, doing logic puzzles. I'm looking at the laundry dripping on the line, the laundry I forgot, catching up on the inevitable dishes that twenty-two people use and thinking of ten years passed. Of new lives — baby goats, new hatched chicks, new planted perennials, new children, boys brought home to the farm and introduced to a herd of brothers and a place. Of loss — the pets buried under the Japanese maple, the ewe with the retained placenta we couldn't save, the foster son we wanted to keep but could not, the dog, the cats, the cats of friends without good dirt to bury in, Eric's grandparents. I'm remembering good days and bad, new things and new trials and chances taken. Phil-the-former-housemate will be back for a visit this week, and we're open for new foster placements. The sheep and Xote the guard donkey return on Friday. The pile of laundry and dishes and things to plant and prune and weed grows smaller and larger but remains. It is a life in a place, just like yours, except it's mine, and from one thing and another, ten years have passed. And I'm looking forward to the next ten.

It is tempting to despair of all action. And sometimes those who despair are right. But sometimes they aren't, and this, I think, is an important and central point for everyone who hits those moments when they simply don't believe society will self-correct in any measure from its impending ecological disaster. I should be clear — I don't believe it will self-correct in every measure, or even as much as I wish desperately it would. But I also do not believe that what one does to mitigate suffering, soften impacts, make life livable or plan for a better outcome is wasted.

I'd tell you why I believe this, but I think the best ever articulation of this reason, the reason I talk about rationing and rational possible responses to depletion and limitation even when they may not happen, was made by Thomas Princen, author of the wonderful and intellectually illuminating book *The Logic of Sufficiency*. He writes:

> I take heart not in the occasional environmental law passed, the tightening of one country's automobile efficiency standards, the international agreement on ozone or timber or toxic substances, but in the hard cases, those little-noticed but nontrivial instances of restrained timber cutting or shortened lobster fishing or community rejection of full automobility. And I take heart in, of all places sites like the Middle East or Sri Lana and the Koreas. I discovered in my earlier research on international conflict resolution that however intractable an intersocietal conflict may be, there are always people working on the solution. Pick the direst time in the Middle East conflict, for example, and you can find someone hidden away in a basement drawing up maps for the water and sewer lines, the lines that wil connect the two societies and that must be built *when peace is reached*, as inconceivable as that is at the time. Someone else is sketching the constitution for the new country, the one that is also inconceivable at the time. And someone else is outlining the terms of trade for the as yet unproduced goods that will traverse the two societies' border. We do not hear about these people because it is the nature of their work, including the dangers of their activities that make it so. Surrounded by intense conflict, hatred and violence, these people appear the fool, idealists who do not know or can not accept the reality of their societies' situation. If they really knew that situation, others would say, they would be "realists"; they

would concentrate their efforts on hard bargaining, economic incentives and military force. But in practice, when the threshold is passed, when leaders shake hands or a jailed dissident is freed or families from the two sides join together, everyone casts about for new ways to organize.

My prognosis, foolish and idealistic as it may seem to some, is that that threshold, that day of biophysical reckoning, is near. And with it, serious questioning about humans' patterns of material provisioning, their production, their consumption, their work and their play. Then the premises of modern industrial societies — capitalist, socialist, communist — will crumble. Efficiency will provide little guidance because it so readily translates to continuing material throughput. A little intensification here, some specialization there just will not make things better. A feedlot is still a feedlot, a conveyor belt still a conveyor belt. When it becomes obvious that efficiency-driven societies can no longer continue their excesses, displace their costs, postpone their investments in natural capital, when it is obvious they can no longer grow their way out of climate change and species extinction and aquifer depletion and the bioaccumulation of persistent toxic substances, people everywhere will indeed be casting about. Some will gravitate to the extremes — religious fundamentalism, survivalist homesteading, totalitarian government. Many, though, will seek paths that are familiar, if not prevalent. Notions of moderation and prudence and stewardship will stand up, as if they were just waiting to be noticed, waiting for their time, even though, in many realms, they were already there. (pp. 359–60)

Princen is not, if you meet him, a wide-eyed optimist in the sense that we think of it — he's a professor of natural resource and environmental policy at the University of Michigan. His book isn't a feel-good

crunchy narrative but a close examination of the economic and ecological impact of the ideas of efficiency in energy and economics and
examples of restraint. And yet I think his kind of optimism is available
to us, and should be. It is not inevitable that the leaders who have been
making war will make peace — we know it isn't. But it is possible.

We have closed off a great number of options — and that's a profound disappointment. In my lifetime it would have been possible to
do a great deal to make the realities of depletion and climate change a
great deal less severe, and we didn't. Now our options are less palatable,
less appealing, more painful — the choices are harder, the results are
going to be a lot worse. From the fact that my parents' generation and
those who came before them tried to address these issues and failed, it
would be easy to conclude that failure is inevitable. And if you set up
success as outside the realm of real possibility — few constraints on climate change, not having to radically change our lives — failure will be
inevitable.

But we also know that human history contains many instances of
the unthinkable becoming thinkable, sometimes quite rapidly. There are
any number of examples — who would have believed that slavery, the
basis of a huge portion of our economy, could be done away with in
the US? Who would have believed that truth and reconciliation and
change could have brought an end to apartheid? Growing up as I did
in an America where my mother and stepmother had to keep an empty
room for my stepmother to pretend to sleep in, so that the landlord and
the courts that could take my mother's children away from her would
not know that she was a lesbian, who would have believed that by the
time all their children were grown, my mother and stepmother would be
married in both their church and their state?

Change happens — it happens slowly, painfully, incrementally, while
rapidly, agonizingly, ripping things apart as it goes. It never goes fast
enough, it never comes exactly as we predict, but when it does come, the
strategies that enable us to go forward are desperately needed. It is quite
possible that the two warring leaders will never shake hands and will
continue to lay waste to the others' countries. It is certain that without
strategies for negotiating peace, they will continue to do so until everything is destroyed. And it is also possible that, given those interventions,

they may yet make an inconceivable peace and a place to begin going forward from.

I keep going forward — ten years seemed impossibly distant when we began, now it is the blink of an eye. We have chosen our place and our dream and will work toward it, toward a decent and humane future with all our power. It is just an ordinary life, and it is the most important thing in the world — a plan, an idea, a dream, a whole and complete life.

I didn't know that this would be my path — I didn't call it Adapting in Place or making a new American dream or any of those things that I sometimes call it now. It was just making my way. All of us do that work — we make our way, and in making our way, we choose our future, make the maps that will guide our posterity and inscribe either hope or despair on the future. It can be hard to remember what we're doing — that we're changing the world. That you too are changing the world if you so choose.

So call me a lunatic optimist — I'm good with that. But damn it, take time to consider before you abandon lunatic optimism, before you assume that we will never change, or only for the worse. Consider once, consider twice, consider a third time and consider anyway doing the work that would enable us not to march to our doom, or not as quickly, or not as many. If my strategy is not for you, find another, one that suits you, a map you can make in your basement if you need to, a garden you can grow behind your house, a life you can live with and that your children can inherit as you also make the plans for the day when the maps come into the light and the gardens stretch out in front yards and your children grow in them as far as your eyes can see.

Profile 6

Gerri

By Gerri Surname

I'm an urban, well-educated African American woman with wanderlust. As a child, I spent Saturday afternoons in my hometown library poring over geography books and novels about faraway places. In college I studied communications and Latin American studies so that I could report global breaking news as a foreign correspondent. Later I joined the US diplomatic corps and for twenty years lived all over the world. I loved packing up and moving out, savoring new cultures, exploring what was around the next corner or across the ocean.

One year, I took a sabbatical term at Pendle Hill, a Quaker residential community in England, and it was there that I became fully aware of the value of Adapting in Place. During its eighty-one years in existence, this spiritual learning center had developed and achieved substantial sufficiency. Residents shared in planting, cultivating and harvesting organic vegetables on the twenty-three acres that provided the bulk of our daily meals.

Until this experience, my attitude about food was: Food? Well, I liked it, knew it was produced "out there," and I was glad that anonymous somebodies out there did the work for me so that I could buy and enjoy it. My time at Pendle Hill awakened a slow but profound change in my attitude about food systems. (It also taught me a lot about the joys and challenges of living in community; but that's another story.)

Since I had lived a rather nomadic life, I had never considered the possibility of having a permanent "home base." Yet the more I read about peak oil and climate instability, the more convinced I was that I needed to reorganize my life to prepare for these conditions. In 2000 my husband Ray and I purchased a 1930s-vintage bungalow with a flat, north-facing backyard in Washington, DC. I retired from the State Department in 2007 and set about developing sufficiency skills, with food production as the central focus.

Off to the garden

There was one problem: I had next to nothing in my background to prepare me to carry out any agricultural tasks — despite having grown up in Minnesota, leading producer of soy, wheat and corn. So the summer of 2007 found me standing in my sunny backyard, seed packets in one hand and a gardening book in the other, wondering what to do next. Each gardening book I consulted contradicted the other. That year I planted kale — my first food from seed — and monitored it warily throughout the growing season. Since other green plants grew near it and nothing ever fully resembled kale, I ended up harvesting none of it.

The experienced gardeners I approached were, unfortunately for me, not particularly adept at transmitting their knowledge. My pointed questions as to soil, seeds and growing techniques were met with either a laconic or a meandering response that ended in — "Well, it depends."

To a neophyte gardener such as myself, "It depends" was the most frustrating and discouraging phrase in the English language. As a beginner, I wanted — and sought — certainty. Clearly I needed help!

Some form of salvation came in the local Master Gardener course I began in the winter of 2008. Here in Washington, DC, the course operates from the Cooperative Extension Service of the University of the District of Columbia. This seventeen-session, science-based program on the principles of plant cultivation and maintenance appealed to my structured mind. The substantive lectures and demonstrations by university professors, garden columnists and working farmers gave me a solid knowledge base and boosted my confidence in my potential to be a good gardener.

But I was still surprised by the answer most of these expert lecturers gave to my specific questions: "It depends."

Even though I had completed the Master Gardener course, I was still on the low end of the learning curve. I benefited from volunteering at two new urban farms in DC. These farms have a major youth teaching emphasis, and working there was part of the fifty-hour volunteer requirement needed for certification as a Master Gardener.

By late summer 2009, my gardening skills had improved and my own newly expanded backyard garden produced a bumper harvest. Canning, dehydrating and cold-room storage activities continued into the fall. I do not yet have any real sense of mastery, but I am proud of these hard-won accomplishments. I have also begun to share my experiences.

Reaching out

I believe some of the most critical work of Adapting in Place is outreach, engaging the people around you. The growing numbers of our fellow citizens facing disruption and poverty need practical support and alternatives. Those of us who know about and are using adaptive practices are honor-bound to share these alternatives with others. How to do this?

I live in a mixed-race neighborhood with a significant population of African-Americans. The language of peak oil, depletion and energy descent is alienating for many minorities. It can suggest continued — or even increased — deprivation and sacrifice, a reality that is already too present in communities of color.

As a trained communicator, it has been a challenge to find appealing and hopeful ways to talk about AIP within my community. But I have found that keeping a local focus and tapping into the resilience that has always been a part of minority communities facilitates outreach and education.

A few years ago, I started doing neighborhood public presentations on peak oil and its implications for our community. To prepare, I researched our local history and found out that tobacco, rye, oats, peas, flax, wheat and potatoes had been widely grown in our northeast DC quadrant in the nineteenth century. Even into the early twentieth century, residents were applying for permits for barns, chicken coops and stables. So at one time, our community had the capability of substantially feeding itself — and I believe it could do so again. A few enthusiastic neighbors who attended my presentations also wanted to go further, with a tentative plan to contribute to a Metro-area food shed map and to survey our other community assets.

Going forward

As for where the future will find me, I'm not really sure. My husband and I, Midwesterners both, often long for the relative safety and stability of the region where we grew up; we miss the pine forests and the lakes. Although I don't love Washington — it's a congested, expensive city, with immense economic and racial divides — it does have decent public transportation (we are a car-less family) and free museums. Slowly, I am developing roots here. These days, I'm inspired by the new aging-in-place "urban villages" springing up everywhere. There are eight in Washington, DC, alone. Tweak a few details, shift the focus, and you have a model for intergenerational Adapting in Place; one that doesn't necessarily depend on familial relationships — important since many of us are childless or located far away from biological family members. The urban village concept acknowledges that we're not all moving en masse "back to the land," and it offers a vision of livable cities with warmer human connections at all points in our lives.

It has been a big psychic shift for me, after having spent much of my working life in an international arena, to refocus my priorities within an intensely local setting. Nevertheless, when, not so many years ago, I put seeds in the ground in my own backyard garden, I felt like a "world citizen" in a different way — joining a long succession of people attending to and caring for the land that reaches far to the past and extends into the future. Cultivating vegetables and flowers is teaching me humility, patience (most of the time, anyway), persistence and close observation — qualities needed everywhere and at all times.

AIP is new terrain that challenges us to thrive within limits, but to also shape those limits through values. We will need to be guided by a willingness and ability to improvise, to innovate according to circumstances, and to do so with style and a spirit of adventure. Now, will I be able to organize in my lifetime a neighborhood solar co-op … or start that community kitchen … or sign up my neighbors for a food-buying club? Well, it depends….

Index

About the author

SHARON ASTYK is a writer, teacher, blogger and small farmer. A former academic, her unfinished doctoral dissertation focused on the ecological and demographic catastrophes explored in Early Modern Literature. Abandoning Shakespeare to work on the ecological and demographic catastrophes of the 21st century, she began by running a small CSA and right now seems to write books, including *Depletion & Abundance: Life on the New Home Front* (New Society  Publishers 2008) and *Independence Days: A Guide to Sustainable Food Storage and Preservation* (New Society Publishers 2009). In her copious spare time, she raises vegetables, fruit, livestock, children and havoc with her husband in rural upstate New York.

If you have enjoyed *Making Home*, you might also enjoy other

BOOKS TO BUILD A NEW SOCIETY

Our books provide positive solutions for people who want to make a difference. We specialize in:

Sustainable Living • Green Building • Peak Oil
Renewable Energy • Environment & Economy
Natural Building & Appropriate Technology
Progressive Leadership • Resistance and Community
Educational & Parenting Resources

New Society Publishers

ENVIRONMENTAL BENEFITS STATEMENT

New Society Publishers has chosen to produce this book on recycled paper made with **100% post consumer waste,** processed chlorine free, and old growth free.

For every 5,000 books printed, New Society saves the following resources:[1]

33	Trees
3,020	Pounds of Solid Waste
3,322	Gallons of Water
4,334	Kilowatt Hours of Electricity
5,489	Pounds of Greenhouse Gases
24	Pounds of HAPs, VOCs, and AOX Combined
8	Cubic Yards of Landfill Space

[1]Environmental benefits are calculated based on research done by the Environmental Defense Fund and other members of the Paper Task Force who study the environmental impacts of the paper industry.

For a full list of NSP's titles, please call 1-800-567-6772 *or check out our website* at:

www.newsociety.com